AF478957

REMEMBERING DEFEAT

REMEMBERING DEFEAT

ANDREW WOLPERT

Civil War and Civic Memory
in Ancient Athens

THE JOHNS HOPKINS UNIVERSITY PRESS
BALTIMORE AND LONDON

The Johns Hopkins University Press
2715 North Charles Street
Baltimore, Maryland 21218-4363
www.press.jhu.edu

LIBRARY OF CONGRESS CATALOGING-IN-PUBLICATION DATA
Wolpert, Andrew.
  Remembering defeat : Civil War and civic memory in
Ancient Athens / Andrew Wolpert.
      p.   cm.
Includes bibliographical references and index.
  ISBN 0-8018-6790-8
  1. Athens (Greece)—History—Thirty Tyrants, 404–403 B.C.
2. Greece—History—Spartan and Theban Supremacies,
404–362 B.C. 3. Greece—History—Macedonian Expansion,
359–323 B.C. 4. Democracy—Greece. I. Title.
  DF231.3.W65 2002
  938—dc21

2001000950

A catalog record for this book is available from the British Library.

Victoriae

CONTENTS

ACKNOWLEDGMENTS

Completion of this project was made possible by a Loeb Faculty Grant, Harvard University, and by a Summer Research Grant, University of Wisconsin. Preliminary drafts were read at the meetings of the APA and CAMWS as well as at the University of Chicago, the University of Durham, Harvard University, and the University of Washington. I would like to thank the audiences for their comments and the members of each department for their gracious hospitality. I am also grateful to the late Arthur Adkins, Danielle Allen, Ed Carawan, David Cohen, Carolyn Higbie, Ian Morris, Greg Nagy, Josh Ober, Victoria Pagán, Peter Rhodes, Richard Saller, and Laura Slatkin for reading chapters from various versions of the manuscript and for their suggestions and criticisms. They are, of course, not responsible for any shortcomings of the final version. Thanks are also owed to Maura Burnett of the Johns Hopkins University Press for her care and attention in the preparation of the book. Part 1 began at the University of Wisconsin. Part 2 started as a dissertation project at the University of Chicago under the title "Rebuilding the Walls of Athens" and since then has undergone revision first in Cambridge, Massachusetts, and then in Madison, Wisconsin. The main premise remains the same: The Athenians struggled to make sense of the painful years of civil war by selectively remembering the past. Unless otherwise noted, translations are adapted from the Loeb Classical Series.

Finally, I owe an enormous debt of gratitude to my parents and my mother-in-law for all their support along the way, including proofing the preliminary manuscript. I can only repay them by offering the same encouragement to their grandson, Abraham Ricardo. This book is dedicated to Victoria, who has helped me with the project in every possible way, from beginning to end, and who knows more than anyone else why the topic has captured my attention for so long.

INTRODUCTION

In 404 B.C.E., the Peloponnesian War finally came to an end when the Athenians, starved into submission, were forced to accept Sparta's terms of surrender. Shortly afterward, a group of thirty conspirators with Spartan backing overthrew the democracy and established a narrow oligarchy. Within the course of thirteen months, the oligarchs killed more than 5 percent of the citizen population and proceeded to terrorize the rest of the community by confiscating property and by banishing from the city all who were not members of their government. After regaining control of Athens, the democratic resistance agreed to an amnesty that protected the collaborators from prosecution for all but the most flagrant crimes. The Athenians, however, could not simply forget the past. Evident in speeches delivered in public at civic settings shortly after the reconciliation of 403, a residue of anger, fear, and distrust remained in the community. Yet Athens did not sink into a cycle of bloodshed such as occurred elsewhere in Greece. In fact the city remained remarkably stable until Macedon dissolved the democracy nearly a century later.

The reader of Thucydides cannot help but be surprised at the outcome of the Athenian civil war. We are taught by the Corcyraean revolution the difficulty of stopping violence once *stasis* erupts (Thuc. 3.69–85, 4.46–48). Athens stands in stark contrast. If Thucydides wrote much of his work after the Peloponnesian War, perhaps he expected his account of Corcyra to draw to the reader's attention the uniqueness of Athens.[1] But even if this is not the case, Corcyra is a vivid reminder to us of the stakes in the Athenian reconciliation and of the consequences were it to fail.

Civil war was widespread in the rest of Greece (Gehrke 1985). For this reason, much of fourth-century philosophy was devoted to the question of how to prevent *stasis*.[2] But the philosophers did not attempt to explain what citizens must do to restore civic harmony should a city suffer from *stasis*; they were more concerned with discovering a blueprint to prevent it from happening in the first place. Still, civil strife continued to occur, and the victims, bystanders, and collaborators were forced to carry on after brutal atrocities. With such concerns in mind, I have set out to examine how the Athenians were able to do what Corcyra and most other Greek cities could not, convinced that the answer can help us better understand the nature of Athenian democracy and show us how a community can repair the damages of a bitter civil war and heal its divisions.

Historians have advanced many explanations for the success of the reconciliation: the terms of the agreement, the political condition of the Greek world, the social and economic problems of Athens.[3] They have shown that revenge and retribution were not viable options, but the Athenians could have simply dismissed pragmatic considerations in order to obtain private satisfaction for past grievances. Causal explanations present the reconciliation as a *fait accompli,* as if there were only one possible outcome to the civil war.[4] But as Corcyra shows, pragmatic considerations do not always lead a people to chose the course of action that best serves its interests.

Whatever the reasons for reconciliation, Athens had to become a community again, and relations between the democrats and former oligarchs had to be normalized. When the Spartans demolished the Long Walls, the Athenians became vulnerable from within and without. Oligarchs in collusion with Lysander seized this opportunity to overthrow the democracy. In the period after the oligarchy of the Thirty, Athens struggled to regain its autonomy. The Athenians rebuilt the walls to protect their city from foreign threats, and they attempted to restore civic harmony. They could not simply pick up the pieces and continue where they had left off. They needed to redefine who they were, or, to echo Loraux (1986), they needed to "reinvent" Athens.

Rather than explain why the reconciliation was successful, this study examines the civic speeches and public commemorations of the early fourth century to consider how the Athenians confronted the troubling memories of defeat and civil war and how they reconciled themselves to an agreement that allowed past crimes to go unpunished. This approach helps us better appreciate changes in Athenian ideology as well as the fragility of the reconciliation. The scope of this study is roughly the first generation after the Thirty, from the peace treaty of 403 to the formation of the Second Athenian League in 378/7. A precise date to mark its end remains elusive, since the reconciliation was not a single act but a process by which the Athenians gradually (and only partially) accepted the reintegration of their city. Over time, hostilities faded and new concerns and fears dominated Athens. The Second Athenian League did much to turn attention away from the rule of the Thirty, but, as late as the 350s to the 330s, speakers referred to the civil war.[5] The oligarchs had left an indelible mark on the city.

There are only a few extant speeches for early fourth-century Athens, but those of Andocides, Isocrates, and Lysias that have survived provide significant and meaningful statements about the civil war and reconciliation. Even when the actions of Thirty did not pertain to a particular dispute, litigants still found it useful to mention them. So too the speaker of the funeral oration had to incorporate defeat into his history of Athens. Using new methods and theories on Athenian law, I consider such references to defeat and civil war within the social and cultural context of the reconciliation. And by drawing from recent works on collective and social memory from fields outside of classics as well as from historical studies on civil war and reconciliation for other periods and regions, including Argentina, France, and Israel, this study places the aftermath of the Athenian civil war in a wider context to show what is distinctive about the Athenian experience.

Most ancient texts—such as the history of Thucydides, the dialogues of Plato, the epideictic speeches of Isocrates, and the philosophical treatises of Aristotle—were intended for an elite audience and articulate an elite ideology. This is not to say that such authors failed to express attitudes that average citizens also endorsed; rather, it is difficult to determine when their thoughts would have appealed both to an elite audience and to a broad range of the Athenian citizenry. Speeches, on the other hand— whether delivered in the Assembly, Council, and law courts or at the public funerals of soldiers—were addressed to audiences fairly representative of the citizenry.[6] They therefore had to express values and beliefs widely shared among the Athenians.[7] The stakes in deliberative and forensic oratory were too high for a speaker to risk professing values that the audience did not endorse. Failure before the Assembly could mean the loss of political power, and failure in the courts could result in financial loss, exile, or even death. Although the speaker of the funeral oration did not face such risks, he was chosen by the city (Thuc. 2.34.6), so he was likely to give a speech that had popular appeal. His reputation depended upon delivering a eulogy pertaining as much to Athens, its might, and the democracy as it did to the dead. The funeral oration thus reveals how the Athenians preferred to view themselves and their city (Loraux 1986: 17–76).

Although the public speaker had to use arguments that appealed to his audience, he did not have to rely exclusively on popular values. The extant orations may even show signs of influence from historians and philosophers.[8] Nevertheless, a speaker who articulates intellectual ideas does so because he believes that they will persuade his audience. Hence I choose the term *civic discourse* to refer to speeches delivered in a civic setting to a mass audience, whether at an official public ceremony or in one of the political institutions of the city. Civic discourse, after all, cannot be reduced to the lowest common denominator, and this perhaps explains much of the difficulty in interpreting the orators. Since both the masses and the elite participated in the political affairs of the city, speakers used a complex network of beliefs and attitudes to appeal to a diverse and even heterogeneous audience. Speakers, for example, sometimes professed elite values, used aristocratic language, and claimed special privileges because of their status.[9] To favor a litigant because of his wealth certainly conflicts with democratic principles. It would be a mistake, however, to conclude that the democracy simply accepted aristocratic principles and failed to develop a language of its own. As democracy developed, the Athenians transformed elite ideals and redirected aristocratic ambition in ways that served the interests of the community, such as in the performance of liturgies.[10]

Yet representational studies such as this have their limits. In his review of recent work on the Athenian economy, Morris (1994a: 360) observes, "Where Hellenists have faced squarely the agendas behind our sources, we seem to be trapped in a bloodless, intellectualized realm of competing discourses, where . . . our data always come to us already implicated in elite acts of representation." With this in mind, we realize that we cannot learn from the speeches what actually happened. They do not reveal whether the litigants acted for the reasons they stated or, for that matter, whether they even did what they said they did.[11] We cannot, for example, use the speeches to answer the most fundamental question concerning the civil war, that is, the composition of the factions. How many citizens joined the men of Piraeus? What were their occupations? Did they receive substantial support from the elite or were they composed mainly of the poor? The speeches do not give us any substantial clues. But for the present study, these limitations are not problematic, since we are concerned precisely with the maintenance of the "bloodless discourses." As long as confrontation remained for the most part confined to an intellectualized realm, the reconciliation prevailed. Were the Athenians to break free from civic discourse, then civil war would resume.

For the very same reasons the Attic orators are such useful sources for the study of values and beliefs expressed in civic discourse, they offer us the opportunity to explore how the Athenians collectively remembered their past. Halbwachs (1992: 52–53, 168–69) argues that every memory, even that of an individual, is a form of social memory, since people live in social groupings and inevitably orient their memories around their relationships with others. He further suggests that, since memories of the past are reconstructed in the present, representations of the past invariably reveal the needs and concerns of the present. It is this suggestion concerning the politicization of the past which has drawn so much attention in recent years to his theories on collective memory.[12] Yet two problems limit the usefulness of such studies. First, collective memory reveals only how a particular individual or group of individuals represents the past at a particular moment. It is therefore difficult to assess long-term trends through such studies of collective memory. But this limitation is actually a strength of this approach. It prevents us from constructing static models of society and allows us to recognize change and disruption in society. And as we shall see, conflicting, contradictory, and competing images of the past often exist simultaneously.

The second problem is more serious. How can one determine the extent to which a particular representation of the past is shared by other individuals? To what extent can memory be collective? For this reason, many modern studies of collective memory focus on commemorative monuments.[13] By examining the discussions of legislators to commemorate an event, the decisions of architects about how to construct the monument, and the experiences of the people who visit it, we can explore the politics of representing the past and investigate the extent to which a particular representation of the past unites or divides people. For Athens, this problem is less serious, given the extensive participation of ordinary citizens in the political affairs of the community. Just as the stakes were too high for public speakers to risk professing values and beliefs that were not commonly shared among their fellow citizens, in the same way they tended to depict the past as their audience preferred to imagine it. The corpus of Attic orators is therefore an ideal source for the study of collective memory.

As speakers selectively invoked the past, appealing to Athenian anger and fear, the reconciliation was transformed from a symbol of compromise into a symbol of victory. The democratic exiles were remembered as loyal citizens who had fought for the good of the city, and the complicity of the demos was passed over in silence. The aid that the Thirty received from a significant portion of the population and the failure of many to assist in the resistance were either denied or downplayed. It was as if the Thirty were solely responsible for the civil war. One could even say that the Athenians accomplished a kind of erasure of the past: amnesty. In the end, 403 was a watershed year for Athens not because institutional arrangements were drastically reconfigured but because the Athenians made a concerted effort to distance themselves from the period of civil war and to rid the community of the ill effects of the oligarchy. So in the same historical period, new procedures for enacting laws were implemented, which are hailed as the democracy's greatest achievement, and Socrates was executed, which is considered one of its worst mistakes. Rather than view these decisions as contradictory, we should instead recognize that both were attempts to insure that Athens would remain stable.

Part One sets forth the historical setting of the restored democracy. Chapter 1 focuses on the narrative accounts of the civil war: Xenophon's *Hellenica*, Aristotle's *Athenaion Politeia*, Diodorus Siculus, and Plutarch's *Alcibiades* and *Lysander*.[14] They amply attest to the campaign of violence that the Thirty carried out, and they show that the civil war had so fractured the community that reconciliation was difficult to sustain. Chapter 2 outlines the laws and decrees enacted after the restoration of the democracy. Although historians conclude that the moderates prevailed, Athenians had different views about how they could best prevent civil war, who should be allowed to be full members of the community, and what direction the democracy should take. Chapter 3 examines the court cases of the restored democracy, including the trials of Eratosthenes (one of the leaders of the oligarchy) and of Socrates. Athenian law, in general, and the terms of the reconciliation, in particular, were so elastic that Athenians could easily use the courts to gain satisfaction for crimes committed during the civil war. Rules, laws, and procedures were not enough to prevent recrimination, unless the juries that heard the cases and the litigants who pursued their grievances were also committed to the principles of reconciliation. In other words, the agreement had to extend beyond the plane of law and become incorporated within the ideology of the community.

For this reason, the focus shifts in Part Two to representations of the defeat and civil war in civic discourse. Chapter 4 explores the cultural significance of the amnesty. Just as the courts could not prevent the agreement from becoming a source of conflict, the memory of the civil war could either promote reconciliation or provoke hostilities. But as the Athenians selectively remembered the past, they constructed images of the amnesty which glossed over conflict. In Chapter 5, I discuss how individual speakers manipulated representations of the factions of the civil war either to depict themselves as loyal democrats and legitimize their own political positions or to contest the positions of others. Although the past was a source of controversy, few were beyond reproach.

Since speakers could more easily cast aspersions on their enemies than prove them, it was difficult to divide the community again into two warring factions. And as litigants praised the men of Piraeus, whether to win the juries' sympathy or to deny their opponents' claims to this title, they made the democratic exiles appear more unique, thereby rendering it more difficult for any single citizen to claim this praise for himself. In a sense, the Athenians democratized the men of Piraeus. The Athenian people as a whole, not a small faction or a select group of individuals, was responsible for the restoration the democracy. Accusations of complicity and cowardice simultaneously fueled and released the tensions between the various members of the restored democracy.

Chapter 6 considers how representations of the oligarchic rule allowed the Athenians to alleviate anxiety about the lasting consequences of the period of civil unrest. By heaping reproach on the oligarchs and blaming them for Athenian misfortunes, they bracketed the civil war from Athenian past and future, thereby reassuring themselves that Athens would not again experience either defeat by a foreign army or an oligarchic uprising from within the city. The more Athenians depicted the oligarchs as utter villains, the easier it was for them to encroach on aristocratic ideals and claim them for the demos. Using the Thirty as proof that oligarchy was not a viable alternative, the Athenians forcefully asserted democratic values in civic discourse. They convinced themselves that as long as Athens remained democratic they could restore its greatness. Thus, civil war gave the democracy a new legitimacy.

This study helps ancient historians and classicists better appreciate the significance of the events of the early fourth century for the development of the Athenian democracy. It puts an end to two misconceptions: (1) following the Peloponnesian War, the Athenians retreated from the so-called radical democracy of the fifth century, and (2) the success of the restored democracy was an inevitable outcome of the civil war. In addition, it offers a new approach to the study of Athenian law and society. Recent studies have collectively examined speeches from the corpus of Attic orators (420–320) to answer general questions about Athenian values and beliefs or the workings of the democracy, and they assume long periods of continuity.[15] Although the synchronic approach permits otherwise impossible investigations, such as Ober's work on relations between the masses and the elite or Loraux's study of the funeral oration, it also creates a static picture of society.[16] By exploring how the Athenians responded to a particular historical event, I show how Athens changed. Rather than conclude that the democracy was generally stable, I argue

that dissension and division—even when resolved, suppressed, or mitigated—were never very far from the surface. The Athens of Lysias was a
very different city from that of either Pericles or Demosthenes. Using
Lysias's speeches to draw general conclusions about rhetorical *topoi* and
their function in the courts is misleading, since the speeches were delivered to address problems and concerns unique to early-fourth-century
Athens and are not easily extrapolated to other periods.

Finally, this study draws on literature that concerns more recent civil
wars, in part because comparisons to the present are inevitable, even
when suppressed. With such comparisons brought to the forefront, we
are forced to confront assumptions that would otherwise remain implicit, and we are prevented from discounting explanations that seem
unbelievable or unlikely.[17] Comparison is useful also because the Athenian reaction to the Thirty—no matter how unique or exceptional—can
help us better appreciate and contextualize how others come to terms
with the disturbing and unsettling events of their past.

THE HISTORICAL SETTING

1 ⚔ CIVIL WAR

When Theramenes arrived, Critias stood up and spoke as follows:
"Members of the Council, if any of you thinks that more people are
being put to death than is right, let him reflect that these things always
take place where governments are changed. Moreover, it is necessary
that those who are changing the government here to an oligarchy
should have the most enemies, both because Athens is the most
populous of Greek cities and because the people have been reared in
freedom for the longest time. Now since we believe that democracy is
an unbearable form of government for men like ourselves and you,
and since we are convinced that the people would never be friendly to
the Lacedaemonians, our preservers, while the aristocrats would
continue to be loyal to them, for these reasons we are establishing the
present government with the approval of the Lacedaemonians. And if
we find anyone opposed to the oligarchy, we get rid of him if we can.
But, most of all, we consider it right to punish anyone of our own
number who is harming this order of things."

XEN. HELL. 2.3.24–26

Sources for the civil war are numerous and detailed; examined collectively, however, they provide a confused and contradictory picture of the surrender, the rule of the Thirty,
and the restoration of the democracy.[1] No doubt many of the variations
are due to the different genres of the works as well as the personal
idiosyncrasies of the different authors who selectively recorded and omit-
ted information in their accounts. But they also stem from the politics of
reconciliation. Using the civil war as a weapon in civic discourse, Athenians delved into the past either to establish their own identity and legitimize their own political positions or to contest those of others. Highly
politicized and emotionally charged, this discourse not only had an impact on how the Athenians understood the Thirty and their rule, but it
also shaped the content and form of the subsequent historical narratives.
The politics of reconciliation became so intertwined with the events of
the civil war that it is now nearly impossible to disentangle the two.

The narrative accounts of the civil war—Xenophon's *Hellenica,* Aristotle's *Athenaion Politeia,* Diodorus Siculus, and Plutarch's *Alcibiades* and *Lysander*—often offer interpretations of the events that are just as tendentious as those of the orators. One can easily find inconsistencies and contradictions in the works of each of these authors, and, when compared, their accounts are sometimes irreconcilable. Since corroborating evidence is often lacking, historians decide which to accept on the basis of probability, reliability of the author, and internal coherence. Nevertheless, these accounts provide the necessary context to consider statements about the civil war found in Attic oratory. And even though many specific details remain in doubt and others will never be known, the general framework is certain.

Defeat at Aegospotami forced the Athenians to accept Spartan terms. Surrender put an end to the Athenian empire and left Athens vulnerable to outside interference. Although the Athenians later conflated surrender and dissolution of the democracy, these events were separate and distinct. Several months after the surrender, oligarchs came to power thanks to Lysander, who helped them overthrow the democracy. For thirteen months they ruled Athens and carried out a campaign of violence to rid the community of the democracy and its supporters. Regardless of the sequence of events—whether the Spartan garrison was installed before or after Theramenes' execution—violence was systemic to the oligarchs' rule. Most surprising is the lukewarm response the democratic exiles received from their fellow citizens. Few Athenians rallied behind their cause, and most who joined them waited until the later stages of the war. At the same time, there was remarkably little dissension within the ranks of the citizens who remained in the city. Even after the extreme measures of the Thirty and the Ten who followed them, the Three Thousand continued to favor oligarchy until they were forced to reach an agreement with the democratic resistance, thanks again to Spartan intervention. Just as the Spartans had imposed terms of surrender on the Athenians, so too they imposed terms of reconciliation.

DEFEAT

It is easy—perhaps too easy—for any account of the Athenian surrender to emphasize the ironic and tragic elements. Despite the destruction of the Athenian forces in Sicily, the subsequent revolt of its allies, and the oligarchic revolution of 411, Athens was able to overcome these difficulties and hold out against what must have appeared to be insurmountable obstacles. Implementing emergency financial and political measures, the Athenians rebuilt their fleet and restored the democracy. They won significant naval victories against Peloponnesian fleets, twice forcing Sparta to sue unsuccessfully for peace.[2] In hindsight, we know that the Athenians miscalculated. But at the time, the war was far from over. Even the second offer, made after Arginusae, would have required the Athenians to abandon much of their empire. They were recuperating from their losses and regaining (albeit slowly) their control of the Aegean, and they preferred instead to risk all and rejected the Spartan overtures.[3]

Then, in 405, the situation changed decisively when Lysander, the only Spartan commander capable of defeating the Athenians at sea, attempted to block the route of the grain ships heading from the Pontus to Athens (Xen. *Hell.* 2.1.17–19). He entered the Hellespont and took Lampsacus by force. The Athenian commanders responded quickly. Setting sail with 180 ships from Sestos, they anchored the fleet on the other side of the Hellespont at Aegospotami, about three kilometers from Lampsacus.[4] Although the site lacked a harbor and could not provide the force with adequate supplies, the generals, eager to attack the Spartans, stationed the fleet there because of its proximity to Lampsacus.[5] By a remarkable coincidence, Alcibiades was also in that region, living in exile in a castle not far from Aegospotami, and it is at this point in the narrative of the battle that our two principal sources, Xenophon and Diodorus, begin to differ.[6]

According to Xenophon, Alcibiades ventured into the camp in order to recommend unsuccessfully to the Athenian commanders that they return to Sestos, where there was a harbor to protect the fleet and sufficient supplies for the crew (*Hell.* 2.1.25). According to Diodorus, he informed the commanders that he was on friendly terms with Thracian kings who were willing to provide him with troops to finish the war. Hoping that he would be permitted to return to Athens if he should win a great victory, he asked for a share of the command and promised either to force the Spartans to fight at sea or to attack them by land with Thracian troops (13.105.3–4). Wylie (1986: 127–30) considers Diodorus's depiction of Alcibiades more convincing because he appears in the camp for self-serving reasons. In Xenophon's narrative, Alcibiades enters the camp unannounced and, without asking for anything in return, merely points out to the generals what they must have already known. Finding Diodorus's portrayal "as hostile as Xenophon's is naïve," Strauss (1983: 26 n. 11) agrees with Lotze (1964: 35) that a combination of the two is more likely.

Yet nowhere does Xenophon explicitly or implicitly state Alcibiades' motives. He only mentions the advice that Alcibiades gave and leaves it to the reader to determine the reasons for his appearance in the Athenian camp at such a critical moment in the war. Recalled from Sicily in 415 to answer charges of impiety, Alcibiades first sought refuge in Sparta, where he helped the Spartans in their war effort until he soon lost favor. Next received by Tissaphernes, he planned a return to Athens. He fueled oligarchic conspiracies by promising Persian support should the Athenians change their constitution. Then once the Four Hundred came to power in 411, he won the favor of the Athenian fleet stationed at Samos and was elected general. And because of his naval victories, the Athenians welcomed him back after the democracy was restored. But then he was blamed for the loss at Notium, and he left Athens once again, only to die in exile. Given Alcibiades' record, it would not have required a cynical reader to infer even from Xenophon's account that he was seeking to promote his own interests when he came forward to warn the generals about their tactical mistake.[7]

Since in both accounts it is the failure of the generals to listen to Alcibiades that caused the destruction of the fleet, Xenophon's portrayal of Alcibiades is only unconvincing if one doubts his explanation for the defeat. After rejecting Alcibiades' advice, Xenophon tells us, the Athenian commanders continued to position the fleet for battle every morning. The Spartan forces remained in their harbor, with the exception of some scout ships sent by Lysander to observe Athenian activity. When the Athenians returned to the beach, they dispersed to search for supplies. As each day passed, they went further from the camp out of necessity and grew more careless out of disdain for the Spartans. Then, on the fifth day, Lysander set his fleet against the Athenian camp while the Athenians were searching for provisions. Conon saw the Spartans approaching and signaled to the Athenians to return to their ships as quickly as possible. The *Paralus,* along with eight other ships, escaped thanks to Conon, but the rest were captured while still on the beach (*Hell.* 2.1.26–28).

In Diodorus's account, the disaster is as devastating as in Xenophon's, but it is not as humiliating. Since Lysander would not accept battle and the Athenians had difficulty obtaining necessary supplies, Philocles decided on the day he was in command to set sail with thirty triremes, and he ordered the rest to follow.[8] Learning of this plan from deserters, Lysander sailed out with his entire fleet and attacked the thirty triremes before the rest were even manned.[9] As he forced Philocles to turn back, he ordered a Spartan contingent to land on the beach. Now that the Athenians were being attacked by land and sea, they were thrown into confusion. Many fled the ships and the camp, and, as a result of this general panic, only ten triremes escaped (13.106.1–6).

Although contemporary scholarship favors Diodorus,[10] corroborating evidence is inconclusive. In some forensic speeches delivered shortly after Aegospotami, litigants mention a "naval battle" at which fighting took place and address the jurors in ways that imply that a substantial number of them were present at Aegospotami. Some conclude that such statements support Diodorus's account, because he describes a battle and reports how many Athenians fled, whereas Xenophon states that practically the entire fleet was captured without a fight and that only the *Paralus* returned to Athens.[11] Yet, far from providing an accurate description, litigants selectively remembered Aegospotami so as to deny responsibility for the defeat. By mentioning fighting and by referring to it as a battle, they made the loss appear less embarrassing.[12] But even if we dismiss the possibility of rhetorical embellishment and take these statements at face value, they are simply too general and too imprecise, proving only that the Athenians suffered a major defeat.

Litigants also had rhetorical reasons for addressing the jurors as survivors of Aegospotami which prevent us from drawing conclusions about the composition of the courts. When the litigant was present at Aegospotami, he could use such an address to establish a personal connection with the jurors and therefore render them sympathetic to his arguments.[13] This was a rhetorical device intended to trigger a favorable emotional response in the jurors so that they would hear his case as his supporters and allies rather than as an impartial body. For this device to be effective, it did not matter whether the jurors had in fact been present at Aegospotami. What mattered was that the litigant appealed to them as if they had shared the same experiences. Such an address also served to promote the fiction of continuity and consistency in Athenian policies, programs, and institutions.[14] It was a way to assert that the Athenian people collectively took part in every officially sanctioned act. It was to say that the same people who manned the triremes voted in the Assembly and delivered the verdict in the courts, thus allowing Athenians to believe that the demos ruled Athens.[15]

Both Xenophon and Diodorus leave out important information and are open to many questions, making it difficult to decide whose version to accept.[16] Yet they agree on one detail that suggests Xenophon's account is the likelier: the extent of the defeat. The Athenians had suffered such a loss only twice before. But in contrast to Aegospotami, the previous defeats—the destruction of the fleet in Egypt in 454 and in Sicily in 413—were not caused by one battle on one day but by the failure to retreat after a series of losses, setbacks, and miscalculations extending over a period of months and even years. In Diodorus's version, the Athenian commanders were preparing to move the fleet. Why then didn't more Athenian triremes escape? Perhaps there was panic and a lack of communication in the camp. Not expecting the Spartans to attack, the sailors grew complacent and overconfident. Yet if they were on the beach preparing to embark, it is surprising that only 10 out of 180 ships escaped. If, however, most of the crew was away from the camp, as Xenophon states, the capture of practically the entire fleet appears plausible. There is even a precedent. While the Athenian crew was searching for food in Eretria, the Spartan fleet attacked and captured 22 of 36 ships (Thuc. 8.95). But given the size of the fleet stationed at Aegospotami, no account can explain adequately the Athenians' serious tactical mistake. Even at Eretria, although the fleet was much smaller and therefore more vulnerable, over a third of the Athenian ships escaped. Only 5 percent escaped from Aegospotami.

SURRENDER

Whether the cause of the defeat was as Xenophon or Diodorus narrates, the consequences were still the same. Aegospotami sealed the fate of Athens. Conon headed to Cyprus while the crew of the *Paralus* sailed directly to Athens.[17] And with a rare display of drama, Xenophon reports how the Athenians reacted to the news:

> It was at night that the *Paralus* arrived at Athens. As the news of the disaster was told, one man passed it on to another, and a sound of wailing arose and extended first from Piraeus, then along the Long Walls until it reached the city. That night no one slept. They mourned for the lost, but more still for their own fate. They thought that they themselves would now be dealt with as they had dealt with others—with the Melians, colonists of Sparta, after they had besieged and conquered Melos, with the people of Histiaea, of Scione, of Torone, of Aegina and many other states. (Xen. *Hell.* 2.2.3 tr. R. Warner)

On the next day, the Assembly passed a decree to prepare the city for a siege, which included blocking up all harbors except one, repairing the walls, and stationing guards (*Hell.* 2.2.4). Clearly, the Athenians were desperate. With all their resources spent, they could not now build another fleet. Perhaps they could prevent Sparta from taking their city by force, but their efforts were useless against a blockade.

Following the battle, Lysander returned to the camp at Lampsacus, where it was decided to execute the Athenian prisoners.[18] Next he secured Spartan control of the Black Sea, a necessary step to cut off Athenian grain supply and to insure the success of the blockade. After Byzantium and Chalcedon had expelled the Athenian garrisons and received him, Lysander installed a harmost for those cities. The Athenians stationed in that region did not suffer the same fate as those captured at Aegospotami; Lysander permitted them to return to Athens in order to increase the population of the city and reduce the food supply that much faster (Xen. *Hell.* 2.2.1–2). He next set out for the Aegean, where he met fierce opposition from the people of Samos, who had killed the aristocrats after the battle of Aegospotami and were now refusing to surrender to Sparta. Because of their loyalty, the Athenians later honored them with citizenship.[19] The rest of the cities, however, received Lysander, and he proceeded to interfere in their internal affairs, abolishing democracies, installing Spartan harmosts, and establishing narrow oligarchies comprised of ten local citizens (decarchies). He continued to spare Athenians as he had done at Byzantium and Chalcedon, but he warned them that they would be killed if they were found outside of Athens. And on his way to Athens, he restored the exiled populations to Aegina, Melos, and Scione.[20]

Leaving a contingent of 40 ships in Samos to continue the siege there and 10 ships with Eteonicus to carry out operations in Thrace, Lysander sailed to Athens with 150 ships. Around October he joined Agis, who was already stationed at Decelea, and Pausanias, who was marching to Attica with a full levy of Spartan and Peloponnesian troops (excluding Argos).[21] This was the first time since the sixth century that both Spartan kings took part in the same campaign, no doubt for the purpose of ending the war as quickly as possible (Krentz 1982: 30). Yet despite this massive display of manpower, the Athenians refused to yield, probably because they expected surrender to result in the destruction of the city, the execution of the adult men, and the enslavement of the rest of the population.[22] And so once it had become clear that they could not achieve a quick surrender, Pausanias returned to Sparta and Lysander to Samos, after decreeing the death penalty for blockade-runners. With the remaining land and naval forces, Agis prevented grain from entering the city and waited for the blockade to starve the Athenians into submission.[23] Now it was just a matter of time before Athens surrendered.

Sometime in November, as their supplies started to run out, the Athenians initiated negotiations. They sent ambassadors to Agis to propose a treaty that would make Athens an ally of Sparta but would allow them to keep the Long Walls and the fortifications of Piraeus intact. Agis informed them that they would have to go to Sparta because he did not have the authority to conclude such an agreement. But when the ambassadors reached Sellasia, the ephors refused to allow them to enter Sparta, telling them not to return until they brought acceptable terms of surrender.[24] Next the Spartans proposed a surrender that would have left the democracy intact and would have permitted the Athenians to keep Lemnos, Imbros, and Scyros as long as they agreed to tear down ten stades (approximately six thousand feet) of each of the Long Walls. Fearing that the Spartans intended to enslave them, the Athenians were unwilling to accept even these terms, and when Archestratus spoke in favor of the Spartan demands, he was arrested. The Athenians then passed a decree forbidding anyone from proposing the dismantling of the walls.[25]

Then, according to Xenophon, Theramenes took a central role in the negotiations. He was already a controversial figure for his actions prior to Aegospotami because, like Alcibiades, he switched sides when the political climate changed. He helped orchestrate the overthrow of the democracy in 411, was a leading member of the Four Hundred, and when the oligarchy began to lose favor he took part in establishing the Five Thousand. Then, serving as trierarch during the battle of Arginusae, he shifted responsibility for the failure to recover capsized sailors from himself to the generals, which led to the illegal execution of six of them.[26] According to Lysias, Theramenes was elected general shortly after the Arginusae Affair, but the jury rejected him at his *dokimasia* because they doubted his loyalty to the democracy (13.10). His subsequent involvement in the surrender to Sparta and the rule of the Thirty only added to his notoriety. But since he lost favor with his fellow oligarchs and was executed as a traitor to their cause, there was also room for an apologetic tradition to emerge.

Xenophon's portrayal of Theramenes is mixed.[27] Although he consistently characterizes Theramenes negatively for his conduct before the civil war, he gives a sympathetic depiction of his death at the hands of Critias (esp. Xen. *Hell.* 2.3.52–56). But perhaps this says more about Critias than it does about Theramenes: he was so despicable and so depraved that he made even Theramenes look heroic.[28] Aristotle and Diodorus, on the other hand, are unambiguous. Aristotle praises Theramenes for his good judgment and considers him one of the best Athenian statesmen (*Ath. Pol.* 28.5, 32.2). Diodorus views Theramenes' involvement in the Arginusae Affair positively (13.98–101), fails to mention his role in the negotiations for surrender (13.107), and invents his opposition to the overthrow of the Athenian democracy (14.3.4–7). Modern accounts, not surprisingly, replicate the ancient debate. Some view Theramenes as a self-serving opportunist who justifiably earned the nickname *kothornos* (buskin).[29] Others believe he was motivated by conviction and patriotism, participating in the oligarchic revolutions in order to establish a moderate government and, when the oligarchies became too extreme, opposing them.[30]

For the tradition hostile to Theramenes, his involvement in the peace negotiations is viewed only negatively. According to Xenophon, Theramenes offered to go to Lysander to find out whether the Spartans demanded the demolition of the walls in order to reduce the Athenians to slavery or to establish their good faith.[31] According to Lysias, he promised to negotiate a peace that would not require them to tear down the walls, surrender the ships, or hand over hostages, and he promised to extract an additional (unspecified) concession from the Spartans (13.9). But he refused to tell the Assembly how he would accomplish these goals, alleging that his mission required secrecy.[32] Since the Spartans had just rejected a similar treaty, it seems doubtful that Theramenes would offer to negotiate what he could not deliver. He ran the risk of angering the Athenians if he returned unsuccessful, especially after Archestratus was imprisoned for merely speaking in favor of the Spartan demands. Moreover, secrecy was of little use in the negotiations once the Spartans had already made their demands clear. However, secrecy could help him avoid Athenian wrath if he was planning to renege on his promise and concede what they opposed.[33] For an audience aware of what follows next, Lysias's account is filled with irony. Theramenes stepped forward with a plan that, on the surface, appeared to be helpful to his fellow citizens but in fact provided him the means to betray them.

In any event, the Assembly approved his proposal, and, as Xenophon explains, he stayed with Lysander for three months so that famine would force the Athenians to accept whatever terms were proposed. On his return, he informed the Assembly that Lysander first detained him and then instructed him to go to Sparta because the ephors alone had the authority on such matters. The Assembly then chose Theramenes to lead an embassy of ten to Sparta and made them *autokratores*.[34] Lysias too insists that Theramenes deliberately delayed, but he places Theramenes in Sparta and explicitly imputes negative motives.[35] Theramenes remained in Sparta to compel the Athenians to accept a peace that would require them to dismantle the fortifications of Piraeus and to give up the democracy (Lys. 12.70, 13.11). Although these accounts are clearly tendentious, most historians believe that Theramenes intentionally delayed returning to Athens.[36]

Krentz (1982: 36–41) suggests that Theramenes delayed because he believed the Athenians still had a chance to avoid defeat. If Darius died before the Athenians surrendered, perhaps Artaxerxes would become the new king and change Persian policy. Sparta would then be forced to end its siege and send the fleet to Ionia. And so, as Theramenes waited, hoping that Darius would die, he used his time with the Spartan general to persuade him that generous terms were in Sparta's interest, because then Athens could check Thebes. This suggestion explains why Theramenes needed to negotiate secretly. Green (1991: 9–10), however, has argued convincingly that the Spartans had the most to gain from delay. Why negotiate when they could wait for Athenian supplies to run out and force them to accept whatever terms they demanded? Sparta had already committed to a long siege. Why give in to Athens now that the siege was working and Athens was most helpless? Moreover, Lysander gave the same answer to Theramenes that Agis had given to the first embassy: he did not have the power to negotiate surrender. Why would Lysander have permitted Theramenes to remain in his camp for so long, knowing that he could not arrange a peace, unless he had wanted to stall the negotiations? Perhaps then we should accept the explanation that Theramenes gave to the Assembly and that Xenophon dismisses. Lysander first detained Theramenes, and then, after months of delay, he told Theramenes that he lacked the authority to negotiate.[37]

Some evidence suggests that Lysander wanted Athens destroyed but then changed his mind.[38] Yet none of the sources indicates that Theramenes was responsible. Furthermore, the final terms were not better than those that the Spartans offered even before Theramenes' embassy. Despite the ingenuity of modern accounts that present his mission as a diplomatic victory, the simplest explanation is that he failed to extract any additional concessions. Serving as a messenger of Spartan demands rather than the triumphant broker of peace, he was merely part of the delay that caused the deaths of more Athenians before the city finally capitulated. Still, they elected him to head another embassy, not because he had returned successful but because they no longer expected to gain better terms than those that Sparta had already offered and, after so many months of the blockade, they could no longer hold out. And so this time they instructed Theramenes to go directly to Sparta and gave him and his fellow ambassadors the title *autokratores,* a further indication that they were prepared to accept Spartan demands. For the apologetic tradition that later emerged, Theramenes' failure in the negotiations was a source of embarrassment, which explains why Aristotle and Diodorus omit discussion of his involvement. In the end, it was Sparta that had the final say, and any leniency that Athens received was only because it served Spartan interests.

When Theramenes and his fellow ambassadors arrived at Sellasia, the ephors stopped them just as they had done before. But this time they permitted the Athenians to enter Sparta, because they had come with full power and because they proposed acceptable terms. Since the Athenians were now willing to surrender unconditionally, the surrender could proceed. The ephors called an Assembly, at which some of the allies, especially Corinth and Thebes, spoke in favor of destroying Athens.[39] The Spartans, however, rejected this idea. In Xenophon, they said that they would not enslave a city that had performed great services for the Greeks (*Hell.* 2.2.20). In Justin, the Spartans—although not known for their rhetorical skill—responded with a rather vivid and powerful metaphor: they would not pluck out one of Greece's two eyes (5.8.4). And while these accounts stress Spartan generosity, self-serving motives better explain their decision. Now that Athens was no longer a threat, Sparta had to worry about Corinth and Thebes as possible rivals.[40] And perhaps revenge was not the only reason these two cities wanted Athens destroyed. If spared, Athens would increase Spartan power and potentially provide the Spartans with resources to use against them.

Sparta prevailed. The ephors published a decree spelling out the specific terms, and all that remained was for the commander in the field to determine how many ships the Athenians could keep (Plut. *Lys.* 14.4). Notwithstanding some minor variations in the sources (Table 1),[41] the conditions were

(1) the destruction of the Long Walls and the walls of Piraeus;
(2) the surrender of the fleet, except for twelve ships;
(3) the return of Athenian exiles;
(4) an alliance with Sparta;[42] and
(5) the surrender of all foreign land, except on Lemnos, Imbros, and Scyros.[43]

Aristotle and Diodorus mention an additional clause concerning the ancestral constitution (*patrios politeia*). Shortly after the surrender, the Athenians engaged in a dispute over their constitution, with democrats and oligarchs insisting on particular arrangements by appealing to the *patrios politeia*.[44] And since the other sources do not include this condition, the question arises as to whether Aristotle and Diodorus project the conflict back to the surrender.

TABLE I   SOURCES ON SURRENDER

	Destruction of Long Walls and walls Piraeus	Surrender of fleet	Return of exiles	Alliance with Sparta	Surrender of foreign land	*Patrios politea*
Lysias 13.14, 34	x	x				
Andociedes 3.11–12 (cf. 1.80; 3-31)	x	x[a]	x		x[b]	
Xenophon, *Hellenica* 2.2.20		x[a]	x	x		
Aristotle, *Athenaion Politeia* 34.3						x
Diodorus Siculus 13.07.4	x[c]	x[d]		x	x	x[e]
Plutarch, *Lysander* 14.4–5	x	x	x		x	

[a]Except 12 ships. [b]Except on Lemnos, Imbros, and Scyros. [c]Deadline for Demolition, 14.3.6. [d]Except 10 ships. [e]4.31.2.

Some accept their statements and conclude that the peace had a formal constitutional requirement.[45] Others consider this evidence unreliable and suggest that the treaty might have contained a clause—but one worded differently from that in Aristotle and Diodorus—to guarantee that Athens would remain autonomous (e.g., *kata ta patria, autonomous kata ta patria,* or *politeuesthai ten patrion politeian*).[46] Since none of the authors list all the conditions that historians unanimously accept as authentic (Conditions 1–5), absence of the *patrios politeia* clause in the other sources is insufficient reason to dismiss Aristotle and Diodorus.[47] And yet, if the Spartans had wanted to impose constitutional demands on the Athenians, they could have been more specific. Lysander installed decarchies and harmosts elsewhere. Why not also in Athens? Perhaps the Spartans avoided meddling directly in the internal affairs of Athens because they had already alienated some of their allies by sparing the city; so they inserted this ambiguous phrase either to stir up dissension or to justify subsequent involvement.

Subsequent actions, however, do not suggest that Sparta was reluctant to interfere in Athenian internal affairs. And although Diodorus includes the *patrios politeia* clause, he states that Lysander later returned to Athens after the surrender and justified the overthrow of the democracy only for the failure of the Athenians to demolish the walls according to the schedule (14.3.6). Why didn't Lysander also mention the Athenian failure to implement the constitution provision? (Adeleye 1976: 11). Given that *patrios politeia* is a vague expression, one that at the very least implies autonomy, it is more likely that the clause, if it was part of the treaty, was a concession rather than a demand, which conspirators later used to justify overthrowing the democracy. The Spartans did not demand the dissolution of the democracy as a condition of surrender, but when conspirators sought to overthrow the democracy, they did not hesitate to help.

And so Theramenes and his fellow ambassadors returned to Athens with an agreement that spared the city and its inhabitants but left it crippled and them defenseless. On their arrival, they found the Athenians anxiously waiting for news because many were dying from the famine and they feared that the mission was unsuccessful. Acting as the spokesperson for the embassy, Theramenes recommended to the Assembly that they obey the Spartans and tear down their walls. There were still some who opposed the treaty, but the majority voted in favor of it (*Hell.* 2.2.23). In March 404, less than a year after the destruction of the Athenian fleet at Aegospotami and some twenty-seven years after the beginning of the war, Athens surrendered: "Lysander sailed into the Peiraieus and the exiles returned and they began to raze the walls to the music of pipe-girls, with great enthusiasm, thinking that day to be the beginning of freedom for Greece."[10]

Sparta, however, had already shown in its dealings with its allies as well as with the former members of the Delian League—not to mention with Persia—that such optimism was misplaced. Soon the Athenian civil war would reveal Sparta's willingness to interfere in the internal affairs of Greek cities on the mainland. The surrender marked not the freedom of Greece but the beginning of Spartan hegemony.

RULE OF THE THIRTY

The discrepancies in the sources for the civil war are much more serious than those for the defeat and surrender. Whether the fleet was destroyed as Xenophon or Diodorus describes, the results were still the same: Sparta captured some 170 Athenian triremes and proceeded to blockade Athens. We can view Theramenes' mission to Lysander either as a success or a failure; nonetheless, the Athenians demolished their walls and surrendered their fleet. So for the civil war, Xenophon's sequence of events is incompatible with Aristotle's.[49] Yet which version we adopt ultimately determines how we understand the rule of the Thirty. Many historians have explained why one source should be preferred over another.[50] But once we stop trying to establish a definitive sequence of events, we can find significant agreement in our sources which is worth emphasizing. They are in complete accord about the brutality of the oligarchy: violence created, sustained, and destroyed the regime. But unlike Xenophon, who represents the reign of terror as senseless, and Aristotle, who shows it to be a reaction to internal and external threats, I argue that it was systemic. The Thirty depended upon violence to seize power, to rid the community of the previous political culture, and to block opposition. A historical narrative cannot explain this brutal fact adequately because it links events in a chain that both explicitly and implicitly presents each new event as a development from that which preceded it.

Let us start with Xenophon because he provides a more detailed narrative of the civil war than Aristotle, and, for that matter, his coverage of the Athenian civil war is far greater than for any other event in the *Hellenica* (Dillery 1995: 139, 146). According to Xenophon, thirty citizens were chosen to draft the ancestral laws (*patrioi nomoi*) as soon as the Long Walls and the fortifications of Piraeus had been destroyed (see Table 2).[51] Failing to do so, the Thirty appointed a new Council and new magistrates, and were, in effect, illegally ruling Athens. They brought to trial and executed people who had acted as sycophants under the democracy and who had harmed the *kaloikagothoi*.[52] At first, many Athenians were pleased. Next, as Xenophon explains, the Thirty considered how they could rule Athens as they saw fit. Using as a pretext their need to remove the wicked (*poneroi*) in order to establish their constitution, they persuaded the Spartans to install a garrison in Athens. Once Callibius had arrived with Spartan troops, the Thirty won him over and changed their policy. At this point, Xenophon interrupts his narrative again to explain their motivation: they wanted Callibius to approve of everything that they might do. And now that they had the support of the Spartan commander, they arrested not the *poneroi* but those who would object to being excluded from the oligarchy or who, if they opposed the oligarchy, would be able to gather many supporters (*Hell.* 2.3.11–14). So in Xenophon's account, the Thirty requested the Spartan garrison not in response to growing opposition (their actions up to this point were still popular),

TABLE 2   RULE OF THE THIRTY

Xenophon *Hellenica 2*	Aristotle *Athenaion Politeia*
Selection of the Thirty to draft laws; appointment of a new Council and new magistrates (3.11)	Acceptance of Dracontides' motion on the Thirty; appointment of a new Council and new magistrates (34.3–35.1)
Execution of sycophants (3.12)	Laws abolished; execution of sycophants (35.2–3)
Arrival of Spartan garrison (3.14)	Execution of the elite and seizure of their possessions (35.4)
Execution of potential opponents (3.14)	Theramenes' opposition (36.1)
Break between Critias and Theramenes (3.15)	Enrollment of the Three Thousand. Theramenes speaks out again (36.1–2)
Many unjust executions. Theramenes speaks out again (3.17)	Thrasybulus seizes Phyle (37.1)
Enrollment of the Three Thousand. Disarming of the disfranchised. Escalation of violence (3.18–22)	Trial and execution of Theramenes (37.1)
Trial and execution of Theramenes (3.23–56)	Disarming of the disfranchised (37.2)
Expulsion of disfranchised (4.1)	Escalation of violence (37.2)
Thrasybulus seizes Phyle (4.2). Execution of the Eleusinians (4.8–10)	Arrival of Spartan garrison (37.2)
Battle of Munichia (4.10–22)	Battle of Munichia (38.1)
Replaced by the Ten, the Thirty retreat to Eleusis (4.23–24)	The Ten replace the Thirty (38.1)

Note: Cf. Rhodes (1981: 416–19).

but so they could prevent opposition from emerging as they made the oligarchy even more extreme and further restricted participation.

Here begins the quarrel between Critias and Theramenes. Because the Athenians had exiled him and because he desired revenge, Critias was eager for more killings, whereas Theramenes argued, unsuccessfully, that it was unfair to kill a man who had never harmed the *kaloikagothoi* just because the demos had honored him. The Thirty continued their unjust executions, which sparked opposition and prompted Theramenes to speak out again. He told them that the regime could not survive unless more were allowed to participate. Fearing that the Athenians might rally behind Theramenes, Critias and the rest of the Thirty isolated him. They enrolled three thousand Athenians—a small number, to which Theramenes objected—to participate in their government, and with the help of the Spartan garrison they then disarmed the rest of the population so that, as Xenophon infers, they could do as they pleased. They killed many, some because of personal enmity and others for their property. And in order to pay the Spartan guards for their services, the Thirty decided that each of them should seize one metic. The metics were executed and their property confiscated.[53]

When Theramenes objected, Critias placed him on trial before the Council, but this act did not have the desired effect. Far from siding with Critias, the Council actually applauded after hearing Theramenes defend himself. And so Critias brought in the Spartan guards and declared that he was removing Theramenes' name from the list of the Three Thousand, an act that permitted the Thirty to execute him without the assent of its Council (*Hell.* 2.3.23–51). Here, Xenophon again interrupts the narrative to suggest a motive for their next measures. Believing that with Theramenes gone they could act like tyrants without fear, the Thirty expelled from the city and seized the property of all who were not enrolled in the Three Thousand. Many fled to Piraeus, and some driven from there went next to Megara and Thebes.[54] This event, in Xenophon's sequence, immediately precedes and implicitly propels the democratic resistance (see Table 2). Afterward, the momentum moves in favor of the democratic exiles and the action moves from the city to the periphery and back to the city as the exiles regain control of Athens. Thebes was, after all, where Thrasybulus, who would eventually defeat the oligarchs, set out with his band of democratic exiles. First they seized Phyle, a fortress on the Boeotian border, and next moved on to Piraeus. Then the Thirty retreated to Eleusis, and afterward the democratic resistance reached an agreement with the oligarchs, who were still holding out in Athens.

The effect of Xenophon's narrative is as follows: it presents the Thirty as becoming increasingly violent as their control over Athens grew stronger. They terrorized the community to satisfy their baseless desires. Four times Xenophon states that they silenced opposition and strengthened their power so that they could do as they pleased (*Hell.* 2.3.13, 14, 21, 4.1).

After they removed each obstacle, their measures became more extreme. In addition, Xenophon makes the Thirty responsible for the reign of terror. They were not implementing Spartan policy; rather, they had to gain Callibius's trust so that they could use the Spartan guards to carry out their radical plans.[55] And when Councilmen sided with Theramenes—who objected not for ideological or moral reasons but because he believed the measures would destabilize the regime—they executed him without the Council's assent.[56]

Finally, the exiles did not cause the violence, they responded to it. As the Thirty became more extreme, the democratic resistance gained strength. Ostwald (1986: 483) finds Xenophon's sequence difficult to accept because it relies on motivations that were "too naïve and simplistic to explain why and by what steps the Thirty veered from a reasonable policy that had the approval of respectable upper-class citizens to embark on a program of repressive oligarchy." In Xenophon, only a lust for unbridled power and bloodshed motivated the Thirty. They were, as Dillery (1995: 147) explains, "the paradigm of the bad community that fails."

Let us now turn to Aristotle's narrative (see Table 2). In some instances he provides more information on the internal political maneuverings than Xenophon, but there are also glaring omissions in his compressed account. Unlike Xenophon, Aristotle mentions Lysander's assistance in the establishment of the Thirty, but Critias is completely absent in his account. He also fails to comment on the expulsion of the disfranchised or discuss the seizure of metics and their property. And from his very first reference to Theramenes and his involvement in the civil war, one can see how ready he is to disassociate Theramenes from the Thirty. The Athenians, as Aristotle explains, were divided into three factions as they attempted to implement the *patrios politeia* clause. There were those seeking to preserve the democracy, those aiming at oligarchy, and a group under the leadership of Theramenes which was attempting to restore the ancestral constitution. The latter included Archinus, Anytus, Cleitophon, Phormisius, and many others (*Ath. Pol.* 34.3).

Diodorus mentions a conflict over the ancestral constitution as well, but, in contrast to Aristotle, he states that they were divided into two factions, democrats and oligarchs (14.3.3). And although Lysias mentions a threefold division, he does not depict three separate and distinct political factions but three groups acting in collusion.[57] In Lysias, the oligarchs prevailed because of a three-pronged attack against the democracy, and Theramenes was no better—and for that matter no worse—than the others.

In Aristotle the threefold division has a very different effect. It removes Theramenes from the factionalism that paved the road for the Thirty.[58] The democratic and oligarchic factions interpreted the treaty to suit their own interests, and as result they were responsible for the overthrow of the democracy. Theramenes, on the other hand, sought to protect Athens since he was in favor of the ancestral constitution, which was, by default, in Athenian interest. Striking too is the list of Athenians whom Aristotle mentions in connection with Theramenes: Archinus, Anytus, Cleitophon, and Phormisius. Although Cleitophon added the rider to the decree that established the Four Hundred, none whom Aristotle groups with Theramenes became a member of the Thirty. Archinus, Anytus, and Phormisius even served in the democratic army.[59]

In the end, the oligarchic conspirators prevailed, thanks to Lysander, who arrived with the Peloponnesian fleet and compelled the Athenians to vote in favor of Dracontides' motion to establish the Thirty.[60] But for what purpose? If Diodorus is correct, as is most likely, they were granted the power to act as a provisional government and to draft new laws.[61] Aristotle, however, says only that the Thirty disregarded the other "regulations,"[62] and that they gained control of the city by appointing a new Council of Five Hundred along with other officials, including the Ten to oversee Piraeus, the Eleven to supervise the prisons, and three hundred lash-bearers to serve as their attendants.[63] He does not make it clear whether the Thirty illegally usurped this power or whether the motion legally authorized it (Adeleye 1976: 14). Under the pretense of restoring the ancestral constitution, the Thirty next tore down the laws of Ephialtes and Archestratus in front of the Areopagus and abolished certain Solonian laws.[64] They executed sycophants, and Aristotle, like Xenophon, states that these first measures were favorably received (*Ath. Pol.* 35. 3).

Then the Thirty arrested and executed not the wicked but citizens who were distinguished for their wealth, birth, or reputation. Fearing that they might oppose the oligarchy, the Thirty killed these citizens so that they could rule unimpeded, and also so that they could acquire the possessions of those they killed (Arist. *Ath. Pol.* 35.4). Although Xenophon places the installation of the Spartan garrison before the execution of potential opponents and indicates that the Spartan garrison made the reign of terror possible, there is no intermediary event in Aristotle's account between the execution of sycophants and the execution of potential opponents (Table 2). In Aristotle, the Thirty do not need outside support to escalate the violence.

Next Theramenes objected to this change in policy and recommended to his colleagues that they allow more of the better citizens to participate in the regime. In Xenophon, the Thirty feared that Theramenes might gain popular support; in Aristotle, their fears were realized. Theramenes' suggestions became known to the many who began to take his side, thus forcing the Thirty to act. They agreed to enroll three thousand Athenians, and, as in Xenophon, Theramenes criticized them for restricting participation to such a small number. For a long time, they delayed publishing the list, and every time they were ready to do so they began to add and remove names from it (Arist. *Ath. Pol.* 36.1–2).

Next Aristotle records Thrasybulus's occupation of Phyle, after which follows the execution of Theramenes, the disarming of the disfranchised, escalation of violence, and then the arrival of the Spartan garrison (*Ath. Pol.* 37.1–2). Here the differences between the two narratives are most striking (see Table 3). Whereas Xenophon places the occupation of Phyle after the trial and execution of Theramenes, Aristotle places it before, thus depicting the Thirty as becoming more violent because the opposition was successful. The Spartan garrison was installed not to allow the Thirty to rule as they pleased (as in Xenophon) but in response to Thrasybulus. The Thirty escalated the violence not out of a lust for power or bloodshed but in order to crush the growing opposition. Aristotle's sequence of events also serves to remove Theramenes from the Thirty before they committed some of their more notorious actions. He died before the disarming of the disfranchised, before the escalation of violence, and before the installation of the Spartan garrison.

Some find Aristotle's account unsatisfactory because it places the call for the Spartan garrison too late in the narrative.[65] Since Thrasybulus had successfully seized Phyle, presumably the Thirty were now in a vulnerable position. Although they did not yet have outside reinforcements, if we accept Aristotle, they were still able to execute Theramenes and disarm the disfranchised without any serious opposition.

More problematic, I believe, is how Aristotle exteriorizes the Thirty's violence, locating it outside the regime, as if the reign of terror was merely a response to outside opposition as it widened and grew in popularity. He makes it too easy to take the next step and blame the democratic exiles for the excesses of the Thirty. So for example, Krentz (1982: 130) concludes, "If Thrasybulus had not acted, one suspects that far, far fewer than 1,500 would have died." One could just as easily conclude that fewer citizens would have died if the Thirty had not carried out such repressive acts and had not caused opposition to form. But this too misses

TABLE 3   SEQUENCE OF EVENTS

Xenophon *Hellenica 2*	Aristotle *Athenaion Politeia*
Arrival of Spartan garrison (3.14)	Thrasybulus seizes Phyle (37.1)
Escalation of violence (3.21–22)	Execution of Theramenes (37.1)
Execution of Theramenes (3.23–56)	Escalation of violence (37.2)
Thrasybulus seizes Phyle (4.2)	Arrival of Spartan garrison (37.2)

Note: Adapted from Adeleye (1976: 17).

the point. It is not a question of whether violence caused opposition or vice versa; both positions imply that it was possible for the Thirty to rule Athens peacefully and that the ill effects of their rule were avoidable. Instead, we need to recognize that violence and opposition were inextricably linked to the regime. Once the conspirators had seized control of Athens, they had to secure their rule by reshaping the political culture from a democracy, in which the citizens participated extensively in the affairs of the city, to a narrow oligarchy, which excluded a large share of the citizens from the political sphere and demanded obedience from the rest. This could not be done without eliminating the opposition and silencing the survivors so that they would accept their new political role as subjects. Fear, force, and intimidation provided the Thirty the necessary means for this repoliticization of Athens.[66]

So we should consider the actions of the oligarchs in such a light. First they killed popular leaders. Then, given the restrictive nature of their regime, the violence intensified as the Thirty both created and responded to a growing pool of opposition and potential opposition. They indiscriminately exiled and murdered citizens and metics, political opponents and personal enemies, whether as part of an effort to crush the resistance, increase their revenues, or—as the Athenians would later claim—to satiate their greed. They barred from the city all who were not enrolled in the Three Thousand, thereby disfranchising practically the entire population of Athens. By the end of their rule, which lasted perhaps eight months, the Thirty had killed as many as 1,500 Athenians, not to mention the number of non-Athenians.[67] Although this figure pales in comparison to numbers from the twentieth century, more than 5 percent of the citizenry was killed in less than a year, according to conservative estimates.[68] Most Athenians must have experienced a personal loss, if not of a family member or relative, then of a friend, associate, or neighbor.

So too the Thirty carried out their war against the very institutions of the democracy. As has already been mentioned, the laws before the Areopagus were physically torn down, an act signaling the repeal of Ephialtes' reforms, and Solonian laws the Thirty claimed were ambiguous were abolished.[69] In addition, honors bestowed on *proxenoi* were revoked (Walbank 1978: n. 26, 61, 63, 72, 79).[70] Altering the procedure for trials held in the Council, the Thirty made a mockery of justice: "The Thirty sat on the benches where the *prytaneis* [presiding officials] now sit. Two tables were placed in front of them, and the vote had to be deposited not in urns, but placed openly on these tables with the vote to convict on the further one: so how could any of them be saved? In a word, all who entered the Council for trial were sentenced to death and no one was acquitted, except this man Agoratus. He was released as a 'benefactor'" (Lys. 13.37–38).

Certainly the Thirty used such occasions to force as many as possible to participate in their crimes, but equally important was their open and conspicuous deviation from previous legal procedures. By inverting democratic law, they declared the democracy no longer valid. Such displays showed the Athenians that the old rules no longer applied and warned them of the danger of voicing any dissent. The Thirty were above the law, and questions of justice, fairness, and innocence were no longer relevant. According to Plutarch, they even changed the direction of the Assembly so that the Pnyx no longer faced the sea because they blamed Athenian naval power for the rise of the democracy.[71] They literally turned their backs on the democracy. Some suggest that they may have been attempting to model their constitution after Sparta's.[72] Before the oligarchs seized power, five leaders called "ephors" organized their operations (Lys. 12.43–47). The Thirty were the same size as the Spartan *gerousia* (council), and perhaps they later enrolled three thousand Athenians to match the size of Sparta's population. The Thirty even implemented new laws, but we can only guess how far their plans extended beyond dissolving the democracy and eliminating their enemies.[73]

Still, these actions reveal clearly that it was not enough for the Thirty to eliminate their opposition; they needed to efface the democratic culture deeply embedded within the various religious, social, and political institutions of Athens. Whether they be festivals such as the City Dionysia and the Panathenaia, the public burials of soldiers fallen in war, or the regular meetings of the court, Athenian institutions voiced democratic ideology. Democracy had become central to the life of the community, making it impossible for the Thirty to dissolve the democracy without also drastically altering these institutions. The landscape was also an enemy to their regime, but obliteration of the past was difficult for the Thirty to achieve. With the numerous temples, public buildings, and stelai recording public decisions and memorials of past battles, from the Acropolis to the Agora, from the Kerameikos to Piraeus, there were simply too many visible reminders of the democracy and its empire.

The democracy had become so entrenched that the oligarchy, by its very nature, required brute force, which inevitably escalated and proliferated into all aspects of Athenian life. To focus narrowly on the sequence of a specific event, such as the installation of the Spartan garrison, diminishes this fact. At every stage of the oligarchy—from the outset of the regime to its demise—the oligarchs depended upon violence, which provided them the means to establish and temporarily secure their narrow rule. Violence also fueled opposition and led to the collapse of their regime.

DEMOCRATIC RESISTANCE

According to Diodorus, the Spartans were pleased with the state of affairs because the possibility that Athens would regain its strength was diminished (14.6.1). To further assist the Thirty, they announced a general prohibition against the harboring of Athenian exiles, demanded that they be surrendered to the Thirty no matter where in Greece they were presently residing, and imposed a penalty on those who violated the prohibition.[74] But for whatever momentary advantage Sparta gained from weakening Athens, it came at a high price. Already angry at Sparta for sparing Athens, for dividing the war booty unfairly, and for meddling in Athenian internal affairs, some allies were now ready to break more openly.[75] Megara and Argos ignored the Spartan decree and gave many exiles protection, whereas Thebes brazenly responded with its own decree, making it illegal for any Theban to refuse the exiles aid.[76] Help was also found in Chalcis, Elis, and Oropus at various points in the civil war.[77]

In the winter of 403, Thrasybulus began his campaign to overthrow the Thirty.[78] He and his band of seventy exiles set out from Thebes and seized Phyle. The Thirty responded quickly. First they marched out with the Three Thousand and the cavalry, and they immediately assaulted the fortress but without success.[79] Afterward they attempted to blockade the democratic force, but a snowstorm hampered their operations and they were forced to retreat back to Athens, with the exiles attacking their rear. The Thirty then stationed the Spartan guards and two divisions of the cavalry near Phyle to protect the farms in that region.[80] According to

Xenophon, the democratic force had increased to seven hundred (*Hell.* 2.4.5). Perhaps these reinforcements arrived within a month of Thrasybulus's seizure of Phyle. Still, the democratic army did not include many more than one hundred Athenian citizens; the rest were metics, foreigners, and mercenaries (Krentz 1982: 83–84 with n. 54).

Next, Thrasybulus defeated the Spartan guards in a surprise attack. During the night, he stationed his men outside the enemy's camp in the deme of Acharnae, and, in the morning as the enemy was waking, the democrats attacked, killing over 120 hoplites.[81] With the help of the cavalry and the consent of the Three Thousand, the Thirty then carried out some of their most brutal acts. According to Xenophon, they killed the Eleusinians because they wanted a place to retreat. His description of the massacre deserves to be quoted in full:

> After this the Thirty no longer regarded their position as secure. They now wanted to take over Eleusis for themselves so as to have a place to retire to if that became necessary. So Critias and the rest of the Thirty ordered out the cavalry and went with them to Eleusis, and held a review of the people there with the cavalry all round them. They pretended that they wanted to check the numbers of the population so as to find out what size of a garrison would be needed, and ordered everyone to register his name. As each man registered, he was to go out from the gate in the wall in the direction of the sea. They then posted cavalry detachments on the shore at each side of the gate and, as each man came out, he was seized and bound by the servants in attendance on the cavalry. When they had all been seized the Thirty ordered Lysimachus, the commander of the cavalry, to take them to Athens and hand them over to the Eleven.
>
> Next day they called a meeting in the Odeum of all the hoplites and cavalry whose names were on the list, and Critias rose and spoke as follows: "My friends, we are organizing this government in your interests as well as in our own. It is right that, just as you share in the privileges, so you should share in the dangers. And so, in order that you may have the same hopes and same fears as we have, you must now pass the death sentence on these men of Eleusis who have been captured."
>
> He then showed them where to vote and gave instructions that the votes were to be cast openly and in full view. One half of the Odeum had been filled with Spartan troops, all carrying their arms. It was a way of doing things which caused pleasure to those citizens whose one thought was of their own advantage. (Xen. *Hell.* 2.4.8–10 tr. R. Warner)

Elsewhere, Xenophon emphasizes important events of the civil war through extended speeches, as in the trial of Theramenes. Because he relies primarily on narrative to recount the massacre of the Eleusinians and because he gives a thorough, step-by-step description of the very procedure that the Thirty used, his reliability is more certain here.[82] According to Diodorus, the Thirty killed not only the Eleusinians but also the Salaminians (cf. Lys. 12.52, 13.44). And, in contrast to Xenophon, Diodorus places these killings prior to the Battle of Acharnae and asserts that the Thirty committed them because they feared that the communities were siding with the exiles (14.32.4). Both, however, agree that the victories of the democratic army caused the oligarchy to unravel.

However, only a few Athenians had joined the democratic resistance, and, although the exiles remained outnumbered by the oligarchic forces, these victories emboldened them. With an army of one thousand, Thrasybulus set out during the night for Piraeus, where his daring continued to pay off.[83] When they reached Piraeus, the Thirty sent out the Spartan garrison as well as their own cavalry and hoplites. Since they lacked the numbers to man the walls and prevent the oligarchic forces from entering the port, the exiles retreated to the hill of Munichia. There they were joined by residents of Piraeus who served as light-armed troops. Then, in a set battle, the exiles delivered a crushing defeat to the oligarchs. Critias fell, the oligarchic forces retreated, and the democrats now firmly controlled Piraeus.[84] It is impossible to determine how many volunteered, but the sources indicate that the resistance had a wide-ranging appeal. Citizens, metics, foreigners, and even slaves joined the ranks.[85] Lysias, for example, later claimed that he provided the exiles three hundred mercenaries, two hundred shields, and two thousand drachmas, perhaps even when they were still at Phyle.[86]

Immediately following the capture of Piraeus, the Three Thousand deposed the Thirty, who withdrew to Eleusis, and they elected the Ten, who ruled Athens for a few months (Xen. *Hell.* 2.4.23–24). Although Aristotle (*Ath. Pol.* 38.1) and Diodorus (14.33.5) state that the Ten continued the war against the wishes of the Three Thousand, who were eager to reconcile with the democratic faction (cf. Lys. 12.54, 92–94), their claims lack credibility.[87] They require us to believe that the Ten duped the Three Thousand into thinking that they had elected moderates so that once in power the Ten could contravene their instructions. The suggestion of Cloché (1916) is more economical: despite some minor dissent within the ranks, the Three Thousand continued to support the oligarchy and remained committed to the war until Pausanias interceded. The men of the city did not remove the Thirty and elect the Ten because they had a sudden change of heart about the war; rather, they removed the Thirty because of their failure to defeat the democrats, and they elected the Ten because they thought the war effort might be more successful under new leadership.

Once in power, the Ten pursued an aggressive policy against the exiles. They sent out the cavalry to protect the countryside from democratic incursions and to prevent the men of Piraeus from foraging for food. During a patrol, they killed some people of Aexone who were heading to their farms. In response, the men of Piraeus killed Callistratus, a cavalryman whom they had captured, and, as they began preparations to take the city by force, the men of the city and the Thirty in Eleusis sent separate envoys to Sparta to request additional aid (Xen. *Hell.* 2.4.26–28).[88] Meanwhile the Ten killed Demaretus as part of their effort to check dissension within the city (Arist. *Ath. Pol.* 38.2). The Spartans agreed to loan the oligarchs one hundred talents, and Lysander marched to Athens with a Peloponnesian army, where his brother, Libys, met him with the fleet in order to blockade Piraeus.

Then, as the blockade was beginning to show signs of success, with the men of Piraeus desperate and the men of the city gaining confidence, Pausanias arrived with additional troops. He first led his soldiers into battle against the democratic army, but after a minor victory he reversed Spartan policy and initiated negotiations. He had the men of Piraeus send envoys to Sparta together with some private individuals from the city, Cephisophon and Meletus. When the Ten learned of these developments, they sent their own envoys to Sparta to insist that the democrats surrender Piraeus and Munichia. The Spartan Assembly, however, decided to send a commission to Athens; this commission worked with Pausanias to arrange a peace between the two factions. After they had reached an agreement, the civil war was formally concluded on 12 Boedromion (October 403) as Thrasybulus led the men of Piraeus in a solemn procession to the Acropolis, thus symbolically declaring the restoration of the democracy.[89]

Although the Athenians later praised the men of Piraeus for the generous terms of reconciliation (see Chapter 2), pressure from Sparta better explains why they agreed to a peace that protected oligarchs and oligarchic sympathizers from prosecution for their conduct during the civil war.[90] As we have seen, Sparta's meddling in Athenian affairs had already angered some of its allies. Now matters were becoming even worse. The Boeotians and Corinthians refused to join in Pausanias's cam-

paign (Xen. *Hell.* 2.4.30), and further intervention threatened to antago-
nize still other allies. By reconciling the warring factions, Pausanias not
only (temporarily) checked dissension within the Peloponnesian League
but also insured that Athens would remain too divided to threaten Spartan hegemony. Even though Pausanias had signaled to the factions his
willingness to accommodate the democrats, envoys from the Ten came
to Sparta demanding that the democrats surrender their strongholds.
Still, the Ten had no choice but to agree to the restoration of the democracy, because they were utterly dependent upon Sparta for assistance.
Likewise, the men of Piraeus could not demand that the oligarchs receive
harsher treatment. If they refused to accept the agreement, Sparta had
sufficient manpower in place to crush them. So in the autumn of 403,
after thirteen months of bloodshed, the two factions were forced to
accept a peace that was not their own. Yet somehow the reconciliation
was remarkably peaceful.

2 ʡ RESTORATION OF THE DEMOCRACY

It is agreed that there are three types of government in the world: tyranny, oligarchy, and democracy. Tyrannies and oligarchies are governed according to the tempers of the rulers, but democracies according to established laws. And be assured, men of Athens, that in a democracy the laws protect the body of the citizen and the constitution of the city, whereas suspicion and armed guards protect tyrants and oligarchs. Oligarchs and any who have a government based upon inequality must, therefore, guard against those who attempt revolution by the law of force. But you, who have a government based upon equality and law, must guard against those whose words or lives violate the laws. Hence, you will only be strong when you have good laws and the revolutionary attempts of lawless men have ceased.

AESCH. I.4–5

After the restoration of the democracy, the Athenians engaged in a flurry of legislative activity, of which the new procedures for enacting laws had perhaps the greatest long-term impact on the shape of the democracy. But for our purposes, what appears most striking is how such measures became a way for the Athenians to deny that the civil war had lasting repercussions, to break from the period of civil unrest, and to redefine the community as one that was again founded on law and democracy. It is not coincidental that they began searching for the laws of Draco and Solon immediately after the Four Hundred and completed the compilation after the Thirty. The call for Athenians to adhere to the laws and to restore the ancestral constitution (*patrios politeia*) was part of a concerted and contested effort to reclaim the city.

Certainly, the violence carried out by the Thirty gave the Athenians a newfound respect for rules, procedures, and laws. And, when examined collectively, the laws and decrees enacted after the civil war suggest that moderation and restraint prevailed. On the other hand, when examined individually, these measures clearly reveal the different lessons that the Athenians had learned from the civil war and their still serious disagreements that were capable of disrupting the peace. Even as a consensus was forming over the need to avoid civil war and to prevent oligarchic conspirators from overthrowing the democracy, the Athenians had different views about how they could best prevent civil war, who should be allowed full membership in the community, and what direction the democracy should take. The agreement Pausanias worked out between the warring factions was merely the first step in reconciliation, and, as subsequent measures reveal, it was not free from division.

THE RECONCILIATION AGREEMENT

As with the events of the civil war, it is difficult to reconstruct the terms of the agreement. None of the sources details all of the provisions. The orators tend either to allude generally to the reconciliation or to offer tendentious interpretations, claiming that its provisions applied even when they did not fall within the parameters of their cases. While they amply attest to the high regard in which the Athenians held the agreement, they hinder those attempting to determine its purpose. Even Aristotle, who provides the most extended discussion, fails to mention all of the agreement's clauses. He only briefly refers to the amnesty, even though it was in the end the most important provision, and his language is sometimes vague, ambiguous, and misleading. Perhaps most surprising is Aristotle's failure to mention the provision for the restoration of the democracy. But, in all fairness, many of the ambiguities are not the fault of Aristotle but derive from either his sources or the original language of the agreement (Rhodes 1981: 420, 463–64). These are, however, still serious obstacles in our attempt to understand why the reconciliation succeeded if it hinged on the terms of the agreement. But once we recognize that the reconciliation was an ongoing process and that Athenian understanding of the agreement changed and evolved over time, the intent of the drafters matters less than how Athenians subsequently interpreted and applied its terms.

Most of the agreement concerns the settlement of Eleusis by the oligarchs and their supporters with only two clauses specifying the terms of amnesty (Arist. *Ath. Pol.* 39.1–6). This imbalance is troubling if the main purpose of the agreement was to reconcile the democrats with the oligarchs. On the other hand, the establishment of two separate and autonomous communities within Attica may have been its main purpose. The men of the city who did not want to live in Athens—whether because they did not trust the men of Piraeus to adhere to their oaths or because they did not want to share power with the democrats—were permitted to settle in Eleusis, where they possessed full civic rights, had full control over their own revenues, and were not subject to the legislation of the restored democracy. The temple of Eleusis belonged to both communities, but travel between Athens and Eleusis was permitted only during the celebration of the mysteries. Both communities were required to contribute funds to the Spartan alliance, and they were individually responsible for their war debts. In addition, the new settlers had the right to purchase property in Eleusis. If the current owner did not find a buyer's offer acceptable, the owner and buyer were each to select three appraisers, who would determine a fair price. The current residents of Eleusis could remain provided that the new settlers were willing to accept them into the community.

The agreement also specified a time frame for emigration to Eleusis. Those who stayed in Athens during the civil war had ten days after the peace was sworn to register and then ten more days to take up residence in Eleusis. Those who were abroad had the same number of days to register and take up residence upon their return. Finally, anyone who settled in Eleusis could return to Athens and hold office after registering for residence in the city. Aristotle fails to explain why the settlers retained this right or how the registration took place, but presumably they could return to Athens because they remained Athenian citizens even though Eleusis was otherwise a separate community.[1]

It is also revealing that the agreement took the form not of a law or a decree but a treaty, the terms of which the Athenians swore to adhere to.[2] Since laws and decrees concern domestic affairs and treaties regulate relations between cities, the status of the agreement as a treaty reveals as much as its content. The war was over, but the Athenians would continue to be divided, almost as though they were from two different cities. If the men of the city had departed from Athens in large numbers, the main concern would have been keeping the peace between Athens and Eleusis.

But, after swearing their oaths, many delayed registering for residence in Eleusis. Archinus took advantage of this opportunity and cut short the deadline in order to force many of them to stay in Athens (Arist. *Ath. Pol.* 40.1). Although he violated the agreement, Aristotle praises him for insuring that more from the city party would remain in Athens (*Ath. Pol.* 40.2), thereby strengthening their position in the restored democracy. Archinus made the restored democracy more conservative than it might otherwise have been and potentially more internally divisive, but he also made Athens more capable of responding to external threats because of the additional population. So, in 401/0, when the democrats heard that the oligarchs were hiring mercenaries, they marched out against Eleusis and destroyed the stronghold. The survivors were permitted to return to Athens, and the amnesty was extended to them.[3] Thereafter, the only clauses that still mattered concerned reconciliation. Ironically, a treaty—which many ancient and modern commentators have praised for peacefully ending the civil war—is called an agreement of reconciliation because the Athenians could not live peacefully in two separate communities as mandated by that very same treaty.

Unlike Eleusis, which was intended to be a safe haven for the oligarchs and which was granted complete autonomy in its internal affairs, Athens was delivered over to the men of Piraeus on the condition that they share power with the men of the city. The agreement therefore imposed restrictions on those living in Athens for the prosecution of offenses committed during the civil war: "Suits of murder [*dikai phonou*] are to be according to the ancestral laws if someone killed or wounded another by his own hands [*autocheiria*]. But it is not permitted for anyone to remember the wrongs [*me mnesikakein*] of another which happened in the past except in the case of the Thirty, the Ten, the Eleven, and the governors of Piraeus,[4] and not even in their case if they render account [*euthyna*]."[5] This passage is notoriously difficult to interpret. The clause on homicide (*dikai phonou*) appears unconnected to the amnesty (*me mnesikakein*) mentioned in the following sentence, but as Cloché (1915: 259–61) and Bonner (1924) have shown, it must be an exception to the amnesty. The reference to wounding in a clause on homicide is also unclear unless it concerns wounding with the intent to kill (*traumatos ek pronoias*), because that was the only form of wounding which was tried by the Areopagus and subject to the same procedure as homicide.[6] Simply, the amnesty granted impunity for all wrongs except murder and attempted murder by one's own hands, and it was extended to all Athenians, even those in the innermost circle of the oligarchy after rendering account.

The agreement also specified that movable property confiscated during the civil war should be returned to the original owner, provided it was unsold. If sold, it remained with the purchaser. Immovable property, whether sold or unsold, was returned to the owner.[7] The Council was prohibited from receiving the summary warrant or arrest (*endeixis* or *apagoge*) of any individual except in the case of exiles who illegally returned to Athens (And. 1.91). Even the Thirty and the other officials of the oligarchy could gain residency in Athens and participate in the amnesty after rendering account (*euthyna*) of their past actions. The governors of

Piraeus were to render account before a court of men who held property in Piraeus, and the Thirty, the Eleven, and the Ten were to do so before a court of men who held property in the city.[8] The property qualification provides proof that the civil war sparked class tensions. Certainly, wealthy and socially prominent Athenians supported the democrats and opposed the Thirty, but none of the *thetes* participated in the oligarchy. Unless they were considered more strident in their opposition and less likely to give the oligarchs a sympathetic hearing, there would have been no reason to prohibit them from serving on the review boards.[9] Apparently, this arrangement worked. Rhinon, a member of the Ten, passed his *euthyna* along with his associates, and it is possible that even some of the Thirty were also successful.[10]

Presumably, the purpose of the amnesty was to protect those who were complicit in the crimes of the Thirty by prohibiting prosecution for planning murder (*bouleusis phonou*).[11] The Thirty routinely called upon others to arrest, denounce, and condemn their victims.[12] But for the most part, the Eleven alone carried out the orders of execution. If *autocheiria* was interpreted literally, it is conceivable that only the officials of the oligarchy could have been convicted of murder or attempted murder by their own hands.[13] The exception to the amnesty would then be inconsequential since the Thirty, the Eleven, the Ten, and the governors of Piraeus were already excluded from the amnesty unless they passed their *euthynai*. If, on the other hand, *autocheiria* was interpreted loosely, this provision could conceivably apply to any person who had assisted the Thirty, including practically to every citizen enrolled in the Three Thousand. Moreover, the agreement stated only that there was an amnesty for past crimes; it did not indicate whether crimes committed before the Thirty were also covered. The Athenians, for example, enacted the decree of Patrocleides in 405 as part of an attempt to unify the city after the defeat at Aegospotami. The decree restored citizenship rights to some who had been disfranchised, but it did not allow the return of exiles who had been charged with murder or other serious crimes (And. 1.77–79). Were these exiles allowed to return in 403 under the terms of amnesty? (Loening 1987: 40–41). Given that the agreement gave priority to the concerns of the Thirty and their supporters, it is unlikely that it intended to answer this question.

The Athenians, however, recognized that the agreement had its limitations and instituted additional measures. They passed the law of Diocles, which stated that all laws passed either before or after the civil war were valid.[14] Judicial decisions delivered before the civil war were also valid, but those given under the Thirty were null and void (Dem. 24.56–57). Thus, the Athenians made it clear that the amnesty did not annul penalties meted out before the civil war. The decree of Patrocleides remained in force, and those exiled before the civil war could not return unless formally pardoned. And despite Andocides' specious arguments suggesting otherwise (1.81–88), the law of Diocles did not specify whether new charges could be lodged for offenses committed before the civil war or whether the accused were exempt from prosecution under the terms of the amnesty.

Nevertheless, the Athenians enacted a safeguard to discourage suits in violation of the reconciliation, which at least partially addressed this problem. If a defendant believed that the charge lodged against him was illegal, he could present a *paragraphe* to the appropriate magistrate. The original suit was suspended, and a court heard the arguments of the defendant and the prosecutor in order to decide whether the original charge was lawful. If the court decided that the charge was illegal, the suit was dropped; if not, the prosecutor was permitted to pursue his original suit. The losing party of the *paragraphe* was required to pay a penalty of one-sixth of the sum in dispute.[15] Although the men of the city gained the most from this procedure, it neither prohibited victims of the Thirty from seeking satisfaction through the courts nor insured that the courts would favor the men of the city. And since each jury was free to interpret the amnesty as it saw fit and prosecutors had many different ways of pursuing complaints, the men of the city were still vulnerable to prosecution (see Chapter 3).

Certainly, these measures answered immediate questions concerning the legality of recent laws and judicial decisions which the agreement failed to resolve, but they also symbolically declared the acts of the democracy as lawful in contradistinction to those of the oligarchy. They linked the newly restored democracy to the previous democracy and excised the oligarchy from Athenian past and future. Just as the Thirty subverted Athenian law and drained it of its authorizing force by placing opponents on trial before juries whose verdicts were a foregone conclusion, the democrats reestablished the authority of the democracy by divorcing the courts from illegal measures and mock trials.

While the *paragraphe* gave the former supporters of the Thirty protection and made it more difficult for the victims of the oligarchs to gain satisfaction, it also forced the men of the city to rely on the laws of the democracy for this protection. Thus, they became implicated in promoting democracy and invalidating oligarchy. Under the oligarchy they had helped the Thirty undermine the laws; now, under the restored democracy, they depended upon the laws for their own safety. On the whole, the reconciliation agreement, together with these subsequent measures, provided the men of the city with the most tangible benefits and demanded from the men of Piraeus the most concessions. But, by making such concessions, the democrats increased their stockpile of ideological weapons to use in their campaign to rid the community of the ill effects of the oligarchy. The rule of the Thirty gave the Athenians only negative reasons to shun oligarchy. The measures enacted after the reconciliation gave them positive proof of the benefits of democracy.

THE LAW REFORMS

The law reforms illustrate perhaps most dramatically the importance of this discourse for defining the restored democracy and distancing it from the Thirty. The purpose and the extent of these reforms, however, have long been disputed, and the scholarly debate continues to become more complex. While I will not attempt to resolve some of the more technical questions (such as the location where the work of the *anagrapheis* was displayed), I will show how the compilation of Athenian laws neutralized oligarchic criticisms and how the creation of boards of *nomothetai* in 403 strengthened the democracy. In order to understand the impulse for these revisions, we will first need to explore the debate over the ancestral constitution: (1) why oligarchic conspirators could call into question the democracy in 411 and 404 and (2) why the Athenians could not readily locate their constitution. Then we will consider the work of the *anagrapheis*: (1) which laws were included in their compilation and (2) whether their compilation was part of a comprehensive review of the laws.

In 411, oligarchic conspirators overthrew the democracy by first killing key opponents, then luring the Athenians with promises of a Persian alliance, and finally disguising the illegality of their plans with specious appeals to the ancestral constitution.[16] Pythodorus proposed a motion to elect a committee with the power to prepare whatever motions it believed would serve the interests of the city.[17] Then, to provide the committee further respectability, Cleitophon added a rider that gave it the additional task of searching for the ancestral laws (*patrioi nomoi*) that Cleisthenes had enacted when he established the democracy.[18] Whether or not he intended to restore the Cleisthenic constitution, Cleitophon used this appeal to justify as well as mask conservative reforms that would turn back the clock on the democracy.[19]

The motions of Pythodorus and Cleitophon were approved, and the next Assembly was held outside the walls of Athens at Colonus to discourage attendance by those not involved in the conspiracy.[20] The committee first brought forward a motion to abolish the law against illegal proposals (*graphe paranomon*) so that no one could prevent the Assembly from voting on its revolutionary proposal. After the acceptance of the motion, Pisander then brought forward a proposal that called for the establishment of the Four Hundred with full power to govern as they deemed best, and in one swift move the Assembly approved the proposal and voted the democracy out of existence. The Four Hundred then dissolved the Assembly, and with assistance from armed guards they disbanded the Council.[21]

Although the democracy was restored in 410, the Athenians were concerned about the ease with which the conspirators had carried out their coup. The assassination of democratic leaders and the absence of the most loyal citizens at the fateful meeting of the Assembly outside the city's walls could help them rationalize the oligarchic victory. Yet legal procedures designed to protect the democracy when it was most vulnerable had been to no avail, and equally disturbing were the doubts that the oligarchs had raised about the validity of the existing constitution. Less than a decade later, the Thirty would follow in the path of the Four Hundred and declare their intention to restore the ancestral constitution. The democracy was vulnerable to such criticism for two reasons.

First, Athens had suffered crippling military defeats in 411 and 404, and its future was uncertain. It was easy for critics to fault the present generation and point to the conduct of their forefathers for a solution. Their ancestors, after all, had twice stopped Persian invasions, built an empire, and kept Sparta at bay. If Athens was no longer victorious, it was because the present generation lacked its ancestors' arete (Dover 1974: 107–8). Although in its narrow sense *politeia* can be translated into English as "constitution," it also has a broader sense, which includes "habits," "way of life," and "spirit of the citizenry."[22] The conspirators were therefore suggesting that the Athenians could regain the spirit of their ancestors, which had led to the great victories of the past and which would make them victorious again, if they restored the *politeia* in its narrow sense. They could regain the military prowess of the previous generations if first they restored the ancestral ways for managing the affairs of the city.

Second and more important, a *politeia* (in its narrow sense) existed in Athens neither as a single document nor even as a collection of documents assembled in one location for the expressed purpose of providing Athenians access to information concerning constitutional arrangements. Scattered throughout Attica, laws and decrees were displayed in monumental form, inscribed in wood and stone on *axones, kyrbeis,* and *stelai,* some of which concerned the various political institutions and magistracies. But they did not amount to a constitution.[23]

Moreover, the Athenians did not establish a central archive until the end of the fifth century, and they did so as a direct consequence of the debate over the ancestral constitution.[24] This failure to establish a central archive explains why Cleitophon proposed that the Athenians "search for" the laws of Cleisthenes. The laws were not readily accessible, and it required some work to find them.[25] But until defeat there was no reason for the Athenians to be concerned that they were deviating from ancestral laws. Continual success gave them substantial proof that they were following in the path of their ancestors. After the Sicilian expedition, however, when the democracy was vulnerable to criticism for the recent catastrophe, those who opposed the conspirators' ploys had no way to prove them wrong. They could neither point to recent successes nor readily locate Cleisthenic laws.

So when the democracy was restored in 410, the Athenians appointed a board of *anagrapheis* (transcribers) to "write up" the laws of Solon, and in 399 they finally completed their mission after a brief hiatus during the civil war of 404–3.[26] In order to neutralize (or rather, democratize) appeals to the ancestral constitution, the Athenians intended to determine once and for all which laws they inherited from their ancestors. But the extent of this inquiry remains highly contested for two reasons.

First, which laws did the Athenians consider Solonian? Some of the legislation that the *anagrapheis* collected and inscribed in their first term (410–404) included (1) Draco's homicide law on a stele before the Stoa Basileios (*IG* I³ 104.4–7), (2) laws concerning the Council of Five Hundred (*IG* I³ 105), which therefore postdate Solon, (3) a trierarchic law, (4) some tax laws, and (5) a sacrificial calendar (*IG* I³ 236–41).[27] The sacrificial calendar was erased, perhaps by the Thirty, but it is also possible that it was erased after the reconciliation to make room for a revised version prepared by the *anagrapheis* in their second term (403–399).[28] These fragments must represent only a small fraction of their work, but they show that it was quite extensive. Various suggestions have been advanced to explain why their mission extended beyond the laws of Solon, but the most convincing is that the Athenians simply called all their currently valid laws "Solonian."[29]

Orators frequently portrayed Solon as the founder of the democracy, attributing to him constitutional reforms, which were the hallmark of the fourth-century democracy. Some revisions, such as the creation of boards of the *nomothetai*, were quite recent, but still the Athenians referred to them as Solon's. And, except for the homicide law of Draco, any law could be attributed to Solon, regardless of its date.[30] In 400, for example, Andocides attributed to Solon the decree of Demophantus even though it was passed only a decade before his trial and the version that he had read to the court clearly specified that Demophantus, not Solon, had proposed the motion (1.95–96). It will not suffice to suggest that Andocides referred to the decree as Solon's because it was included in the revised Solonian code, which the *anagrapheis* inscribed on a stele before the Stoa Basileios. If this were the case, Andocides would have better served his interests by quoting from that stele rather than from the original one, which stood in front of the Council (Hansen 1990a: 66–67).

When the democracy was restored in 403, the decree of Teisamenus was passed, which established procedures for making new laws and speci-fied that the laws of Draco and Solon were to be enforced.[31] Rather than view the decree as tacitly referring to the work of the *anagrapheis,* we should recognize that it was first and foremost referring to all the laws of the democracy that were in force before the Thirty seized control of Athens.[32] Shortly afterward, the Athenians enacted the law of Diocles, which specified that all laws passed under the democracy, whether be-fore, during, or after the archonship of Eucleides (403 / 2), were valid. The law of Diocles did not extend the scope of legislation that would now be valid under the restored democracy, nor did it refer to different legislation from that specified by the decree of Teisamenus; rather, it merely re-affirmed this decree.[33]

We need not look far for a reason for the invention of this tradition about Solon. In 411, the oligarchs had accused the Athenians of deviating from the ancestral laws. So in 410, the democrats responded by electing a board of *anagrapheis* to write up all the laws that were valid before the Four Hundred had seized power, but they labeled them the laws of Solon. In many ways, this discourse on the ancient lawgiver operated similarly to the myth of autochthony. Just as the Athenians justified the extensive inclusion of all citizens in political affairs by imagining the demos to be autochthonous, as having always lived in Athens, they situated recent legislation in their past to shield it from present controversies.[34] Under the rubric of Solon, they collapsed the time between the past and present, rendered contemporary legislation ancestral, and superimposed recent victories on Athenian history.[35]

For our purposes, it is irrelevant whether the Athenians believed these claims or whether they knew that the claims were false and were engaging in an elaborate fiction, suspending disbelief to show their support for the democracy and to diffuse the impact of recent criticism.[36] The law reforms were an important stage in the tradition of Solon which continued to develop and grow in the fourth century.[37] Most important is how contemporary laws became Solonian so that the democracy could become the ancestral constitution and critics could not turn to the past to challenge its validity. The future of the democracy, as the law reforms demonstrate, depended upon paving a path for it in the past.

Given their ideological significance, one would expect the reforms to have had a dramatic impact on the shape of Athenian law, which brings us to the second area of contention concerning the *anagrapheis*. Scholars traditionally believed that the work of the *anagrapheis* was part of a comprehensive review of Athenian law for the express purpose of creating a new legal code to be posted on a wall before the Stoa Basileios for permanent display.[38] But the evidence for such a review and display depends entirely on a passage in Andocides which has long been recognized to be misleading.[39] According to Andocides, the Athenians discovered upon the restoration of the democracy in 403 that, under many of the laws of Draco and Solon, citizens could be held liable for their previous actions. They therefore passed the decree of Teisamenus, which called for a review (*dokimasia*) of all the laws; the approved laws were then posted on a wall before the stoa.[40] But the wording of the decree does not agree with Andocides' interpretation. It does not state that all laws must be reviewed; rather, it calls for the review of only additional laws (And. 1.83–84). Until recently it was thought that Andocides was only incorrect to imply that the review was begun anew in 403.[41] Rather than make a claim the jury would surely recognize as false, Andocides confuses the legislative activity of 410–404 with that of 403. He was correct to speak of a review and codification of the laws, but he incorrectly associated these with the decree of Teisamenus in order to persuade the jury that he was immune from prosecution. Certainly, he was more likely to be persuasive if he relied on deception and misleading statements rather than outright lies. The advantage of this interpretation is that it prevents us from accusing either Andocides of poor arguments or the jury of gullibility.

Robertson (1990), however, doubts that a comprehensive revision of

Athenian laws took place even in the first term of the *anagrapheis* (410–404). The problem is that our evidence for their first term depends mostly on Lysias, who insists that the *anagrapheis* had only secretarial responsibilities.[42] And although Andocides speaks of reforms, he does so only for 403, and, what is worse, he is clearly incorrect. One therefore cannot use him as evidence for reforms in the first term. And since the decree of Teisamenus concerns procedures for passing additional legislation, Robertson (1990: 46–52) further argues that the stoa referred to in the decree must be intended not for the permanent display of all laws (as was previously believed) but for the temporary display of additional laws under consideration. Thus, for Robertson, evidence is lacking for both a comprehensive review and a permanent display of the laws. Instead, he argues that the *anagrapheis* were simply instructed to make copies of existing Athenian laws for the new central archive.

Much of his interpretation is quite convincing, but still the evidence is so incomplete that many questions cannot be answered, making it difficult to reach such a definitive conclusion. The fragments of Draco's homicide law, along with the other inscriptions already discussed, reveal that at least some of laws that the *anagrapheis* collected were published on stone. It is quite possible that they were responsible for inscribing these laws as part of a larger project to publish all currently valid laws for permanent display, which was left unfinished when the Thirty seized power.[43] Doubt can easily be cast on the evidence for publication, but for that matter it is uncertain even whether the *anagrapheis* made copies for the new archive. The only proof that we have to link their work with the new archive is the date that it was established, but even that date is disputable.[44]

In the end, it does not really matter whether the *anagrapheis* compiled laws for publication on stone or for the central archive. We know that they collected currently valid laws in order to dispel doubts about the existing constitution and that this compilation was part of an attempt to make the laws easier to locate. And although, as Robertson rightly points out, the evidence for a comprehensive review of the laws is lacking, it is possible that the Athenians revised some of the laws that the *anagrapheis* bought to their attention. Andocides, then, was not outright lying when he spoke of law reforms; rather, he was distorting, exaggerating, and misdating previous legislative activity.[45] In any event, the aftermath of the Four Hundred shows us that Athenian concern about the state of their laws sparked some new legal initiatives.

In the aftermath of the Thirty, similar concerns motivated the Athenians to embark on more significant reforms. The power to implement, revise, and repeal laws (*nomoi*) was transferred from the Assembly to newly created boards called the *nomothetai,* and the Assembly could now only enact decrees (*psephismata*). *Nomoi* were general and permanent rules, and *psephismata* were measures that were either temporary or limited to specific individuals. The *nomothetai* could not initiate proceedings; a motion to implement, revise, or repeal a law was first heard in the Assembly, and only if approved was it then submitted to the *nomothetai* for ratification.[46] In effect, the *nomothetai* had only the power to reject motions passed in the Assembly.[47] Many historians believe that these reforms did not significantly alter the democracy and emphasize the structural continuity from the fifth to the fourth century.[48]

Hansen, in particular, has challenged this position, suggesting that these reforms shifted "sovereignty" from the Assembly to the courts. In contrast to the radical democracy of the fifth century, in which the people ruled through the Assembly, the democracy of the fourth century was ruled by laws and was thus more moderate.[49] Hansen further argues that the reforms were in response to the excesses of the fifth-century democracy: "After the two oligarchic revolutions of 411 and 404 the Athenians restored democracy in 403 / 2; but it was not Periklean democracy that they wanted to return to. Responsibility for the total defeat in the Peloponnesian War was largely laid at the door of the 'demagogues', who, by their misuse of the radical-democratic constitution, had induced the people to adopt false policies."[50] Others also consider the law reforms a defining moment for Athens. Ostwald (1986: 524) ends his book on the Athenian democracy by asserting, "Thus the democracy achieved stability, consistency, and continuity when the higher sovereignty of *nomos* limited the sovereignty of the people." Sealey (1982: 302) goes further: "The Athenians achieved something more valuable and more fundamental than democracy. They achieved the rule of law."

But since many of the same people served as *nomothetai* as attended the Assembly, it is doubtful that this new procedure was a significant brake on the power of the demos.[51] Rather than view these reforms as a conservative development designed to curb democratic excesses, we need to look for an other explanation. Twice oligarchs overthrew the democracy by pressuring the Assembly to vote itself out of existence. The *nomothetai* made it nearly impossible to subvert the democracy from within democratic institutions.[52] Just as litigants appealing to the jurors' desire for stability proclaimed law the solution to the civil war (see Part II), so the *nomothetai* assured the Athenians that the democracy was securely in place.

Doubtless, those who were concerned about past democratic excesses would have welcomed this reform, but it is unlikely that these were the most pressing concerns after all that the oligarchs had done. Rather, the Athenians embarked on law reforms primarily as a response to the Thirty in order to prevent future oligarchic revolutions, and in so doing they established further proof of the connection between democracy and law. Certainly the reforms provided important safeguards for the community, but they were also a significant ideological victory, allowing the Athenians to declare the rule of law to be the defining characteristic of democracy (see epigraph of this chapter). Here I part company with those who emphasize continuity, and I agree with Hansen and Ostwald that 403 was a watershed year for Athens, but not because institutional arrangements were drastically reconfigured; rather, it was the beginning of an age that the Athenians marked as substantially different from the preceding period. Through legislation, they redefined the community as one that was once again founded upon law and democracy, and, as the following chapters will show, this was only one of the many ways that the Athenians distanced themselves from the Thirty.

PARTISAN MEASURES

The law reforms probably sparked little controversy, since they provided important safeguards for all Athenians, regardless of their political views. But legislation did not invariably promote reconciliation, and some measures were quite divisive, particularly those that concerned the status of the former factions—the men of Piraeus and the men of the city. And no matter was more controversial than that of citizenship. When the democratic resistance was stationed in Piraeus, Thrasybulus promised all the foreigners who were fighting alongside the citizens that after the democracy was restored they would receive *isoteleia* (equality of taxation) (Xen. *Hell.* 2.4.25). No doubt he made this promise because they were a substantial portion of his forces and he hoped to increase their zeal for the cause.[53] But when the democracy was restored and Thrasybulus successfully brought forward an even more ambitious proposal, which granted citizenship to all foreigners in the democratic army, including slaves, Archinus suspended it by a *graphe paranomon* (Arist. *Ath. Pol.* 40.2).

Thrasybulus's measure would have strengthened the power of the democratic exiles by swelling their ranks, and so here Archinus's action is consistent with his earlier move of preventing the men of the city from emigrating to Eleusis. Archinus was also responsible for the summary arrest and execution of an individual accused of violating the terms of the amnesty (Arist. *Ath. Pol.* 40.2). But since he had served with the men of Piraeus, it is unlikely that there was a wide ideological gulf between him and Thrasybulus. In fact, Archinus even proposed a motion bestowing honors on the democratic exiles who had seized Phyle. These political moves suggest instead that he was reaching out to members of both factions while simultaneously preventing Thrasybulus from increasing the size of his own political base through grants of citizenship.[54]

Phormisius, on the other hand, aligned himself fully with the men of the city even though he had returned to Athens with Thrasybulus and the democratic exiles. In order to alleviate the fear that they would suffer reprisals at the hands of the men of Piraeus, he proposed that citizenship be restricted to those who owned property (D.H. *Lys.* 32). By disfranchising the poorest Athenians, who were the most adamant supporters of the democratic resistance, the Athenians would have given the men of the city the victory they had failed to achieve in the negotiations to end the civil war. Without the new procedures for enacting laws, the Assembly could have erased the impact of the restoration of the democracy in one rash vote, thus further revealing the importance of the *nomothetai* for the preservation of the democracy. And, although Phormisius's measure was unsuccessful, it shows that the men of the city and their supporters did not simply give up after the reconciliation and accept the restored democracy as a *fait accompli*.

Some were willing to challenge existing arrangements, and they forced the men of Piraeus to rally together in order to protect their own interests. Still the reactionaries were unsuccessful, and the Athenians chose instead to renew Pericles' citizenship law of 451 / 0, which stated that for a child to receive citizenship both parents must be citizens.[55] The message was quite clear: the demos would remain the same as it had been in the fifth century. The Athenians were unwilling to accept either a substantial increase or a substantial decrease in the size of the citizenry. But the failure of Thrasybulus's and Phormisius's proposals does not suggest that the restored democracy was moderate compared to the so-called radical democracy of the fifth century.[56] Such labels serve only to cloud the politics of the reconciliation. The failure of these measures suggests instead that the majority of the Athenians wanted to continue where they had left off before the oligarchs seized power.[57]

In the end, Thrasybulus's promise was not in vain. In the archonship of Xenaenetus, 401/0, the very same year that the Athenians destroyed the oligarchic community of Eleusis, the foreigners who joined the ranks of the democratic exiles were recognized for their part in the struggle and were awarded various honors, including *isoteleia*.[58] A stele was erected listing their names and occupations, which included a farmer, cook, carpenter, gardener, bread-seller, and laborer, to name just a few—yet another forceful reminder that the civil war divided the Athenians along class lines. Some of the recipients may even have been granted citizenship, but probably fewer than would have through Thrasybulus's original bill. Lysias, for example, lived the rest of his life with only *isoteleia* ([Plut.] *X Orat.* 835f–836a), although one would have expected him to have been made a citizen after all the assistance he had provided the exiles.[59]

The Athenians also approved Archinus's motion to honor the one hundred citizens who had occupied Phyle. Each received an olive crown and a sum of less than ten drachmas to be used for sacrifices and dedicatory offerings.[60] In addition, the legitimate children of Athenian citizens who died while fighting the oligarchs received state support, but not the illegitimate children or the children of foreigners and metics, a restriction to which Lysias objected in his speech against Theozotides, the author of the law.[61] On the whole, these measures show that only a small portion of the democratic army was recognized and that their rewards were quite modest.

Initially, it is surprising that the men of Piraeus—who were so regularly praised in civic discourse for their bravery and their willingness to come to terms with the former supporters of the oligarchs—were recognized so begrudgingly. Loraux (1986: 200–201) suggests that they were an embarrassment to the Athenians, in part because their ranks included foreigners and slaves and in part because they had fought a war not against a foreign enemy invading Athenian land but a civil war against fellow Athenians. Why, then, were speakers so effusive in their praise for the men of Piraeus? Far from showing any embarrassment, they held them up as a paradigm of excellence. Speaker after speaker attempted to win the jury's favor by aligning himself with the democratic resistance. Litigants readily offered their service in the democratic army to establish their credibility, while their opponents were clearly placed in the awkward situation of having to explain how they could be at odds with such loyal citizens (see Part II).

In Athens, equality existed among the male citizens not in spite of but because of the inequality that foreigners, slaves, and women were subjected to and the restrictions imposed upon them. Their exclusion allowed for the inclusion of poor men into the political process. Because citizenship was restricted by birth, all citizens could claim to share in a common Athenian ancestry.[62] Birth is what defined the Athenians as equals and gave the poor the same political rights as the rich. If foreigners had been allowed to become citizens in large numbers, then the uniqueness of the Athenian people would have been undermined and the very basis for the democracy called into question.

The failure of Thrasybulus's bill was therefore not a defeat for the democratic faction, but a victory. Likewise, citizens who served in the democratic army did not receive more extravagant rewards, because such displays would have drawn attention to the small number of Athenians who had rallied to restore the democracy. The more particular individuals were honored, the less the Athenians could claim that the men of Piraeus was the demos and that the demos was responsible for the restoration of the democracy. And so the Athenians avoided bestowing greater rewards on the men of Piraeus not out of embarrassment but because of jealousy and because further recognition would have undermined a democratic image of the resistance movement.

Still, Piraeus was a problematic symbol. On the one hand, the development of the democracy was linked to the rise of Athenian naval power, and, even late into the fourth century, the inhabitants of Piraeus could be described as "more democratic" than those of the city (Arist. *Pol.* 1303b7–12). No doubt, they received and retained this reputation at least partially because of the events of 404–403. On the other hand, the harbor was in competition with the city as both a political and economic center, and it could be viewed negatively because it blurred the distinction between Athenian and foreigner. Von Reden (1995: 25) explains: "First, a harbour town upsets the structural subordination of a local deme to the *astu;* secondly, the harbour as the gate to foreign trade calls into question the ideological emphasis on autarky; and, thirdly, the concentration and importance of foreigners, not infrequently linked themselves by the same place of origin, weakens the concept of citizenship status."[63] Therefore, the Athenians avoided depicting the men of Piraeus as standing apart from the demos. They were members of the demos, and since the demos restored the democracy, individual Athenians could only receive modest rewards for the victory.

At the same time, the Athenians did not seriously challenge the status of the men of the city, although they directed their hostility against the cavalry in particular.[64] Cavalry pay decreased from one drachma per day to four obols, and the pay for the mounted archers increased from two obols to eight.[65] Three hundred knights were purposefully selected for a Spartan expedition to Asia because the Athenians wanted to get rid of them (Xen. *Hell.* 3.1.4). In addition, they exiled Xenophon because they feared that, as a former member of the cavalry, he might try to overthrow the restored democracy (Green 1994). No doubt they targeted the cavalry for having remained faithful to the Thirty throughout the civil war and for providing them some of the most important military support.[66] As a result, knights serving in the cavalry after the restoration of the democracy had great difficulty dispelling suspicion about their loyalties. On a cenotaph for Dexileus, a young knight who died at the battle of Corinth in 394, the dates of his birth and death were inscribed (*IG* II² 6217). Since it is so unusual for Attic epitaphs to include dates, Edmonson has suggested in an unpublished paper that this information was provided to show that Dexileus was too young to have served under the Thirty.[67]

Finally, only one other measure was directed against the oligarchs. In 402/1, the Athenians erected a stele listing the property of the Thirty and Eleven, which had been confiscated (Walbank 1982). Presumably this measure did not violate the terms of the amnesty, since only those oligarchs who either did not submit to or did not pass their *euthynai* were subject to these confiscations (Krentz 1982: 123). Moreover, the Athenians at least mitigated the effects of the measure by agreeing to pay the oligarchs' war debt (Arist. *Ath. Pol.* 40.3; Isoc. 7.68). On the whole, the men of the city suffered only a minor backlash in the Assembly for having sided with the Thirty.

Most historians emphasize the stability of early-fourth-century Athens, with some even concluding that the democracy had become more conservative and the gulf between rich and poor had diminished.[68] Civil war had discredited the extremists, and the Athenians had grown weary of factionalism. And since oligarchy was now no longer a viable alternative, the Athenians searched for and found a middle ground. Certainly, the failure of Thrasybulus's and Phormisius's bills shows that the majority was unwilling to either increase or decrease the size of the demos. But we must also remember that Assembly pay was first introduced in the immediate years after the civil war (Arist. *Ath. Pol.* 40.3), a measure that, by all accounts, clearly advanced the democracy. For that matter, the *nomothetai* placed a brake not on popular rule but on oligarchic conspiracies. Far from retreating from democracy, the Athenians continued to cultivate it.[69] It could even be said that Athens was becoming more democratic.[70] Indeed, that was Aristotle's conclusion.[71]

The flurry of legislative activity in the wake of the reconciliation agreement reveals first and foremost that the Athenians did not retreat from politics but again steeped themselves in it in an effort to redefine the community and undo the damages of civil war. Some offered conciliatory measures, but others attempted to gain the victory in the Assembly that they had failed to achieve on the battlefield. Although the more extreme measures failed, this does not suggest that the Athenians gladly accepted compromise; rather, they were in a deadlock. Thus, the success of the reconciliation is all the more remarkable given that it did not put an end to the hostilities that had surfaced during the civil war and that were aggravated by it. These hostilities were merely contained.

3 ⚜ RECRIMINATION

When one of the returning exiles began to violate the amnesty [*mnesikakein*], Archinus brought him before the Council and persuaded the Councilors to execute him without a trial. Archinus told them that now they would show whether they wanted to preserve the democracy and abide by their oaths. If they released him, they would encourage others. But if they executed him, they would make him an example to all—which is what happened. After he was executed, no one ever again violated the amnesty [*mnesikakein*].

ARIST. *ATH. POL.* 40.2 (translation adapted from
K. von Fritz and E. Kapp)

Many of the extant speeches delivered in the first generation after the reconciliation focus on the civil war and the terms of the amnesty.[1] Some went to court, attempting to circumvent the agreement, and others sought satisfaction by alternate means. Sometimes the period of civil unrest was recalled even when it was not directly relevant to the case at hand, and sometimes the defendant was on trial for what he had done under the Thirty, regardless of the actual charges lodged against him. Socrates, for example, was tried, convicted, and executed at least in part because he had been the teacher of Critias and had associated with other members of the Thirty. Others were also targeted for what they had done during the civil war, and some of them paid the consequences.

Clearly, the execution of the unnamed democrat mentioned in the epigraph is not the end of the story. The Athenians did not simply forget past wrongs; rather, they recalled the horrors of the civil war over and over again. It is therefore hard to believe that the Athenians were as scrupulous as Aristotle maintains. And yet, the ancient testimony is unanimous in its praise of the Athenians for the reconciliation.[2] Doubtless, there is some truth to their remarks. Athens did not suffer from a cycle of bloodshed such as had occurred at Corcyra during the Peloponnesian War, and we do not hear of indiscriminate killings by vigilantes. The men of the city were allowed to participate in the restored democracy, and many lived with impunity because of the agreement. Thus, Athens is exemplary compared to other Greek cities that suffered from civil war.[3]

However, the agreement was an imperfect solution to a bitter civil war. At best it created a dangerous stalemate; at worst it laid the foundation for further conflict. Far from putting an end to all hostilities, as Aristotle implies, the agreement itself was a source of controversy and even caused new disagreements, further complicating the social dynamics of the restored democracy. Given the open texture of Athenian law, those unwilling to let bygones be bygones could choose from a variety of different legal procedures in order to seek satisfaction, embarrass their enemies, and dredge up the past without the risk of violating the terms of the amnesty. This was not merely a theoretical possibility. As the extant speeches amply demonstrate, prosecutors were quite creative in their efforts to bypass the agreement. Rules, laws, and procedures were therefore insufficient to prevent recrimination, unless both the jurors and the litigants embraced the principles of reconciliation. In other words, the agreement had to extend beyond the plane of law and become incorporated within the ideology of the community.

ARISTOTLE AND THE SUCCESS OF THE AMNESTY

Attempts to determine whether Aristotle correctly assessed Athenian adherence to the agreement are easily frustrated. In some instances, the Athenians clearly observed its terms. As mentioned in Chapter 2, Rhinon and his associates passed their *euthynai* even though they had served as members of the Ten and even though the Athenians were under no compulsion to permit them to share in the amnesty and to reside in Athens. Rhinon was even later elected general, and he may also have served as treasurer.[4] When Evander was selected by lot to be the eponymous archon for 382 / 1, he was challenged at his scrutiny (*dokimasia*). The challenger asserted that Evander should be rejected since he had served on the Council and in the cavalry of the Thirty (Lys. 26.10). Yet he passed his scrutiny and became archon.[5] In addition, we know that Cephisophon, who had remained in the city during the civil war and had participated in a private delegation to Sparta, was politically active after the democracy was restored. In 403 / 2, he was a member of the Council, where he also served as secretary and possibly *epistates*. Then in 398 / 7, he became treasurer.[6]

Finally, Andocides was allowed to return to Athens after the restoration of the democracy, and when he was charged with impiety in 400 he was acquitted in spite of his checkered past. Since he was absent from Athens during the rule of the Thirty, he could not be directly linked to their crimes. Yet he was only in exile at the time of the civil war because he had previously been accused of participating in the mutilation of the herms and the profanation of the Eleusinian mysteries, and because the Athenians suspected that he had participated in oligarchic conspiracies to overthrow the democracy. Although not a member of the Thirty, he had in the past associated with them, which his prosecutors expected to sway the jury. So in his speech defending himself against the charge of impiety, Andocides was careful to distance himself from the Thirty and to dispel such suspicions about his loyalties (1.101). He depended heavily on the amnesty in order to win an acquittal (80–91), and he even argued that his prosecutors were placing the reconciliation on trial (104–6, 140)—a strategy that would have been useless unless the agreement held weight with the jury.

But we must also bear in mind that these four cases may be exceptional. Rhinon and Cephisophon might have been spared from reprisals because they had helped end the civil war. And by the time Evander was selected to serve as archon in 382, it is possible that much of the resentment against the men of the city had already subsided.[7] Yet he still had to answer accusations about his conduct from some twenty years before. And although Andocides used the amnesty to defend himself, it was technically irrelevant in his case and does not prove that the Athenians faithfully adhered to the agreement in disputes concerning the men of the city.

Moreover, others were clearly not as fortunate as these four men. Menestratus, who had been an informer of the Thirty, was later convicted of murder and executed.[8] Ironically, a vacancy was created for Evander to become the eponymous archon after the previous candidate, Leodamas, had failed his *dokimasia*. Like Evander, Leodamas was accused of having supported the Thirty, but, unlike Evander, he was rejected.[9] So in the very same year and for the very same office, one candidate who was accused of remaining in the city was rejected and another one who responded to the same charge was accepted. Finally, Xenophon and Socrates both paid the consequences. Although Xenophon's assistance to Cyrus or connection to Sparta might have caused the Athenians to exile him, one cannot rule out his involvement in the rule of Thirty as a contributing factor. Socrates will be discussed in greater detail, but it is enough for now to point out that he had lived in Athens for some seventy years without once being placed on trial. It is unlikely that his views or actions suddenly changed in 399, thus compelling the jury to condemn him to death. Rather, the jury at that time viewed him differently because of his connection to the Thirty. What was tolerated before the civil war was no longer possible in its aftermath.

Nevertheless, one cannot disprove Aristotle, because these men were not indicted for crimes committed during the civil war and therefore the terms of the agreement did not formally apply in their cases. Leodamas's rejection might have circumvented the reconciliation agreement, and it could even be argued that it violated the purpose and even the spirit of the agreement, but it did not violate the letter of the law.[10] Technically, he was not on trial for his conduct during the civil war. He was merely undergoing a routine *dokimasia* in order to determine whether he was fit to serve as archon. And, although it is likely that Xenophon and Socrates were convicted at least in part because of their conduct during the civil war, they were in fact placed on trial for crimes committed after the civil war. Even in the case of Menestratus, it was his actions after the civil war which served as the justification for the indictment.[11]

It is therefore tempting to use the extant forensic speeches to further assess Aristotle's judgment, but this path leads only to further unanswerable questions.[12] First, the orators were notoriously deceptive. A litigant would lie, mislead, and deceive the jury if it would help his case. For example, in Lysias 26 the speaker asserts: "If Evander was undergoing a *dokimasia* for the Council and was recorded on the tablets as having served in the cavalry under the Thirty, you would reject him even without an accuser. So now since he has served not only in the cavalry and on the Council, but also appears to have harmed the people, wouldn't you be acting wondrously if you do not treat him the same?" (10). At yet another *dokimasia,* Mantitheus makes the opposite claim, even though he received the speech from the same logographer: "Members of the Council, if I had served in the cavalry of the Thirty, I would not deny it as if I had done something terrible; rather I would deem myself worthy to pass my *dokimasia* after I had shown that no citizen had been harmed by me. And I see that you hold a similar view since many who had served in the cavalry then are now on the Council, while many others have been elected generals and hipparchs" (Lys. 16.8).

Clearly, one of these speakers must be wrong—possibly even both. We therefore cannot trust that litigants reported honestly about Athenian adherence to the agreement. If it served their interests, litigants would provide inaccurate information about previous trials. They would falsely recount why the jury either convicted or acquitted a particular defendant, what procedure was used, and even what crimes the defendant was accused of committing. The speaker of Lysias 26 declares that knights of the Thirty are routinely rejected at their *dokimasiai* for the Council, and Mantitheus insists the opposite to be true.

Second, the outcome of the extant speeches is unknown except for Andocides and Evander, and we do not have in any instance both sides of a dispute concerning the terms of the agreement.[13] Therefore, the arguments of a given speech must be weighed to determine whether the speaker was successful. But even if most of his arguments were insubstantial, the speech did not necessarily fail, because the arguments of the opposing speaker may have been worse, or the verdict contrary to modern—let alone Athenian—expectations.[14]

Third, we have no way of knowing which arguments prevailed upon the jury. Some arguments may have been more effective with some of the jurors and ineffective with others. Fourth, the jurors rarely, if ever, delivered a unanimous verdict. If only thirty jurors had voted differently at the trial of Socrates, he would have been acquitted (Pl. *Ap.* 36a5–6). Finally, it is impossible to determine whether the extant speeches are representative of the types of disputes that arose after the reconciliation, and, if they are, whether such disputes were common and their outcomes typical. Even if it were proven that the verdict for each surviving speech violated the amnesty, one cannot conclude that such violations were frequent under the restored democracy. It is quite possible that these speeches survived because the cases were exceptional and therefore deserved to be recorded.

ATHENIAN LAW AND THE LIMITS OF RECONCILIATION

The forensic speeches are enormously useful for historians because they reveal that Aristotle has qualitatively misjudged the efficacy of the reconciliation agreement. In his recounting of the incident between Archinus and the unnamed democratic exile, he prioritizes substantive law; that is to say, the agreement outlined certain rights that the men of the city possessed, and it was the responsibility of the courts to uphold these rights. This rule-centered paradigm has long held sway in Western jurisprudence, creating serious obstacles for those studying societies lacking a central coercive power that can use force to impose its verdict on the disputants and lacking legal institutions comparable to those in the West.

Legal anthropology has been at the forefront of solving these obstacles with new methods that have shifted the focus from formalist approaches, which view law as an autonomous institution that regulates society, to processual approaches, which explore the dynamics between law and society.[15] In particular, much attention has been given to the legal and extralegal procedures the parties employed to pursue (and not end) their disputes; the resources on which they drew, the norms and beliefs they invoked to justify their actions, and the assistance they received from kin and friends.[16] Legal studies have even shown that formalist assumptions fail to account for the complexity of social control in modern societies.[17] Drawing on such works, recent studies of Athenian law focus more heavily on the social dynamics of the dispute and give greater attention to the procedures that litigants employed to pursue their claims.[18] For our purposes, these new approaches help us better understand why the terms of the agreement could not ensure the success of the reconciliation.

We must begin by recognizing that law is not the only outlet for grieved parties seeking satisfaction. As Roberts (1976: 666) explains: "Most important, perhaps, is the fact that even where judicial institutions are found they do not always enjoy the unchallenged pre-eminence in the business of dispute settlement which our courts claim and manage to exercise. Fighting and other forms of self-help, resort to supernatural agencies, the use of shaming and ridicule, or the unilateral withdrawal of essential forms of co-operation may all constitute equally approved and effective means of handling conflict." For anthropologists it is quite easy to explore these extralegal venues for settling disputes, because they can gather the evidence themselves. But for historians this task is much more difficult, because their evidence depends either on the accidental survival of past remains or on the choices that others have made. Previous generations decide what information is worthy to preserve for the future generations and in what format this information should be preserved, and until recently the priority has always been to record state documents and state decisions.

For example, Thompson (1975) uses anonymous letters of blackmail published in the *London Gazette* as evidence for social protest in eighteenth-century England, which had previously been unrecognized. The writers seek payment from individuals from the upper orders as recompense for either a private or a social grievance, and often for both in the same letter. Quite threatening, they express a virulent animosity for the landed aristocracy. Yet the letters survive only because the authorities were offering rewards to those individuals who could provide information leading to arrests. Hence they were quoted verbatim, with the original spelling preserved. Without these letters, Thompson (1975: 304) suggests, one could too easily assume that "England between 1750 and 1810 was always a land of moderate consensus."

Rosenzweig (1983) draws similar conclusions about consensus in Worcester, Massachusetts. As industry consolidated from 1870 to 1920, conventional expressions of class conflict—whether through union activity, strikes, or radical parties—were minimal compared to those of other industrial cities for the same period in American history. Rosenzweig argues, however, that a consensus between the industrialists and the working class did not exist. Although the workers did not openly confront the industrialists, they carved out for themselves an alternative culture in the saloons and parks and in their celebration of national holidays, which differed from the demands imposed on them in their work: efficiency, individualism, propriety, and discipline. As industrialists attempted to regulate leisure time and leisure space, the workers frustrated their efforts through evasion, group pressure, and even the legal system. Although they did not seriously challenge the industrialists' vision of work, the workers preserved their own vision of leisure. Rosenzweig's study shows us that we cannot assume consensus where there is the absence of conflict. Between consensus and conflict lies a whole range of alternative responses, varying in the degree that assent and dissent are vocalized. Therefore, just because the Athenians did not openly violate the reconciliation agreement, we cannot conclude that the men of the city and the men of Piraeus lived harmoniously under the restored democracy.

One last comparison further illustrates the extent to which animosity can be expressed outside of the court of law. In the introduction to his study of Germany and Japan after World Word II, Buruma (1994: 3) recalls how he and the children of his town in the Netherlands avoided particular shops because the owners had collaborated with the Germans: "Our teachers told us stories of German wickedness and their own acts of bravery. Every member of the older generation, it appeared, had been in the resistance. That is to say, everybody except for the butcher on the corner of the high street, who had been a collaborator; one didn't go shopping there. And then there was the woman at the tobacconist; she had had a German lover. One didn't go there either." This is a passive and silent form of disapproval, but the social and economic impact can be quite significant for those who are shunned. It also makes explicit that the collaborators are not full members of the community and thus informally undoes the impact of formal amnesties and formal pardons. They may escape prison for political reasons beyond the control of the local inhabitants, but the collaborators cannot escape from social censure. For Athens, most of our information on the reconciliation comes from the orators, and therefore we cannot so readily uncover such extralegal remedies to conflict. After all, the speeches were written for parties that addressed their grievances in the courts. However, some evidence suggests that the Athenians sought satisfaction in other ways.

In Isocrates 18, the speaker accuses Callimachus of lodging a complaint first against Patrocles and then against Lysimachus for an offense committed during the civil war so that the two parties would then be compelled to pay him in order to prevent their quarrel from appearing in court. Afterward, Callimachus publicly accused the speaker. He went to crowds around Athens and spoke in workshops, where he revealed how the speaker had helped Patrocles and Lysimachus defraud him of his money. Friends of the speaker suggested that he settle out of court, and, even though he agreed to arbitration, Callimachus violated the settlement and a jury eventually heard their dispute (7–12). It is irrelevant whether Callimachus was a sycophant who was blackmailing the speaker or whether his accusations had merit. Callimachus's violation of the settlement suggests the latter is correct. Either way, this incident shows that at least one individual defamed his enemies by spreading rumors around town about their conduct during the civil war.[19] It is interesting that Callimachus spoke to the poorer segments of Athenian society, no doubt because he expected them to be a more receptive audience. Perhaps Callimachus's accusations were true, or perhaps he was angry at the speaker for other reasons and used the civil war to harm him. Regardless, he was able to embarrass the speaker publicly without even bringing the case to a jury, which may explain why the speaker's friends encouraged him to settle out of court and why he yielded to their recommendation. He and his friends feared not only that a jury would side against him should he allow the dispute to be heard in court, but also that Callimachus had already turned public opinion against the speaker and that he would suffer more public humiliation unless Callimachus were appeased.

Even more important, the speeches show that Athenian law provided the men of Piraeus ample opportunities to seek revenge, regardless of the constraints imposed on them by the provisions of the amnesty and regardless of the intent of its drafters. Even after the compilation of the laws from 410 to 399, Athenian law remained amateur and unsystematic:[20] there were no judges to prevent litigants from introducing irrelevant material; litigants, even in public cases, acted in private capacities; the jury was composed of citizens from all classes and occupations and was untrained in law; and the verdict was rendered without deliberation.[21] Since Athenian law lacked jurists, judges, and clearly defined statutes, a system of precedent did not develop. As a result, statutes did not function as rules the jury applied to the evidence of the case. Statutes were themselves a form of evidence, and, like other forms of evidence, they served to persuade the jury.[22] And since statutes did not normally include definitions, Cohen (1991: 209) suggests that "the only applicable definitions of the offenses were those residing in the collective consciousness of the community, as manifested through the five hundred or more citizens who happened to be sitting on a particular day to hear a particular case." Or as Bateman (1958: 279) concludes, "The intention of the lawgiver is whatever the logographer can establish with adequate probability; and so, too, it seems, is the letter of the law."

Athenian law was thus highly elastic, which in turn prevented the reconciliation agreement from remaining static and its meaning from staying fixed. "In theory," Todd (1993:91) states, "the Amnesty guaranteed [the oligarchic supporters] statutory protection; but where the immediate as well as the ultimate source of law is public opinion, that statutory protection can only be valuable so long as it remains popular to keep the Amnesty." One court could give a strict interpretation of the amnesty, serving to protect the former oligarchs, while another a loose interpretation, assisting those seeking redress. Hence, the amnesty could promote reconciliation only if the Athenians who served on the juries chose to interpret it in a conciliatory way. Yet they alone could not guarantee its success. Even if the juries consistently upheld the provisions of the amnesty, a litigant confident in his rhetorical skills could always offer a new interpretation or challenge an existing interpretation. And, as long as litigants came forward with claims that called into question its terms, the agreement remained divisive. Reconciliation, therefore, depended on the goodwill of not only the jury but also the litigants.

For example, Andocides insisted that the amnesty granted him immunity from prosecution even though he was absent from the civil war (1.80–88). In Lysias 13, however, the speaker argues that Agoratus was not protected from prosecution since the agreement was between the men of Piraeus and the men of the city while they were both members of the Piraeus party. Only if an oath had been taken between the men of Piraeus and the men of Piraeus, so the prosecutor insists, would Agoratus have immunity.[23] If the speaker were correct, then the agreement would apply neither to Andocides, who was absent from Athens, nor to Agoratus, who was a member of the same faction as the prosecutor. But given that even modern commentators disagree about the validity of this argument, we should not be surprised if the jurors who heard the case also reached different conclusions.[24] Each juror had to decide for himself whether this interpretation was sensible. Moreover, one jury might deliver a verdict supporting the speaker's interpretation while another might give a verdict rejecting it. Far from preventing antagonisms from erupting, the amnesty was itself a source of contention. It did not end hostilities; rather, it redirected, rechanneled, and reconfigured them.

Even when the defendant was not on trial for a crime committed during the civil war, the case could easily center on the civil war. The courts, after all, had no mechanism to prevent the litigants from introducing irrelevant or inadmissible arguments. But even the suggestion that statements on the civil war could be irrelevant or inadmissible misses the point. Character was an integral component of the litigant's argument.[25] The litigant commented on his past actions in order to establish his own credibility while he recounted all spheres of his opponent's life in order to undermine his credibility. Hence, speakers were careful to show that they had gladly performed services for the city, because a loyal citizen was more believable than a citizen who avoided doing his duty.[26] Past conduct was important because it established a pattern and helped the jury determine whether it was probable that the defendant committed the crime with which he was charged. If the prosecutor convinced the jurors that the defendant had repeatedly violated Athenian laws and behaved inappropriately, then the prosecutor was more likely to convince the jury that the defendant was guilty of the charge lodged against him. Character, therefore, was part of the evidence the jury assessed to determine the guilt or innocence of the defendant. As Cohen (1995: 191) explains:

> The courts did not reach decisions purely through the interpretation of legal norms and principles and their application to a particular transaction. Rather, Athenian courts, as they responded to the speakers' competing attempts to frame the case within a particular characterization of the community's normative repertoire, appear to have rendered judgment in regard to representations about the totality of the transaction of which that particular act was a part. This process by its very nature focussed upon judgments about the political, social and moral context of the relations of the parties and, therefore, upon what sort of person each of the parties was. On this view, much of the judicial rhetoric

which has been too readily dismissed as "irrelevant" or a "perversion of
legal process" is in reality central to the process of judgment as the
Athenians conceived it.

So as disputes were heard again in the courts after the restoration of the
democracy, it was not only unavoidable but even necessary for litigants to
recall the civil war, given the nature of Athenian law. A litigant—whether
he was guilty or innocent of any misconduct—placed himself unneces-
sarily at a disadvantage if he did not tell the jury how he had behaved
during the civil war.

Finally, the reconciliation agreement had a limited impact because
the grieved parties had alternate ways of pursuing their claims. In Athens,
the prosecutor did not simply decide what offense the defendant committed and lodge a charge against him accordingly. In many instances, he
had a whole range of procedures from which to choose for a particular offense, and, as Osborne (1985b) has shown, the prosecutor decided which
procedure to use on the basis of his wealth, status, and confidence in his
case. The law courts were a "public stage" to regulate, not end, conflicts.
Sometimes the prosecutor attempted to convict the defendant for the
same crime through different procedures, and sometimes the same parties appeared again in the courts with new complaints.[27]

The dispute between Meidias and Demosthenes lasted at least eigh-
teen years. Between 364 / 3 and 347 / 6, they charged each other with slan-
der, desertion, and wrongful conduct concerning the festival, and the
dispute was carried out through many different legal proceedings: *anti-
dosis, probole, dokimasia,* and private arbitration.[28] The amnesty prevented
the grieved parties from lodging certain kind of charges, but they still had
other procedures from which they could choose that did not violate the
agreement. Moreover, the courts constrained litigants, forcing them to
narrate their conflict in a fashion appropriate for the legal forum. But
their private motives for bringing their cases to court may have differed
substantially from those they asserted in public.[29] Thus, even for those
cases in which the Thirty and the democratic resistance were not mentioned, the disputes may have appeared in court because of events that
took place during the civil war.

THE PAST ON TRIAL

The trials in which the civil war received the focus of attention amply
show that the amnesty was of limited effectiveness. Although they cannot tell us the extent to which reconciliation was contested, these trials

reveal how some Athenians could dredge up the civil war regardless of the terms of the agreement. We must also bear in mind that the litigants may have had ulterior reasons for lodging their particular complaints. Their quarrels may have begun either before or after the civil war, but they focused on the civil war because it provided them the best opportunity to settle the score with their enemies. Regardless of the litigants' motives, these trials reveal that the past was far from settled; otherwise the speakers would have directed their attention to other matters.

Murder

Lysias 12

Although the defendants in Lysias 12 and 13 were not prosecuted for murder under the traditional procedure of homicide (*dike phonou*), they are classified together because both focus primarily on the question of murder. Lysias 12 is perhaps the most extraordinary speech in all of the logographer's corpus. It is the only extant speech that Lysias delivered for himself and the only extant speech given at a trial in which the defendant was a former member of the Thirty. But since the case is so exceptional, its authenticity has been called into question.[30] No other source tells us that Eratosthenes underwent a *euthyna*. Given that he had been a member of the Thirty, it seems doubtful that he would have taken such a risk. It is also difficult to understand how Lysias was able to deliver a speech in court on his own behalf when he was only a metic.

However, there is evidence, although of questionable reliability, indicating that at least one of the Thirty passed his *euthyna* (see Chapter 2 n. 10). And perhaps Lysias was able to speak on his own behalf by the grant of *isoteleia*, or because he prosecuted Eratosthenes before Thrasybulus's citizenship law was annulled, or maybe the decree honoring metics (*IG* II[2] 10) gave him the right to speak in court.[31] Although I am wary of rejecting this speech merely because it is exceptional, its authenticity does not matter for our purposes. Even if it were a political pamphlet, it is still useful in showing how the Athenians depicted the rule of the Thirty (see Part 2). And because the prosecution of Eratosthenes falls within the terms of the agreement, we do not need to rely on this speech to show how Athenians circumvented the amnesty.

It has also been debated whether Lysias wrote the speech for Eratosthenes' *euthyna* in 403/2 or whether it was intended for a *dike phonou* sometime after Eratosthenes had passed his *euthyna*. But since Lysias does not attempt to prove that Eratosthenes was guilty of murder *autocheiria*, the speech must be from his *euthyna*.[32] In the speech, Lysias describes how his brother Polemarchus was arrested by Eratosthenes and then executed (16–17). He argues that Eratosthenes willingly arrested Polemarchus even though he knew what was to happen and even though Eratosthenes could easily have allowed him to escape without risking any harm to himself (26–34). In addition, Lysias responds to Eratosthenes' claim of being a moderate oligarch aligned with Theramenes and opposed to the extreme policies of the Thirty. Lysias argues that Theramenes was no better than the rest of the Thirty, and he depicts the oligarchs as utterly depraved individuals, united in their villainy. A vote against Eratosthenes was therefore a vote against the Thirty (62–78).

Although the outcome is unknown, Lysias 1 concerns the murder of an adulterer named Eratosthenes. If the Eratosthenes of Lysias 1 and 12 were the same man, then he must have passed his *euthyna*, only later to be killed by Euphiletus for sleeping with his wife. Yet it would be hard to explain why Euphiletus does not explicitly mention in Lysias 1 that Eratosthenes (the adulterer) had served as a member of the Thirty, and so we can safely conclude that the two cannot be the same.[33] It is therefore best to avoid further speculation on the outcome of Lysias 12.

Lysias 13

Sometime between 400 and 398, Dionysius initiated the procedure of *apagoge* against Agoratus for the murder of his brother Dionysodorus.[34] The brother-in-law of the deceased assisted Dionysius and was the speaker of Lysias 13. The two probably waited so long because of the amnesty, but, after the successful conviction of Menestratus by the very same procedure, they decided to proceed.[35] There were perhaps as many as four different ways that *apagoge* could be used against murderers.[36] But in the case of Agoratus, Dionysius could have arrested him only in one of two ways: either by *apagoge phonou* or by *apagoge kakourgon*.[37]

According to Demosthenes, a suspected murderer could be arrested and prosecuted if he was found entering either holy places or the agora (23.80). No doubt the purpose was to protect public areas from the pollution of the murderer. The defendant was not charged with murder but with the illegal entry into prohibited areas (Gagarin 1979: 314–15). This procedure—if it were in place at the time of the restored democracy— would not have violated the amnesty because the defendant was charged with a crime that took place after the civil war. Therefore, it is tempting to conclude that Dionysius must have initiated an *apagoge phonou* against Agoratus. On the other hand, a murderer was also subject to arrest on the grounds that he was a wrongdoer (*apagoge kakourgon*). If he confessed, he was summarily executed. If he did not, a trial took place. Although this procedure was particularly useful against foreigners and metics so that they could not flee before the trial, it could even be used against Athenians.[38] It is not entirely clear whether a conviction by this procedure would have violated the amnesty, but we cannot dismiss it on these grounds. It is always possible that Dionysius did not proceed in strict accord with the reconciliation agreement.

Attempts to prove which type of *apagoge* Dionysius used yield only inconclusive results. The speaker of Lysias 13 neither refers to Agoratus as a wrongdoer (*kakourgos*) nor mentions that Agoratus had entered a prohibited area. It is certainly evident that a person accused of murder is a wrongdoer, and it is also not surprising that the speaker would have focused on the question of murder even if Agoratus was formally charged with violating some debarment.[39] After all, the debarment depended on whether he was in fact guilty of murder. Perhaps Dionysius even mentioned in his speech (which has not survived) that Agoratus illegally entered a prohibited area.

The Eleven's requiring Dionysius to add the phrase *ep' autophoroi* has also been used as evidence to deduce which procedure was used.[40] The meaning of this phrase ranges from "caught in the act," to "manifestly." It was often used for thieves who either were caught while committing burglary or were later found with the stolen goods in their possession.[41] According to the speaker of Lysias 13, the phrase was added to help the prosecution since it was obvious that Agoratus was "manifestly" responsible for the murder. Agoratus, however, insisted that the prosecution must prove that he was "caught in the act" (85–87). Unfortunately, the opposing arguments attempting to explain why this phrase was added to the charge are equally probable whether Dionysius proceeded by *apagoge kakourgon* or *apagoge phonou*. But whichever procedure he chose, he did so because he was more likely to win a conviction. By bringing an *apagoge*, he had to prove only that Agoratus was guilty of murder *ep' autophoroi*. If, on the other hand, Dionysius had initiated a *dike phonou,* he would have had to prove that Agoratus was guilty of murder "by his own hands" (*autocheiria*), a much more difficult case to make.

Other than Lysias 12, no other extant speech gives as vivid an account of the civil war. The speaker of Lysias 13 attempts not only to prove that Agoratus was responsible for the murder of his brother-in-law but also to place squarely on his shoulders responsibility for the Athenian surrender, the overthrow of the democracy, and the crimes of the Thirty. He recalls the mood of Athens when Theramenes returned from Sparta with conditions of surrender. Dionysodorus, Strombichides, and some other

loyal generals opposed him because they believed that these concessions would cause the destruction of the democracy. But oligarchic conspirators put a stop to them by persuading Agoratus to act as an informer. After the democrats were arrested because of his false accusations,
Athens surrendered and the Thirty seized power. The speaker insists that
Agoratus could have avoided denouncing these men if he had wanted.
Many people offered to smuggle him out of the city, but he preferred to
help the Thirty. Hence, Agoratus was manifestly responsible for their
deaths. With much detail, the speaker describes the sad scene of his
brother-in-law in prison and how the Thirty tried and executed Dionysodorus along with the other loyal generals (12–36). The speaker also
responds to Agoratus's attempt to portray himself as a member of the
democratic resistance. He recounts how the men of Piraeus were so
convinced of his treachery that they refused to associate with him and
how he barely escaped from being summarily executed. The speaker
even claims that when the democrats won the war Agoratus was driven
away as he attempted to take part in the victory procession to the Acropolis (77–80).

Impiety

Within the course of a year, three defendants were placed on trial for
impiety: Socrates, Andocides, and Nicomachus. Each of these trials is
enormously important in its own right. The trial of Socrates forces us to
consider the part he played in the oligarchic revolutions as well as to
question the extent to which freedom of speech was tolerated under the
democracy. From the trials of Andocides and Nicomachus we gain valuable information about the compilation of the laws, and, as with Socrates,
their past activities clearly aroused much concern among the Athenians.
In addition, a defendant was placed on trial a few years later for illegally
removing a sacred olive stump (Lys. 7), and the question of impiety
figures prominently in another case, although only a small portion of it
survives (Lys. 5).

Connor (1991: 50) suggests that religious issues were prominent in
399. Although the corpus of Attic orators does not allow us to gauge
whether more individuals were prosecuted for impiety in 399 compared
to other years, the frequency of such important trials in the span of one
year is quite significant, and it is not accidental that all three concern
impiety. Just as the Athenians crafted new laws and new political institutions to prevent future oligarchic conspiracies, they used the courts to
purge the city of dangerous individuals. Impiety provided the Athenians

an easy way to understand the period of civil unrest. Citizens who had violated the laws of the gods were also responsible for Athenian political troubles. What better way to ensure the success of the restored democracy than by removing them and their pollution from the city?

Socrates

No trial under the restored democracy is more notorious than that of Socrates. In 399, Meletus, together with Anytus and Lycon, indicted him for impiety. They accused Socrates of refusing to recognize the gods of the city, of introducing new divinities, and of corrupting the youth.[42] It would be easy to dismiss their charges as groundless and to conclude that Socrates was unjustly executed. Yet in 346/5, more than fifty years after his execution, Aeschines declared in a court of law, "Did you kill Socrates the sophist, men of Athens, because he was shown to have taught Critias, one of the Thirty who overthrew the democracy, and will Demosthenes take your comrades from you and will he exact such a penalty from private citizens and from men loyal to the demos because they exercised their equal right to speak?"[43] This comparison would have been counterproductive had the jury not believed that Socrates deserved the punishment he received.[44] We should therefore be wary of later testimony claiming the Athenians subsequently regretted his execution, and we should also recognize that his conviction was more typical than we may want to believe.[45] It was typical not because other intellectuals suffered a similar punishment but because the Athenians were willing to punish any individual whom they considered a threat to the community. As Wallace (1994: 144) remarks, "Sokrates' execution was just one of many, done for the good of Athens. There is no reason why we should single him out for our especial horror."[46]

It would also seem reasonable to infer from Aeschines that many of the jurors who voted to convict Socrates made their decision at least in part because of his connection with Critias.[47] Xenophon even states that Socrates' accuser mentioned his association with Critias and Alcibiades (*Mem.* 1.2.12). Some, however, dismiss this evidence for the following reasons: (1) the amnesty would have prevented the prosecutors from mentioning Critias and the jury from condemning Socrates because of his association with Critias; (2) Xenophon is drawing from a pamphlet written by Polycrates and not from a speech of one of Socrates' accusers; and (3) if the accusers had mentioned Critias, then surely Socrates would have responded to this accusation in the *Apology*.[48] Yet these objections are unfounded.[49] Critias is mentioned several times in extant speeches.[50] Even though the prosecutors formally charged Socrates with impiety, the amnesty did not prevent them from discussing any other aspect of his life which they thought would influence the jury. Given Socrates' association with Critias, it would be most surprising if they failed to mention Critias, as such restraint is completely absent in the corpus of Attic orators. Finally, even if the *Apology* were historically accurate, it cannot be used to reconstruct the arguments of the prosecution.

Socrates could have had a number of reasons not to discuss his involvement with Critias, and in fact the *Apology* implicitly responds to such accusations. Socrates discusses how he disobeyed the Thirty's order to arrest Leon (Pl. *Ap.* 32c4–d8), and he mentions that he was a friend of Chaerephon, who was a member of the democratic resistance (21a1–3). Yet he neither prevented the arrest of Leon nor joined the men of Piraeus. Perhaps even more damning, many in his circle had participated in the mutilation of the herms, the profanation of the mysteries, and the oligarchic revolutions of 411 and 404.[51] It was far easier for the prosecution to link Socrates with the oligarchic conspirators than for Socrates to show that he had remained a loyal democrat during the civil war, which could even explain why Critias is not mentioned in the *Apology*.

But did the jury consider Socrates an oligarchic sympathizer? The answer must be yes. In spite of the amnesty, litigants often recalled what their opponents did during the civil war, and defendants were often accused of having remained in the city. Although such accusations were not necessarily sufficient to prove oligarchic sympathies, they certainly created the suspicion and forced the defendants to justify their conduct. Socrates was no exception. The prosecutors needed only to mention that he had stayed in Athens in order to put him on the defensive. And it certainly did not help his cause that they could also remind the jurors that he had been an intimate friend of Critias, along with other young men who had overthrown the democracy. What better proof that Socrates had in fact corrupted the youth? What better reason to fear that a new generation under his influence might follow in the path of Alcibiades and Critias?

For the sake of argument, assume that the jurors did not take into account what Socrates did during or before the civil war. Many of them must still have considered him a serious religious and political threat; otherwise they would not have voted to convict and execute him. It will not do to conclude that they had been tricked. Not even the words of his apologists justify our assuming differently. But why was Socrates considered such a dangerous threat after the restoration of the democracy? Surely he had not changed; rather, Athenian opinion had changed and many no longer considered him harmless. What, then, accounts for this change in Athenian opinion? The conclusion is inescapable: the mood in Athens had changed as a result of the defeat and civil war, and it led the jury to condemn Socrates.

Some suggest that the prosecutors accused Socrates of impiety to avoid violating the amnesty.[52] Although this is certainly a possibility, it would be a mistake to conclude that the charges were only a pretext and that his political beliefs and his associations with Critias and Alcibiades were the real reasons why he was convicted. "Particularly in times of social crisis," Cohen (1991: 228) remarks, "[Athenians] might consider many aspects of religious practice and belief as intimately connected to the public order." At the same time, we cannot dismiss the political component of Socrates' trial. Impiety threatened the community and was therefore political. Whatever the reasons for this religious fear, it reflected a concern for the safety of the city.[53]

Perhaps the most important lesson from the trial of Socrates is that the "rule of law" was a double-edged sword. Only a few years before, the Athenians had embarked on significant law reforms. And although many view the law reforms as the crowning achievement of the democracy, the execution of Socrates is considered to be one of its worst mistakes. The Athenians were not, however, acting inconsistently. Many of them believed that Socrates had taught young men to despise the democracy and to break the laws. The *nomothetai* prevented conspirators from being able to subvert the democracy from within; the execution of Socrates cut off the source of the conspirators. Both, therefore, were attempts to insure that the democracy would remain stable by ridding the community of lawlessness.

Many ask why Socrates was executed in 399 and not in 403, after the restoration of the democracy, or why not in 401, after the destruction of the oligarchic stronghold in Eleusis, and why the Athenians chose Socrates and not others. These are the wrong questions to ask. The reconciliation was under constant negotiation and renegotiation. Somehow, as the Athenians acquitted and convicted citizens of crimes they deemed dangerous to the community, they were able to maintain the reconciliation. The death of Socrates serves to remind us just how fragile the peace was.

Andocides 1

In the summer of 415, shortly before the Athenians launched the Sicilian expedition, nearly all the herms of Athens were mutilated in the course of one evening. Convinced that they were destroyed to undermine the expedition and to overthrow the democracy, the Athenians began an inquiry to find out who was responsible. During their investigation, they learned that Alcibiades and some other young men had parodied the Eleusinian mysteries. Andocides was named as a participant in these crimes, but he was granted immunity for providing information against his accomplices.[54] Afterward, the decree of Isotimides was enacted, which prohibited those who had committed impiety from entering either holy places or the agora. Rather than endure the humiliation, Andocides decided to go into exile.[55] He returned to Athens shortly after the restoration of the democracy but soon became enmeshed in a quarrel with Callias. According to Andocides, they came into conflict over the daughter of Epilycus. In order to stop Andocides from claiming her, Callias had Cephisius accuse Andocides of impiety for participating in the Eleusinian mysteries when he was prohibited from doing so by the decree of Isotimides. He expected Andocides to go into exile rather than stand trial. But when Andocides failed to do so, Callias next accused him of illegally placing a suppliant's branch on the altar at the temple of Eleusis. He promised to dismiss the charge if Andocides would give up his claim to the woman, but Andocides refused (71–72, 110–23). So Callias proceeded with his accusations, and the trial took place in 400.[56]

Although Andocides was accused of offenses committed after the restoration of the democracy, he devotes much of his attention to the preceding period. He insists that he never committed an act of impiety, that he never admitted his guilt, and that he never acted as an informer (10). Moreover, he interprets the amnesty and the law reforms as invalidating the decree of Isotimides. Therefore, even if he were guilty of an offense, it was no longer actionable since the decree had been annulled. Doubtless, Andocides included this second argument because his innocence was far-fetched. If, however, he had admitted his guilt and relied solely on the amnesty for his defense, there was then the danger that the jury would convict him regardless of legal niceties. Therefore he asserts that he was simultaneously innocent of wrongdoing and immune from prosecution. In addition, he maintains that he was and would continue to be a loyal democrat. Although he could not point to any services that he had performed during the civil war, he declares that the Thirty would have killed him if he had entered the city because they considered him a serious threat to their rule. Thus he renders his absence from Athens as proof of his loyalty (101–2).

If the dispute began as Andocides maintains, it shows how the civil war could become the focus of attention even when it was not the cause of the quarrel. Although the dispute was over Epilycus's daughter, it was Andocides' past that was on trial. He had to defend not merely his actions in 415 but also his absence from Athens when the democratic exiles needed his support. Given Socrates' conviction, it may seem remarkable that Andocides was acquitted, but Andocides shows a willingness in his speech to defer to popular opinion in order to win an acquittal.

Lysias 30

In 399, the speaker of Lysias 30 prosecuted Nicomachus for offenses committed while he was serving as an *anagrapheus*. It is uncertain what type of procedure the prosecutor initiated, but the title of the speech in the manuscript indicates that it was delivered at a *euthyna*. However, because the prosecutor accuses Nicomachus of failing to submit his accounts (5), it seems unlikely that he would make such a claim if it were a *euthyna*. Moreover, the title in the manuscript wrongly identifies Nicomachus as a secretary (*grammateus*). It is more likely that the prosecutor initiated an *eisangelia,* that is, a proceeding of impeachment to remove Nicomachus from office because of misconduct (Todd 1996: 104–6).

The prosecutor alleges that Nicomachus was instructed to complete the job within four months, but he extended his term for six years, during which time he received daily pay and usurped the power of lawgiver (*nomothetes*). Then, after the restoration of the democracy, he was reappointed and held the office for four years, even though he could have surrendered his post in thirty days and should have submitted to a *euthyna* (2–5). The prosecutor accuses Nicomachus of impiety for inscribing more sacrifices on the tablets than were ordained, thus bankrupting the city and forcing the Athenians to abandon some of their ancestral rites (18–22). In addition, the prosecutor alleges that Nicomachus helped oligarchic conspirators overthrow the democracy by furnishing a law that they used to eliminate Cleophon, as well as other prominent Athenians, including Strombichides.[57] But he is also careful to justify these accusations. He says that he would have passed over Nicomachus's conduct during the civil war had he not learned that Nicomachus would attempt to present himself as a democrat and would use his exile as proof of his loyalty (16). Since Nicomachus decided unjustly to remember the wrongs of others (*mnesikakein*), it was only fair that the jury hear about his crimes (9).

Dokimasiai

Every candidate for public office had to undergo a scrutiny (*dokimasia*), which for most offices took place only in the law courts. Candidates for the archonship first had a *dokimasia* in the Council and then a second one in the courts. The vote of the Council was only prejudicial. For candidates for the Council, the outgoing Council alone heard the *dokimasia,* but its decision could be appealed to the courts.[58] The candidate was first asked the names of his parents and grandparents, the location of his family tombs, and the deme to which he belonged; then whether his family had shrines to Apollo and Zeus, and if so where they were located; whether he had treated his parents well and had paid his taxes; and whether he had served on military campaigns. After these questions were answered, anyone could come forward with accusations. If no one came forward, the vote was taken. If an accuser approached, his charges were heard and the candidate then gave his response.[59]

Some believe that the purpose of the *dokimasia* was simply to establish whether the candidate was legally qualified to hold office.[60] Others argue that the *dokimasia* permitted (or at the very least, provided the opportunity for) a general probe into the public and private life of the candidate. [61] This is a difficult matter to settle, because only few speeches from *dokimasiai* of public officials survive, and each concerns a candidate who was accused of either supporting the Thirty during the civil war or failing to help the democrats.[62] Moreover, one cannot prove that the *dokimasia* was intended to probe into a person's entire life simply because the accusers did so in these cases, which are clearly exceptional (Todd 1993: 288–89).

In most instances, the *dokimasia* was probably a formality for the candidate and was quickly completed. But if the candidate were accused of mistreating his parents or failing to serve on military campaigns, many details about his private life would inevitably become the focus of the review (Hunter 1994: 107). Of course the candidate's answers to these questions indicated whether he had suffered *atimia,* but these questions were not simply about formal legal qualifications. Implicit in this series of questions is the idea that only a citizen who acts appropriately deserves the benefits of citizenship. Hence, Athenians who prostituted themselves were prohibited from speaking in the Assembly.[63] And, as mentioned in the previous section, arguments based on character were an essential component of the litigant's case, so it was inevitable, given the type of questions routinely asked at the *dokimasia,* that character could and did become the focus of concern.

Finally, Aristotle does not specify what charges the accuser was permitted to bring forward. In all likelihood, each accuser decided for himself what were appropriate accusations to lodge, and it was the responsibility of the jury hearing that particular *dokimasia* to decide whether the defendant was guilty of the charges lodged against him and whether he should be prohibited from holding office. It is therefore both expected and appropriate for a *dokimasia* sometimes to become a probe into the entire life of the candidate (Adeleye 1983: 300). It is not surprising, therefore, that grieved parties came forward at the *dokimasia* to charge the candidate with misconduct during their civil war and to call into question his loyalty to the democracy. This occasion provided them an excellent opportunity to dredge up the past, to humiliate the candidate, and perhaps even to make him pay for what he had done without fear of violating the amnesty.

Lysias 16 and 25, and *Papyrus Rylands* 489

Lysias 16 and 25 and *Papyrus Rylands* 489 were written for candidates at their *dokimasiai*. Lysias 16 was for Mantitheus to deliver before the outgoing Council. The accuser argues that Mantitheus should not be allowed to serve as Councilor since he was a former knight of the Thirty. In response, Mantitheus maintains that he was too young to have been a knight of the Thirty, and, even if he had served in the cavalry, he would not now be prohibited from holding office. He recounts the services he performed for the city, and he tells the Council that he had lived in exile during part of the civil war. He fails, however, to explain why he and his father returned to the city when the oligarchs were still in power instead of joining the democrats at Phyle or why the Thirty would have allowed them to return (4–5).

Although Lysias 25 is titled "A defense for overthrowing the democracy," internal evidence suggests that it was also written for a candidate to deliver at his *dokimasia*. The speaker mentions the purpose of the *dokimasia* (10) and explains why he is entitled to hold office (14).[64] But unlike Lysias 16, this speech was delivered before a jury. *Papyrus Rylands* 489 was written on behalf of Eryximachus. Although only fragments survive, the arguments of Eryximachus are so similar to those of the speaker in Lysias 25 that it was probably intended for a *dokimasia*. The speaker states the following: Eryximachus performed his liturgies generously so that he could more easily defend himself should he appear in court; his accusers linked him to the Thirty since they could not charge him with committing a crime; and he did not hold any office or arrest anyone during the rule of the Thirty.[65] As with Lysias 25, the office for which Eryximachus was a candidate is unknown.

Lysias 26 and 31

Lysias 26 and 31 were both written for prosecutors. Lysias 26 is notorious for two reasons. First, unlike Mantitheus of Lysias 16, the speaker insists that former knights of the Thirty were not allowed to serve on the Council. Second, he states that the *dokimasia* was instituted to prevent former oligarchs from holding office (Lys. 26.9–10). This assertion has led some to conclude that the *dokimasia* was revised after the restoration of the democracy.[66] In the previous chapter we saw how speakers ascribe contemporary legislation to Solon. Here the speaker of Lysias 26 must be disguising his own interpretation of the *dokimasia* by declaring it to be the intent of the lawgiver.[67] In any event, his argument was ineffective, because Evander was permitted to serve as archon for 382 / 81.

Perhaps the most creative argument comes from Lysias 31. At the *dokimasia* of Philon, the speaker argues that the candidate should be denied the right to serve as archon because he had remained neutral during the civil war. Although the speaker is unable to claim that Philon had participated in the crimes of the Thirty, he still insists that Philon should not be allowed to hold office because he failed to help the demos in its time of need.[68]

Some of the arguments lodged against the candidates are outrageous, and it is quite possible that the jury dismissed these accusations. Still, the *dokimasia* provided a forum for grieved parties to air complaints against candidates for their conduct during the civil war. Although some insist that the *dokimasia* was never intended for such purposes, no legal mechanism was in place to prevent the airing of these accusations.

Damages, Assault, and Other Trials

As mentioned above, Callimachus began proceedings against the speaker of Isocrates 18 for defrauding him of his money. In response, the speaker initiated a *paragraphe* against Callimachus on the grounds that he had violated the terms of the amnesty. The speaker of Isocrates 21 also attempted to recover money of which he was allegedly defrauded during the civil war. There are several additional speeches in which the litigants used the civil war as ammunition against their opponents even though it was not directly relevant to the case. In Isocrates 20, the prosecutor accuses Lochites of battery and describes how, even though Lochites was too young to have assisted the Thirty, he has the same disposition as the oligarchs, and therefore the jury must punish him in order to prevent future oligarchic conspiracies (11). In Lysias 18, the speaker describes the terrible plight of his family during the civil war and how he and his brother risk losing their family estate unless the jury takes pity on them. He mentions the services of his uncle Nicias (2–3), how his father was killed for opposing the Thirty (4–5), and how his other uncle, Diognetus, persuaded Pausanias to favor the democratic resistance (10–12). These and other anecdotal references to the civil war will be discussed in greater detail in Part 2. But for now it is enough to point out that they show the subtle and not-so-subtle ways that litigants used the civil war to their advantage in disputes with their opponents.

Despite the unanimous praise the Athenians have received for their willingness to let bygones be bygones and resolve their differences peacefully, the disputes that appeared in the courts show quite dramatically that the agreement did not put an end to division and conflict. As we have seen, the Thirty carried out a brutal campaign of violence, and so it is not surprising that at least some Athenians sought revenge. No law, no matter how well crafted, and no penalty, no matter how severe, could deter some from airing their complaints. Given the elasticity of Athenian law, grieved parties had ample opportunity to pursue their disputes without even risking the consequences of violating the reconciliation agreement. And as the trial of Socrates shows, some clearly suffered the consequences. Thus, laws, rules, and procedures were clearly not enough to prevent further factionalism and even a new round of civil war. But in the end, the courts were enormously useful in restoring the unity of the community, not because they ended disputes, but because they provided the Athenians a forum to reflect on the past, to explain to themselves and to each other what had happened and where they had gone wrong, and to envision the future of the democracy. One could even say that the courts, together with other political institutions, gave Athenians the opportunity to "reinvent" Athens, that the success of the restored democracy depended upon the willingness of the Athenians to remember the past in ways that promoted reconciliation rather than fueled animosity.

PART TWO

CIVIC MEMORY

4 ⪥ REMEMBERING AMNESTY

It is also worth remembering that, while our ancestors performed
many fine deeds in war, not least of all will the city gain renown for
the reconciliation. Although many cities could be found to have fought
well in war, one could not find another city to have planned better
than ours in civil war. Moreover, most accomplishments done at great
risk are due to luck, but no one could offer another reason for our
moderation towards each other than our wisdom.

ISOC. 18.31–32

The civil war shattered Athenians' notions about their community. With little resistance from the rest of the population, conspirators seized power. They carried out a brutal reign, and when democratic exiles began their campaign to remove the oligarchs, they received only modest support from the rest of the citizens. After all that, Sparta forced the democrats to accept an agreement that allowed the collaborators to participate in the restored democracy, thus sowing the seeds for dissension, division, and conflict. Although ancient testimony presents the reconciliation as a *fait accompli,* the legislation enacted after the restoration of the democracy and the disputes heard in the courts reveal that there were still significant disagreements that disrupted the peace among the citizens.

Yet Athens did not sink again into civil war. We cannot fully appreciate how the Athenians were able to maintain the peace until we consider how they remembered the past and how they fostered images of defeat and civil war in civic discourse that promoted reconciliation, in spite of the anger and animosity that remained in the community. The success of the reconciliation depended on the ability of the Athenians to create narratives about the past which reaffirmed their beliefs in the stability of the democracy, the loyalty of the citizens, and the unity of the demos. Through civic discourse, they distanced themselves from the Thirty while simultaneously constructing a continuity with the democracy of the fifth century.

AMNESTY AS A CULTURAL CONSTRUCT

The wording of the reconciliation agreement is startling—"not to re-member past wrongs"—as if it were possible to mandate a collective forgetting and to enforce such a prohibition; even if it were possible, it is hard to imagine how this erasing of the past would insure the success of the restored democracy. Even more difficult to explain is how the democratic exiles could agree to terms that forced them to abandon the benefits of victory: revenge, retribution, and the dissemination of their version of the civil war.

We could dismiss these questions by reducing *me mnesikakein* to mean simply that oligarchic collaborators were granted impunity for offenses committed during the civil war. As shown in Chapters 2 and 3, the Athenians were prohibited only from initiating certain types of legal procedures. They were not literally prohibited from speaking about the past. Still, it is remarkable that they defined such prohibitions with the term *me mnesikakein,* the meaning of which is even retained in the English derivative, "amnesty." By exploring the cultural significance of this phrase, we can better understand why amnesty had such a strong emotional appeal to the Athenians (regardless of whether they adhered to it) and why they had such confidence in the reconciliation, even though it was imposed on them.

Of course, 403 was not the first time that *me mnesikakein* was used to denote amnesty. In 424, some Megarians began negotiations with the Athenian army in order to prevent their fellow citizens from restoring oligarchic exiles (Thuc. 4.66). Their plans, however, backfired (4.67–73). The exiles returned to Megara, and some who had participated in the plot with the Athenians fled. The rest swore oaths to act in the best interest of the city and not to remember past wrongs. But afterward, the exiles established a narrow oligarchy and compelled the people to condemn some one hundred Megarians who were their personal enemies to death on the grounds that they had collaborated with the Athenians (4.74).

Another amnesty occurred in 422 when the Athenians put an end to the rebellion of the Bottiaeans. Under the terms of the agreement, the generals, Council, and other magistrates promised not to remember wrongs (*IG* I³ 76 l. 15). In 411 the democratic faction of Samos, with help from the Athenian fleet stationed in the area, overthrew the Samian oligarchy. They killed thirty and exiled three of the three hundred who had established the oligarchy. The rest were permitted to live under the democracy with the promise that past wrongs would not be remembered

(Thuc. 8.73). And finally, the Athenians enacted the decree of Patrocleides in 405, allowing citizens to return who had been exiled for various crimes, including participation in the rule of the Four Hundred. The decree stipulated that the official records of the exiles' offenses should be erased, that no one was permitted to possess private copies of these records, and that no one could remember past wrongs (And. 1.79).

In all of these instances, the pledge *me mnesikakein* served as a condition to end *stasis* and to reunite the warring factions. Indeed, the factions would never have agreed to end hostilities if crimes committed during civil war were punishable. *Me mnesikakein* was a necessary concession to allow for the transition from a state of war, in which citizens engaged in violent acts and their victims had no recourse to law, to a state of peace, in which citizens were held liable for the offenses that they committed against their fellow citizens. It was also an admission that the polis had no way of resolving civil war fairly. The only option was to disregard what had happened, welcome both factions back into the community, and move forward. And, as the events of Megara forcefully illustrate, the pledge could last only as long as both factions were willing to abide by it. In those cases in which cessation of hostilities placed one faction in a position of power over the other, there was little to prevent the victors from taking advantage of the situation. And so *me mnesikakein* required not only the consent of both parties but also their continual vigilance, since reconciliation was always renegotiable.

These examples show that the purpose of *me mnesikakein* was to prevent individuals from seeking revenge for the wrongs that they had suffered. The concern was not with the act of recounting the past, but rather with the possibility that someone would retaliate against another by recalling the past. *Me mnesikakein* implies that one can use memory of the past as a weapon against others.[1] Hence, the Athenian reconciliation literally translates as follows: "It is not permitted for any one to recall wrongs *against another*."[2]

But how can one recall a past wrong against another? It is possible only by inflicting a punishment, by forcing the guilty party to pay the consequences for his actions. In a sense, then, to impose a punishment on another is a form of remembering (Allen 2000: esp. 65–72, 202–5). Thus, the Furies are described as "remembering of wrongs."[3] Ever mindful of the crimes that the guilty have committed, the Furies do not cease in their hunt until they have exacted punishment. To remember a wrong is therefore to punish the guilty party. Thus, the names of state debtors are inscribed on stelai for as long as they owe the state, and their names are erased after their debts have been paid. It is also why the decree of Patrocleides calls for the list of exiles to be erased and why no one could keep a copy in his private possession. But in the case of an amnesty, the guilty party need not first pay the penalty before the record of his crimes are erased. He is compelled neither to endure a trial in which his offenses would be recounted nor to compensate the victims for the pain he has caused. Indeed, this is a kind of forgetting.[4]

But *me mnesikakein* was a forgetting not only of crimes but also of factionalism that had divided the community, and it has its origin in Greek notions about citizenship. As Morris argues, the polis emerged in the eighth century as Greeks began to define their communities as groups of "middling" citizens. *To meson,* however, was not a class but "an ideological construct," allowing citizens to locate themselves in the middle and to suppress those traits and characteristics that distinguished them from other citizens. Although it reached its fullest form under democracy, the middling construct was not limited to a specific political system or city. It was expressed in a variety of ways and to different degrees throughout the Greek world in architecture, social and political institutions, and language.[5] So the Spartans named themselves the "same ones" (*homoioi*), and the decrees passed by the Athenian Assembly began, "The people resolved" (*edoxe toi demoi*). The rationale for participation in political affairs depended on this idea of sameness, which characterized those men who possessed citizenship and which distinguished them from those individuals prohibited from politics: slaves, resident aliens, and women.

The idea also left its mark on the public and private space that the citizens occupied. As Vernant (1983: 185) explains, once the agora became the political center of the community: "Now the universe of the city-state is one of egalitarian and reversible relationships according to which all the citizens are defined in relationship to one another as being politically identical. One can say that, in that they have access to this circular space centered on the agora, the citizens enter a political system governed by equilibrium, symmetry, and reciprocity."[6] Such values had an impact even on how the Greeks waged war. Hoplite warfare, although tactically not the most effective method of fighting on the rugged terrain of Greece, was preferred because it gave the most prominent role to the bulk of citizens that made up the hoplite troops and managed the affairs of the polis.[7] For Archilochus, the best warrior was not the tall, lanky general but the short infantry man with feet planted squarely on the ground (fr. 114 W).

The middling construct also shaped Greek views about stability, conflict, and reconciliation, and it helps explain why the Athenians depicted the men of Piraeus as the demos in exile. *Stasis,* although etymologically a neutral word, could mean "faction," "sedition," or "civil war." Finley (1962: 6) notes that "there must be deep significance in the fact that a word which has the original sense of 'station' or 'position,' and which, in abstract logic, could have an equally neutral sense when used in a political context, in practice does nothing of the kind, but immediately takes on the nastiest overtones." To have a position implies the existence of an opposing and conflicting position, and thus of factions. But in a polis in which the citizens are alike, dissension and disagreement should not exist, and when it does, it is an indication of a breakdown. *Stasis* rarely has a neutral sense in a political context because the Greeks would have had to recognize not only that it was inevitable for division to exist within the polis but also that this condition was not necessarily disastrous. Rather than reject their ideal, they viewed politics negatively. "This is a strange contradiction," Loraux (1991: 39) remarks, "particularly since we credit the Greeks with having invented politics."

Greeks therefore constructed screens to avoid envisaging conflict as a necessary and natural part of the polis.[8] At the close of the *Eumenides* (984–87), the chorus prays that Athens never suffer from civil war and that the citizens instead "repay joy with joy in the thought of common love and hate with one heart; for this is the remedy of many woes for mortals." The polis is stable when it acts as one in domestic and foreign matters, with a collective hostility directed outward and a unified *philia* inward. On the shield of Achilles (Hom. *Il.* 18.490–540), this dichotomy is vividly illustrated by the city at war versus the city at peace: two scenes of the same city, just as the obverse and reverse of a coin. The community is mutually dependent upon friendship and hatred.[9] Hostility must remain for two reasons. It unites the citizens not only by directing their energies against a foreign enemy but also by preventing the dissipation of their loyalty. Outward hostility checks the encroachment on communal bonds from within and without. The polis retains a duality, but, by relegating hatred and friendship to separate spheres, the very forces that would otherwise destroy the community thus create unanimity.[10] So in the case of civil war, Greek writers often use the reflexive rather than the reciprocal pronoun: "they fought against themselves" rather than "they fought each other" (Loraux 1991: 49) In a sense then, unanimity is maintained, but now hatred is misdirected inward against the community to destroy it rather than outward to strengthen it.

Thus, once the polis has become fragmented by civil war, compromise is necessary to reunite the factions and to restore the harmony of the community. In such a light, we should consider the concessions the Athenian exiles made to the defeated oligarchs. The victors must compromise precisely because their success creates a dangerous imbalance. If they use their victory to punish the defeated and grant themselves a greater share of power, the polis will remain divided with one faction oppressing the other, such as had occurred at Megara. For the reconciliation to succeed, authority must rest with the whole community, *eis to meson,* and not one faction. Compromise therefore requires the victors to elevate the defeated so that they are on equal terms.[11]

It is not enough for the victors merely to welcome the vanquished back into the community as equal members; they must also abandon even legitimate grievances, because otherwise the courts would become a way for them to perpetuate the war and continue to treat the vanquished as their enemies. Herodotus, for example, explains that the Corinthians took part in the expedition against Samos because the Samians had helped Corcyra. If, however, the Corcyraeans had been on friendly terms with Corinth, the Corinthians would never have held a grudge (*apemnesikakeon*) against the Samians (3.49). They were angry at the Samians not because of what they had done but because of whom they had helped. The lesson is that one only pursues a grievance against one's enemies or the friends of one's enemies. In *Phoenissae* (461–64), Jocasta tells her sons, Eteocles and Polyneices, "When a friend comes face to face to a friend at whom he is angry, he must consider only what brings him there and not hold a memory of previous wrongs" (*kakon de ton prin medenos mneian exein*). *Philia*—whether between friends or citizens—cannot last should one party remember the wrongs that the other had committed. So, in the case of civil war, consensus can only be restored should the citizens forget the wrongs that had caused the polis to be divided into two separate and competing factions.

The purpose of *me mnesikakein* was then to transform the former exiles and collaborators from warring factions into a united citizenry. Prosecution for crimes committed during the civil war was prohibited because such suits threatened to alienate the men of the city, create dissension, and perpetuate their animosities. Not surprisingly, defendants argued that it was necessary for the Athenians to adhere to the agreement at all costs. The nephew of Nicias claimed that the democratic exiles agreed to the amnesty because they desired concord and realized that Athens would soon return to a state of civil war if they sought revenge (Lys. 18.18). Likewise, the speaker of Isocrates 18 asked: "Is it not right for you to fear that if we violate the oaths we will produce the very same condition which required us to make them? In fact, you do not need to learn from others how wonderful unanimity is and terrible civil war; for you have experienced both so fully that you could best teach all others about them."[12]

The choice was simple: *homonoia* or *stasis*. As Andocides would have his jury believe, Athenians forgot past wrongs because they considered it more important to preserve the polis than obtain private satisfaction (1.81). The Athenians were able to curb suspicions only by outlawing vengeance as well as the public airing of legitimate grievances. Lévy (1976: 214) suggests, however, that the harmony these litigants advocated was negative, as it was achieved by adhering to a litany of prohibitions. It did not offer the Athenians positive ways to reunite the community or to restore consensus.

As Hartman (1994b: 15) points out, collective forgetting is a type of memory that by its omissions constructs "a highly selective story." By removing—or, rather, attempting to remove—the civil war from civic memory, the Athenians denied that past conflicts had any bearing on the present and declared the disputes that had divided the city and allowed the Thirty to seize power to be resolved (Lévy 1976: 216). Loraux (1988: 27–28) believes that the purpose of this collective amnesia was to restore a continuity with the past between the restored democracy and the democracy of the fifth century, as if Athens had not experienced a civil war and the Thirty had not ruled. The Athenians desired immediate closure, which was not possible if they actually confronted the past and attempted to come to terms with their anger, fear, and sorrow. The civil war was too recent and too painful. Forgetting provided an easy solution that assured them that the city would remain free from internal dissent as long as the citizens continued to forget.

One could object that such readings stretch the meaning of *me mnesikakein* beyond that intended by the drafters. But, in fact, it is quite common for communities to pass over in silence, omit, or selectively recall painful events of their past. The recent debate on the historiography of the Holocaust, the *Historikerstreit*, has attracted contributions from historians from other areas of expertise (Dominick LaCapra, Pierre Vidal-Naquet, and Hayden White) precisely because the questions raised about the Holocaust have an impact on historiography in general.[13] This research has given rise to new approaches to issues concerning trauma and transference, collective and personal memory, the politics of commemoration, and the limits of historical representation.

But more importantly for our purposes, studies on Holocaust memory help us better appreciate the impulse to forget, and they further illuminate the ideological processes at work. For roughly fifteen to twenty years after World War II, Israel and Germany experienced a suppression of the past; both victim and victimizer desired to forget.[14] It is worth quoting Appelfeld (1994: 150) at length:

> So we learned silence. It was not easy to keep silent. But it was a good way out for all of us. For what, when all is said and done, was there to tell? To us as well it began to sound like something imaginary, which ought not to be believed. Of course there was more in that stillness than merely the inability to translate traumatic sights into normal speech. There was a desire to forget, to bury the bitter memories deep in the bedrock of the soul, in a place where no stranger's eye, not even our own, could get to them. So strong was the desire that we managed to accomplish the impossible. One mustn't talk. One mustn't tell. That was the order of the day, and it did not come just from outside. What didn't we do to conceal the dark secret?

As Appelfeld reveals, there was a deep desire at the personal level to control the effects of the trauma, to end them once and for all by obliterating even the memory of trauma. Perhaps such impulses were not calculated, but nor were they irrational or senseless. The Athenian civil war, of course, was not a trauma on the scale of the Holocaust. But if individuals could block out the past even after such a horrifying experience, an experience that would seem impossible to repress given its magnitude, then we should not be surprised that the Athenians could attempt to do the same after the Thirty.

This impulse to forget also influences how a people collectively recall the past and how the past is commemorated at the national level. On the one hand, the Holocaust provided legitimacy for Israel and a sense of urgency for Zionism. On the other hand, it was a disturbing reminder of weakness for a people which sought to place their nation on equal terms with the United States and Europe. So Israelis turned to antiquity to find examples of Jewish courage and to blot out recent memories of the Jewish victim. Ironically, the fall of Masada most captured Israeli imagination, though it was not passed down through Jewish tradition. It became a foil to the Holocaust: the Jewish hero who held out against all odds to replace the recent and horrifying image of Jews led to gas chambers. Masada came to symbolize the goals and aspirations of the new nation and the willingness of its people to endure all obstacles and fight to the bitter end.

This redemptive image, however, depended upon glossing over those parts of Josephus's narrative that were just as embarrassing as the recent events that the Israelis sought to either forget or downplay in the history of their nation. Josephus consistently referred to the fighters at Masada as Sicarii (i.e., a group of extremists who raided neighboring communities and assassinated their political opponents). Modern accounts, on the other hand, either identify them with the Zealots (i.e., a group headed by Eleazar, son of Simon, which seized Jerusalem and occupied the Temple) or call them freedom fighters and empathize how they heroically withstood the Romans. Thus, the defeat of criminals from antiquity who fought against fellow Jews and who committed suicide without a battle was transformed into a victory for a nation seeking to distance itself from a modern catastrophe.[15]

Those nations that Germany occupied were confronted by an equally vexing problem: how to incorporate in their history the defeat to Germany and the willingness of some to participate in occupation and genocide. Divisions surfaced during the war which were not easy to explain after it had ended. In his study of postwar France, Rousso (1991) shows how the myth of the "Resistance" as a movement that symbolically represented the nation as a whole gained widespread acceptance from 1954 to 1971. It allowed the French to minimize the impact of the Vichy regime on French society and to avoid recognizing that they had experienced a civil war under German occupation. The Resistance became an abstract symbol, extending beyond the various competing movements that had resisted Germany and beyond the individuals who had fought in these movements. At the same time, questions about collaboration, accommodation, and passivity, if not completely disregarded, were safely removed from postwar debates under the cloak of a united resistance.[16] World War II was transformed from a civil war into a foreign war, either by passing over or by ignoring the significance of the divisions under German occupation.[17]

To return to Athens, *me mnesikakein* was not merely a pledge to refrain from certain kinds of prosecutions, nor merely a pledge to restore the harmony of the community by allowing the former exiles and former collaborators to be on equal terms with the members of the democratic resistance. It was also an attempt to distance the restored democracy from the ill effects of the civil war by denying that past divisions still existed. It was an attempt to pass over these divisions in silence. It allowed the Athenians to insist that the civil war never seriously threatened the unity of the Athenian people and that, once the war was over, the democracy could simply continue where it had left off before Athens surrendered to Sparta, before the Thirty seized power, and before the band of democratic exiles marched against Athens.

Hence, *me mnesikakein* was not only a forgetting of past wrongs but also a kind of erasure of the past from civic memory. But to erase the past, even only partially, would be a defeat for the men of Piraeus, because it would deny them important opportunities to assign the civil war democratic meaning (Loraux 1986: 196–201). Perhaps by forgetting past wrongs the democratic exiles failed to use the past to their advantage, that is, to construct the restored democracy as would serve their interests. Even worse, this strategy gave them no assurance that the former supporters of oligarchy would now be loyal democrats and would not again attempt to overthrow the democracy. In a perverse way, the prohibition validated the oligarchy by forbidding certain memories, as if crimes committed by those outside the Thirty and the other groups excluded from the amnesty were justifiable. To restore the community without distinction between the victors and the defeated was to dismiss what was at stake in the civil war. Even more disturbing, to forget was to deny the magnitude of the crimes of the oligarchs and their supporters.

STRATEGIES OF REMEMBERING

No matter how much litigants espoused these various underlying meanings of *me mnesikakein,* they still recounted the civil war over and over again. It is not surprising that prosecutors of former oligarchs and collaborators advocated remembering.[18] Recalling the civil war, they attempted to tap into the jurors' anger and fear in order to convict the defendants. So in his speech against Agoratus, the prosecutor explained how hostilities erupted at the victory procession: "When they reached an agreement and the men of Piraeus made their procession to the Acropolis, Aesimus led them and this man [Agoratus] was so bold that he was actually present! Equipped with heavy armor, he followed in the procession with the hoplites to the city. But when they came to the gates and set their armor down before going inside the city, Aesimus saw Agoratus and approached him. Seizing Agoratus' shield, he hurled it down and told

Agoratus to go to hell! For he said that a murderer must not be in the procession to Athena" (Lys. 13.80–81). The prosecutor provided testimony from witnesses to corroborate his story, but it is impossible to know for certain whether the confrontation actually occurred or how those present reacted. Yet the purpose of this story is clear. He wanted the jury to admire the conduct of Aesimus and to make a stand against Agoratus like Aesimus. Their choice was simple, to follow in the path of the democratic exiles or the henchmen of the oligarchs: honor or shame. The prosecutor offered them the chance to exact vengeance against the Thirty by condemning Agoratus.

In the only extant speech that Lysias wrote for himself to deliver, he asked the jurors to feel the same anger as when they were exiles (Lys. 12.96). He claimed that the crimes of the Thirty against the Athenian people were so terrible that the former oligarchs could not pay fully even if they were executed twice (37). It would be impossible, so Lysias argued, to accuse the Thirty of more outrageous acts than what they had actually committed. So terrible were their crimes against all Athenians that the prosecutor did not have to explain why he initiated the suit against the defendant; rather, the defendant had to explain his hostility against the entire city (1–2). To further arouse the jury's anger, Lysias abruptly concluded his speech by saying, "You have heard, you have seen, you have suffered, you hold the guilty. Give your verdict" (100).[19] The speaker of Lysias 26 told the members of the Council that they would incur the hostility of the Athenian people if they allowed Evander to become archon. Evander might be on trial before them, but they were on trial before the entire city which was watching to learn what view they held (12 14). Likewise, the speaker of Lysias 31 declared that it would be outrageous if Philon, a man whose conduct had established a new standard foreign to democracy (34), were allowed to live in Athens without punishment and even hold office (26).

Even democratic exiles were subjected to such criticism. In his speech against Ergocles, a former exile charged with embezzlement and treason, the prosecutor said that the Athenians should be more angry with Ergocles than with the Thirty because the Thirty were elected to harm the people, whereas the defendant was trusted to promote the interests of the city (Lys. 28.12–14). He offered Ergocles as a substitute for the Thirty. Unable to vent their anger against the former oligarchs, they had on trial an even more despicable criminal, or so the prosecutor would have them believe. In response to charges of having supported the Thirty, the candidate in Lysias 25 asked the jury to imagine what crimes his accusers would have committed if they had been allowed to be members of the oligarchy (30). He suggested that they were no different from the Thirty. Because of the dangers that they suffered in Piraeus, they believed they could do as they pleased and thus were the cause of the suspicion among the Athenians (31–33).

Advocates of remembering further justified prosecution by arousing the jury's fear of civil unrest. Lysias claimed that the trial of Eratosthenes would determine whether the townsmen would rule as tyrants over the city or would live on equal terms with their fellow citizens (12.35). People were watching to find out whether they would be able to plot against the city with impunity (85). If such men escaped, they would be able to destroy the city again (88). Other prosecutors said that the Athenians must protect themselves and stop those who aimed to return Athens to a state of civil war. If the Athenians were to permit former oligarchs to hold office, they would again seize control of Athens (Lys. 26.9). The prosecutor of Ergocles argued that the jury must convict Ergocles because he was planning to establish an oligarchy. By accepting bribes and embezzling money from the people, Ergocles proved himself willing to surrender Athenian walls and ships (Lys. 28.7, 11). He was just like the Thirty, and until such persons were punished for their offenses the danger of civil unrest remained.[20]

Even advocates of forgetting found it useful to recall the past.[21] They mentioned the civil war and the subsequent reconciliation to persuade the jury that the stability of the restored democracy depended upon the continued enforcement of the amnesty. The Thirty showed why the Athenians must avoid civil strife. In addition, these advocates claimed that others would be vulnerable to prosecution if the jury should find in favor of the prosecution.[22] As Andocides argued, "Some come here to learn whether they can trust the established laws and the oaths which you swore to each other, others to test your opinion whether they will be able to act as sycophants without fear, make indictments, lodge information against others, and make arrests" (1.105). If the Athenians violated the agreement, sycophants would spring up and others would face similar charges. The enemies of the restored democracy welcomed such a situation because they expected those citizens who suffered *atimia* as a result of these illegal actions to become their allies. By stirring up dissension, the sycophants were therefore the real threat to the democracy, not those accused of supporting the Thirty (Lys. 25.5, 24, 29–32). Moreover, advocates of forgetting responded to accusations about their own conduct during the civil war by recalling what their opponents had done.[23]

MINDFUL FORGETFULNESS

It was impossible for the Athenians either to remember the past "as it really happened" or to erase the civil war completely from civic memory. Advocates of remembering either passed over in silence or minimized the complicity of the demos, and advocates of forgetting reminded the Athenians of the reasons why they must forget. Remembering and forgetting were not complete in themselves; rather, they were dependent on each other. As Nagy has observed with regard to archaic poetry, "Without the obliteration of what need not be remembered, there cannot be memory."[24] The reverse is also true: memory makes forgetting possible. But the selection of certain memories to forget and others to remember is not innocent, because specific individuals and groups benefit from the selections.

As the Athenians reconstructed the civil war in civic memory, these strategies of reconciliation blended together, which in turn promoted peace. What I call a "mindful forgetfulness" emerged, whereby the reconciliation was transformed from a symbol of compromise into a symbol of victory, the men of the city from supporters of the Thirty into loyal democrats, and the amnesty as promoting, not complicating, justice. Before discussing how public speakers depicted the demos and explained the amnesty, let us first examine how the Athenians rendered the civil war a victory for the demos through commemorative monuments.

Commemorating Compromise

We have already discussed the three decrees passed by the Assembly awarding honors to members of the democratic resistance. Each of the one hundred citizens who were besieged by the Thirty and the Spartans at Phyle received an olive crown and less than ten drachmas per person to use for a sacrifice and an offering. The decree of Theozotides awarded state support to the legitimate children of all Athenians who died while fighting against the oligarchs, and by another decree those metics and foreigners who fought with the democratic exiles were granted limited privileges. These motions were recorded on three stone stelai and were prominently displayed in public. The Athenians did not erect these stelai merely to announce that the motions had passed; they served to commemorate the victory of the democratic exiles, to remind the Athenians who were the winners and who were the losers of the civil war, and to impose a democratic version of the period of civil unrest on Athenian landscape.[25] For the very same reason, the inscriptions in honor of proxenies that the Thirty had destroyed were restored and placed in public for everyone to see. What better way to undo the rule of the Thirty than by erecting monuments to replace those that the Thirty had torn down? These decrees must, therefore, be reexamined so that their significance not only as acts of the Assembly but also as commemorative monuments can be appreciated.

Although the rewards were modest, the language of the decrees does not suggest that the Athenians were reluctant to award the men of Piraeus. On the stele honoring the "heroes of Phyle," the following epigram was inscribed, "Because of the bravery of these men who first set out to depose those ruling the city by unjust laws and placed their bodies in danger, the indigenous Athenian people have granted them crowns" (Aesch. 3.190). The rest of the democratic army was not excluded; rather, the demos singled out the one hundred citizens who fought the combined forces of the Spartans and the Thirty at Phyle for their daring initiative against overwhelming odds. To honor even a fraction of the exiles was to side with the men of Piraeus, and, in fact, the recipients were praised in the inscription for their opposition to the unjust regime. But more importantly, the Athenians legitimized the power of the demos by commemorating the early stages of the uprising. The "heroes of Phyle" were not praised for restoring the democracy but for being the first to resist the oligarchs. The epigraph also makes it clear that the demos now ruled Athens again. It is the demos that bestowed the honors on the heroes of Phyle and was responsible for placing this inscription in public. The heroes of Phyle were now indebted to the people, and the stele served as visible reminder for all that the demos had returned and the democracy had been restored.

In the decree of Theozotides, the sacrifice of all Athenians who died fighting the oligarchs was vividly described "in rather more colorful language than that found in most Attic decrees of this period" (Stroud 1971: 285). Loraux (1986: 201) notes how the description of their deaths as *biaioi thanatoi* violates the traditional language of funerary epigrams, which leads her to conclude that the Athenians had difficulty commemorating the victory of the exiles. I would argue that this emphasis on brutality transformed the Thirty into outsiders, thereby allowing the Athenians to recast the civil war as a foreign war and to claim a victory untainted by *stasis*. By their lawlessness, the oligarchs turned themselves into foreigners and made Athens their enemy. Since they were utter villains willing to violate all norms, the deaths of their victims could be described only as violent. Moreover, the decree awarded the sons of the dead state support, which was an honor normally given only to war orphans. The Athenians magnified the victory of the democratic exiles.

In addition to these stelai, the Athenians set up two other commemorative monuments: the tomb of Thrasybulus in the *demosion sema* and a herm beside the walls of Piraeus, which were rebuilt in 395 / 4. Describing the graves between the Dipylon gate and the Academy, Pausanias gives special attention to that of Thrasybulus. He indicates that his tomb was first, after which were those of Pericles, Chabrias, and Phormio, and he notes that the achievements of Thrasybulus included ending the civil war and persuading the Athenians to adhere to the agreement.[26] His burial in the *demosion sema,* an area "charged with heroic sacrality" (Clairmont 1983: i, 45), would have been inappropriate had the Athenians viewed Thrasybulus as simply the leader of one faction of a violent civil war. But the democrats rejected this image of their leader. By placing his tomb in the public cemetery, they declared that the victory over the oligarchs was a victory for Athens. Thus, they rendered democracy the lawful constitution and the actions of Thirty illegal.

The tomb of the Spartans in the *demosion sema* appears to undermine such an interpretation of the civil war. But in the funeral oration of Lysias, the speaker denied that this privilege was intended to honor the Spartans who died fighting against the democrats. Instead, he suggested that the monument reflected back on the men of Piraeus: "Nevertheless, unafraid of the mass of their opponents, risking their own lives, they set up a trophy over their enemy, and they rendered the tombs of the Spartans which are near this monument as proof of their *arete.* And so, they showed that the city was great instead of run down and that it was harmonious and not in a state of civil unrest, and they rebuilt walls in place of those torn down" (2.63). Rendering the tomb a *mnema* for the democrats and their valor, the speaker failed to mention that it was Athenian citizens who had requested the Spartan troops. Although he implicitly recognized that Athens had been in a state of civil war, he disassociated the men of Piraeus from this struggle. They had fought against a foreign enemy, and they were the ones who had put an end to *stasis.* They were not members of a faction, but loyal citizens seeking to restore the unity of the city. The tomb of the Spartans served as a visible reminder that the civil war had an external component, and it simultaneously obscured the fact that the war was waged between citizens.

Finally, the erection of a herm seems an odd way to commemorate the restoration of the democracy, but, as scholars suggest, herms expressed values fundamental to the democracy. Osborne (1985a: 53) argues,

"The herm takes up the gaze and claims identity with every viewer. This identity is not just identity before death and the gods, it is no less than the democratic claim that men are equal in all their hermaic qualities." As Halperin (1990: 104) remarks, "The erection of herms may be another symptom . . . of the growing sense of masculine self-assertion and the new pride in masculine egalitarianism that accompanied the consolidation of the democracy at Athens." In other words, images such as the herms promoted a radical "middling" construct of the citizen body. Masculinity rather than noble birth or wealth became the justification for participation in politics.

After their mutilation in 415, the herms acquired even greater democratic significance. According to Thucydides, the Athenians believed that oligarchic sympathizers were conspiring to overthrow the democracy, and they went to great lengths to expose them (6.27). When Andocides returned after the restoration of the democracy, his enemies used his involvement to their advantage in their quarrel against him. Although they accused Andocides of committing new offenses, they supported their accusations by reminding the jury of his involvement in the mutilation of the herms. Whether or not the mutilation was in fact part of an oligarchic conspiracy to overthrow the democracy, the herms were now implicated in the civil unrest between the democrats and the oligarchs. Now a symbol of the democratic struggle to rid Athens of oligarchy, they revealed that the democracy was as fragile as these statues.

By erecting a herm beside the rebuilt walls of Piraeus in 395 / 4, the archons commemorated the new fortifications, which would protect Athens once again from foreign invasions.[27] They had repaired the damage inflicted by the Thirty and the Spartans. Juxtaposed beside the new fortifications, the herm was also an image that implicitly contrasted the actions of oligarchs with those of democrats. Oligarchs mutilate herms and conspire with the enemy to tear down Athenian fortifications; democrats erect new herms and rebuild walls. Moreover, this image gave the Athenians a sense of continuity with the fifth-century democracy; they were restoring what the oligarchs had destroyed. Thus the Athenians represented the restoration of the democracy as a victory by dotting the landscape of Athens with such memorials. At the same time, however, these memorials were implicated in the forgetting of the civil war by avoiding explicit references to the many Athenians who failed to come to the aid of the democrats, or did so only in the later stages of the war. Only by passing over in silence the complicity of the demos could the Athenians remember the restoration of the democracy as a victory.

The Demos in Exile

So too in forensic oratory, remembering and forgetting blended together. Prosecutors and defendants, for example, frequently addressed the members of the jury as the men of Piraeus, although some had certainly remained in the city. Often they referred to the period of civil unrest by saying, "you were expelled," "you were in exile," or "you returned."[28] Mantitheus asserted that he had no reason to deny serving on the cavalry of the Thirty, since many others who had done so later became Councilors after the democracy was restored and still others were even elected generals and *hipparchoi* (Lys. 16.8). Despite this assertion, he addressed the members of the Council as if they were all former exiles (6). The one notable exception occurs in Lysias 12. At the end of the speech, Lysias appealed to the jurors by addressing them separately as men of the city and men of Piraeus.[29] He told those who had remained in the city that they too were victims of the Thirty, and he reminded those who had joined the democrats in Piraeus of their sufferings (92–98). But in the very same speech, Lysias also addressed the jurors collectively as men of Piraeus (57–58).

One possible explanation is that this address was a form of flattery which litigants used to win the favor of the jury. The men of the city might even have considered it a compliment to be referred to as if they were former exiles (Adams 1905: 102). But this suggestion does not explain why only once in the extant orations a litigant acknowledged that some members of the jury had remained in the city. Certainly it was useful for a former exile who wanted to win the sympathy of the jurors to address them as the men of Piraeus. By transforming them from a heterogeneous group with differing allegiances into loyal democrats who had actively assisted in the restoration of the democracy, the litigant would create a more receptive jury. Moreover, if the jurors viewed themselves as former exiles, they would be more inclined to vote against the men of the city.

In *P. Oxy.* 1606 ll. 113–18, for example, speaking on behalf of Lysias, who was attempting to recover his property, the litigant declared, "for it would be terrible, men of the jury, if you returned [to Athens] as the victims only to be deprived of your property as if you were the criminals." Sometimes this form of address served to arouse the jury's anger against the opposing litigant. After reminding the jurors how they lost their private property and how they were all expelled together from their fatherland by the Thirty, the prosecutor of Lysias 13 told them that they could obtain satisfaction by punishing the person responsible for their misfortunes, namely Agoratus.[30] It would have been counterproductive for the prosecutor to acknowledge that some members of the court had remained in the city, since this would have served only to point out that they too were vulnerable to prosecution.

Yet on other occasions it would have been useful for litigants to remind the jurors of their vulnerability. In fact, as mentioned above, they sometimes argued that others would face similar charges if the amnesty were violated. By addressing the jurors separately as men of Piraeus and men of the city, the litigants could personalize this danger. However, they did not do so. Instead, they too referred to the jurors as the men of Piraeus.[31] I suggest that litigants avoided pointing out that some members of the jury had remained in the city because they did not want to risk offending those jurors by reminding them of this embarrassing fact. Even when Lysias addressed the men of the city separately, he emphasized that they were victims of the Thirty (12.92–94). But they were praiseworthy only in as much as they were similar to the men of Piraeus.

Litigants, however, did not address the members of the jury collectively as the men of Piraeus merely to avoid embarrassing those jurors who had remained in the city. They could just as easily have done so if they simply avoided referring to them as either the men of Piraeus or the men of the city. To address the jurors as former exiles was to make a statement about the authority of the demos similar to that of other rhetorical tropes. Litigants, for example, often used the second person plural when referring to decrees passed in the Assembly. Although there was certainly an overlap in personnel between the courts and the Assembly, Ober argues that this does not explain why litigants addressed the jurors as if they had all been present at a given meeting of the Assembly. The Athenians preferred to believe that the same men served on the courts as attended the Assembly because it affirmed the power of the demos. Such an address was a fiction that promoted the notion that the law courts and the Assembly acted in accord. If the same people served in both institutions, then both voiced the will of the demos.[32] So, when litigants referred to the jurors as the men of Piraeus, they declared that the former exiles controlled the courts and, by extension, Athens. This address did not undermine the Athenian construct of the ruling demos; rather, it affirmed that the men of Piraeus were the demos.

Both factions of the civil war could not represent the people, because this would require the Athenians to deny that Athens was a community of like-minded citizens and to accept an image of the demos as a group of citizens divided into two opposing factions. The men of the city had stayed in Athens after the oligarchs seized power. If they represented the people, then the Athenians would have had to accept the paradoxical conclusion that at least some members of the demos had supported the Thirty. By removing the men of the city from the demos, the Athenians could assert that the demos had remained unified in spite of the civil war.

Furthermore, by equating the men of Piraeus with the demos, the Athenians constructed a continuity with the past. The oligarchs did not dissolve the democracy. It was in exile with the men of Piraeus, and their return to Athens was equivalent to the restoration of the demos. The reconciliation was not a compromise between the democrats and the oligarchs in the sense that both factions were placed on equal terms. The men of Piraeus ruled Athens, and the men of the city were allowed to participate only if they gave up their former allegiances and again became members of the demos. The Athenians thus transformed the reconciliation into a victory by representing the men of Piraeus as the demos in exile, but this victory was only possible by reintegrating the men of the city so that they no longer existed as a separate faction. Otherwise, they would have served as a reminder that the restored democracy was vulnerable to unrest and the reconciliation was only a compromise.

The Athenians reincorporated the men of the city into the community by forgetting that they had supported the Thirty and by remembering them as victims of the Thirty who opposed the oligarchs after the reign of terror began. But as Cloché has argued, the evidence in fact suggests that, despite some dissension within the ranks, the Three Thousand continued to support the oligarchy. They deposed the Thirty and elected the Ten not because they wanted to reach an agreement with the democratic exiles but because they were dissatisfied with the Thirty's campaign against the exiles. In fact, once the Ten were installed, they sent an embassy to Sparta to request assistance (Xen. *Hell.* 2.4.28). They only later agreed to a reconciliation because of Spartan pressure.

The men of the city undoubtedly benefited from depicting themselves as hostile opponents to the oligarchs. This fiction allowed them to dissociate themselves from the Thirty and their policies and to assert that they were as much responsible for the restoration of the democracy as the men of Piraeus. The candidate of Lysias 25 said: "When you heard that the men of the city were in agreement, you had little hope of return since you considered our harmony to be the greatest obstacle to you in your exile. But when you learned that the Three Thousand were divided [i.e., in a state of *stasis*], the rest of the citizens had been banished from the city, the Thirty were quarreling, and more feared on your behalf than were fighting against you, then you expected to return and punish your enemies" (21–22).

This image of internal dissent promoted a sense of unity in spite of civil war; for opposition to the Thirty existed on all fronts, both inside and outside the city. Whereas the men of Piraeus actively opposed the oligarchs, the Three Thousand were negatively responsible for the restoration of the democracy by virtue of their discord. In funeral orations, speakers always attributed Athenian defeat to their own failure rather than the success of their enemies, thus rendering the Athenians victorious in their defeat (Loraux 1986: 138–41). The image of internal dissent in the funeral oration allowed the Athenians to believe that Athens was militarily superior to its enemies. So this representation of the Three Thousand as deeply divided preserved the integrity of the demos. The men of Piraeus were successful because the oligarchs alienated the entire community. Athens thus remained united in spite of civil war.

Even prosecutors of men who had remained in the city accepted this portrayal of the Three Thousand. At the *dokimasia* of Evander, the plaintiff said that the men of Piraeus, although fewer in numbers, defeated the oligarchs because of dissension within the city (Lys. 26.17–20). In the trial of Eratosthenes, Lysias stated that the Ten replaced the Thirty because a growing number of the citizens within the city desired a reconciliation with the democrats (12.54, 58). At the end of the speech, he said that the men of the city were forced to fight on behalf of the Thirty, and although they did not benefit from the oligarchy they received a share of the infamy (92–94). The prosecutors, however, were not disinterested parties. They depicted the men of the city favorably because they wanted those jurors who had remained in the city to be receptive to their arguments.[33] In order to be successful, they needed to appeal to both former exiles and former oligarchic sympathizers.

Regardless of their motives, the result was the same. By portraying the men of the city as victims of the Thirty and by asserting that internal dissent helped bring down the oligarchy, prosecutors alleviated the fear that the men of the city might attempt to overthrow the restored democracy. Ironically, in their prosecution of individual oligarchs and oligarchic supporters, they helped promote the reintegration of the men of the city as a whole. They declared that virtually all of the Athenian people had opposed the Thirty and thus reduced the body of oligarchic supporters to those groups and individuals who had been excluded from the amnesty in the first place. Although this favorable representation of the men of the city created an obstacle in the long run for those seeking redress for crimes committed during the civil war, it gave the Athenians the assurance that the democrats were again in control of the city and Athens was free from oligarchic factions. The former exiles had their victory, but at a price. Victory was possible only by welcoming the men of the city back into the democratic community.

Amnesty for the Innocent

The amnesty permitted certain crimes committed during the civil war to go unpunished. In other words, it prohibited the application of laws that were otherwise in effect. Suppose an individual committed a crime during the civil war which was covered by the amnesty. If he were prosecuted, the amnesty would require the jury to acquit him even though he was guilty. Certainly this verdict was in accord with the amnesty, but was it just? Rather than recognize that reconciliation required compromise and complicated law, litigants insisted that justice was a simple matter in spite of the amnesty. First, litigants maintained that a just verdict was still easily obtainable. Defendants argued that the amnesty simply added one more reason that the jury must acquit, while prosecutors responded by denying that the amnesty was even relevant. The jurors had only to consider whether the defendant was innocent or guilty. Second, litigants assured the jurors that Athens would remain free from civil strife provided they delivered a just verdict. Defendants claimed that the amnesty prevented *stasis*, while prosecutors maintained that punishing former oligarchs deterred others from plotting against the democracy. If they did not have to choose between justice and advantage, then the jurors did not have to recognize the problems that the reconciliation created and the dangers that confronted the restored democracy.

In a speech probably delivered during the Corinthian War, a litigant accused of failing to pay a fine ended his defense by instructing the jurors to "deem justice above all else, take notice that you even forgive conspicuous wrongs, and do not allow those who are innocent to suffer unjustly the greatest misfortunes because of personal enmity" (Lys. 9.22).[34] It is tempting to believe that the defendant was referring to the amnesty. But, even if he was not, his comments help reveal how the amnesty complicated the verdict. Justice required the jury to acquit the innocent and to convict the guilty. If the defendant committed a wrong, the jury was under oath to observe the laws and punish him. The amnesty, on the other hand, called for the jury to acquit the defendant regardless of his guilt and regardless of the existing laws. Although an acquittal was in accord with the amnesty, this verdict could be considered unjust, because it permitted an individual who had committed a wrong to go unpunished.

At the very least, the amnesty created competing and conflicting claims to justice, thus making it more difficult for the jury to deliver a just verdict. For example, the candidate of Lysias 25 reminded the jurors of their obligation to abide by the amnesty. Yet at the same time, he conceded, "Nevertheless when we see that those responsible for your suffering pay the penalty, remembering what happened to you, we forgive you, but when you manifestly punish the innocent just like the guilty, you will place all of us under suspicion by the same vote."[35] Although technically the jury had to adhere to the amnesty, the candidate argued that noncompliance was pardonable when the defendant was guilty. After all, an individual who commits a crime ought to suffer the consequences. Yet a guilty verdict, however excusable, was still in violation of the amnesty.

Implementing the amnesty created an unresolvable dilemma. Whether the jurors acquitted or convicted a defendant guilty of committing crimes during the civil war, the verdict was problematic. The amnesty required them to deliver an acquittal, but the defendant's actions required a conviction. Recognizing such competing pressures, the defendant of Isocrates 18 said he would prove the prosecution's accusations to be false in order to make the jury more willing to adhere to the amnesty (4). This is an odd assertion, since the innocent did not need amnesty, but it allowed him to maintain that the jury had no choice but to vote in his favor. If the defendant was innocent, the jurors could determine both from his actions and from the amnesty that an acquittal was the just verdict.

By professing their innocence, the men of the city allowed the Athenians to believe that adjudication was uncomplicated despite the amnesty. If only the innocent remained, a jury of ordinary citizens was easily able to deliver a just verdict, since even without the amnesty they had to acquit the innocent. But the amnesty was still necessary. In a city free from oligarchic sympathizers, it insured that the jurors would not, as the candidate of Lysias 25 feared, vent their anger against those who had had no part in the oligarchy. Although public speakers gladly proclaimed their innocence, it seems remarkable that the Athenians could honestly believe that the oligarchic sympathizers had simply vanished after the expulsion of the Thirty. Nevertheless, they had powerful incentives to accept the assertions of any given speaker. If defendants were innocent, then at least for the moment Athenians did not have to recognize that reconciliation demanded sacrifices. There was no danger of further oligarchic uprisings, and the amnesty, far from undermining the laws by permitting past crimes to go unpunished, upheld them by preventing the Athenians from convicting the innocent.

Prosecutors, on the other hand, had to convince the jurors that oligarchic sympathizers remained in Athens even after the expulsion of the Thirty and that justice required them to convict those who had wronged others during the civil war. Not surprisingly, they preferred to detail the crimes of the defendants rather than invoke the amnesty, which allowed them to insist that the jurors were easily able to reach a just verdict regardless of the amnesty. Lysias instructed the jurors that Eratosthenes had to prove either that he did not arrest Polemarchus or that he was right to do so. But Eratosthenes admitted that he had wrongly arrested him, and therefore it was easy for the jury to deliver a just verdict (12.34). In contrast to the Thirty, who killed the innocent without a fair trial, the demos preferred to try according to the laws those who had attempted to destroy the city (82). As no punishment sufficed for such villains, it would be outrageous for the jury not to allow the prosecution to exact from them whatever penalty was sought (84).

In a like manner, the prosecutor of Lysias 13 told the jury that Agoratus must prove either that he did not harm the demos or that he was justified to do so (84). If the jurors failed to punish him, their verdict would serve to convict those whom the Thirty had killed. They must therefore convict Agoratus in order to acquit those whom the Thirty had convicted (92–94). Yet they need not worry that the punishment he sought was too extreme, because Agoratus deserved to die more than once for the crimes he had committed against the Athenian people (91). Such arguments served to alleviate concerns about violating the amnesty. It was their duty, the prosecutor insisted, to convict the guilty (2–3). By implicating Agoratus in the crimes of the Thirty and by reminding the jurors of the atrocities they had suffered, he was using their anger to his advantage.

At the *dokimasia* of Philon, the prosecutor said that the candidate's crimes were so terrible that it was impossible to detail his wickedness in full (Lys. 31.3–4). This claim seems to be an exaggeration, as his main accusation was that Philon had remained neutral during the civil war. And, as the candidate stated in his defense and the prosecutor even conceded, neutrality was not prohibited by the laws. In response to this defense, the prosecutor argued that the Athenians never imagined that anyone would have committed such a grave offense. Otherwise, they would have certainly enacted a law prohibiting neutrality (27–28). He would have the members of the Council believe that they should reject Philon even though he had not violated the established laws. In a sense, he was arguing that the laws did not make an act a crime, but the Athenians intuitively recognized certain acts as crimes and established laws to prescribe penalties for such acts. A just decision was therefore easily obtainable. The members of the Council needed only to consider whether they approved or disapproved of Philon's conduct.

In a section from Lysias 26 that has already been used to illustrate the ambiguities of the reconciliation, the prosecutor attempted to assure the Council that his accusations against Evander did not violate the amnesty (16). Whereas the candidate of Lysias 25 had said that noncompliance was pardonable in the case of the guilty, the prosecutor of Evander declared that the amnesty did not apply to the guilty. Acknowledging that some had remained in the city and engaged in crimes while others had helped restore the democracy, he said that "the demos therefore bestowed on them the greatest honors, selecting them, rather than those men, to serve as their generals, *hipparchs*, and ambassadors, and they never regretted it. Because of those men who had committed many wrongs, they created the *dokimasia*, whereas because of them who were innocent of wrongdoing, they agreed to the reconciliation" (Lys. 26.20). He claimed that the amnesty was designed only to protect the innocent and that the Athenians had every intention of punishing those who had committed crimes during the civil war. At the very least, such individuals would not be permitted to hold public office. Whereas the men of the city maintained their innocence so they could insist that the jury had to acquit them regardless of the amnesty, the prosecutor of Evander asserted that the amnesty was irrelevant and that the Council needed only to consider the question of guilt. Although his assertion was dubious, it allowed him to maintain that the Council had no choice but to forbid Evander from serving as archon.

Thus, defendants and prosecutors denied that the reconciliation complicated the legal process. Both agreed that the jury was able to deliver a just verdict by examining the conduct of the accused. But defendants maintained that the amnesty added one more reason that the jury had to acquit, and prosecutors asserted that it was irrelevant.

CONCLUSION

In many ways, these fictions established a safe framework for the Athenians to work through their anxiety without disrupting the peace. Since they neither significantly expanded nor reduced the citizen roll after the restoration of the democracy, neither faction gained the upper hand. Thrasybulus failed in his efforts to pass a decree that would have given citizenship to the foreigners and metics who had assisted the democratic exiles. The Assembly later passed a similar decree, which probably granted the foreigners special privileges, including *isoteleia,* but not citizenship. Even if some became citizens, probably fewer did than would have through Thrasybulus's bill.

Thus, this stalemate forced the former exiles to reach out to the men of the city. Whether they liked it or not, these men attended the Assembly, sat in the law courts, served on the Council, and held public offices. Speakers had no choice but to construct arguments that would appeal, as they believed, to the citizens whom they were addressing. The result was a reconstruction of the past in civic memory which both sides could tolerate, but the reconciliation was never final because it depended upon the maintenance of these fictions. Had the Athenians decided to reject the representation of the Three Thousand as victims, retribution and division would have been possible consequences. Moreover, their denial that the Thirty had received support from at least some members of the demos prevented them from working through their most troubling memory. At least, however, this avoidance gave the Athenians time to heal their wounds, and time was most needed.

I marvel that Nicomachus deems himself worthy to recall the wrongs [*mnesikakein*] of others in this illegal manner when I will show that he plotted against the demos. Listen to me, men of the jury, for it is right to hear such accusations against the very men who say that they are now loyal to the demos although they once subverted the democracy.

LYS. 30.9

Even if civic memory of the civil war eased the tension between the former factions, conciliatory representations did not prevent accusations and counteraccusations such as the above. At least in some cases, disgruntled citizens advanced favorable representations of their former enemies as a group while they sought satisfaction against specific individuals. Reconciliation at the representational level and retribution in the courts were far from incompatible. Reconciliation could even be used to justify retribution. As we saw in the previous chapter, the speaker of Lysias 26 asserted that many of the citizens who had remained in Athens during the civil war were loyal to the democracy and deserved to be protected by the amnesty, but he then proceeded to explain why Evander was not one of them and should therefore not be allowed to serve as archon (16–20).

Litigants individually manipulated representations of the men of Piraeus and the men of the city to justify either their own inclusion within or the exclusion of their enemies from the ranks of citizens deemed acceptable. Whether appearing in court as prosecutors or defendants, litigants attempted to persuade the jurors that they had remained loyal to the demos during the civil war by presenting themselves as opponents of the Thirty, victims, or, at the very least, innocent bystanders. Opposing litigants countered by challenging their motives, by denying that they had any part in the democratic victory, or by accusing them of involvement in the crimes of the oligarchs. Yet the very same ambiguities that created areas of contention and allowed litigants to make accusations and counteraccusations also helped to promote reconciliation.

Since many were vulnerable to some form of criticism or allegation, it was difficult for any single citizen to appropriate for himself the praise bestowed on the demos for the restoration of the democracy. The ambiguities of the civil war allowed suspect individuals to present themselves as loyal democrats and even to challenge the claims of former exiles. Pointing out their opponents' shortcomings, speakers denied that they represented the men of Piraeus. Although everyone praised the amnesty, no one dared to admit in court to having participated in the oligarchy. As we have seen, it was as if the amnesty protected only the innocent. The men of the city maintained this fiction of innocence to assure the Athenians that they intended to adhere to the laws of the restored democracy. By disavowing past allegiances, they asserted that they would now be loyal to the democracy, despite whatever they might have done in the past.

THE MEN OF PIRAEUS

As a group, the men of Piraeus were considered beyond reproach. Litigants claimed this title to win the sympathy of the jurors, and opposing litigants responded by denying that their opponents deserved to benefit from the high esteem in which the Athenians held the men of Piraeus. Speakers who presented themselves as the men of Piraeus no doubt benefited if the Athenians regarded their deeds as exceptional. More surprising are the strategies of their adversaries. Rather than challenge the status of the former exiles, the opposing speakers conceded that the men of Piraeus deserved special recognition, making it easier for them to attack their opponents without appearing hostile to the democratic exiles. Thus, as litigants praised the men of Piraeus, whether to win the jury's sympathy or to deny their opponents' claims to this title, they depicted the resistance as transcending the sum of its parts. In a sense, the Athenians democratized the men of Piraeus. The Athenian people as a whole, not a small faction or a select group of individuals, were responsible for the restoration of the democracy.

One would expect the men of Piraeus gladly to recount in the law courts how they came to the defense of the democracy, as litigants often told the court about their past services to establish their credibility and to win the jurors' sympathy. Yet, at least in the extant orations, speakers who fought on the side of the democrats during the civil war or assisted them in other capacities offered only scant details about their services. Lysias failed to mention in his speech against Eratosthenes that he had furnished the democrats with mercenaries and equipment. The prosecutor of Agoratus stated that he had joined the exiles in Piraeus, but he did so briefly and only to support his claim that the reconciliation agreement did not protect the defendant (Lys. 13.90).

These omissions are not too surprising, however. Prosecutors in Lysias typically do not provide as many details about themselves as defendants. As Usher (1965: 113) has observed, "The prosecutor is not on trial, and needs to draw attention to himself only to the extent of showing honest and patriotic motives." Since Lysias 12 and 13 both concerned the murder of a relative by the Thirty, perhaps the speakers did not need to provide further proof of their loyalty to the demos or their hostility to the oligarchs. Moreover, each accused the defendant of harming the city and called on the jurors to avenge themselves as well as the dead.[1] By presenting the defendants not as individuals acting independently but as participants in the oligarchy, the prosecutors rendered the crimes of the Thirty against the entire community relevant to their cases. This strategy gave them greater leeway in their accusations, but it also forced them to limit any discussion about themselves.[2] The more each interjected his own personality and character into his speech, the more the case became a personal quarrel between the prosecutor and the defendant and the more difficult it became to argue that the jurors had a stake in its outcome.

Whatever their reasons, it would be hasty to infer from these two cases that the men of Piraeus generally did not comment on their own services. In a fragment of a speech concerning the property of Lysias, the speaker declared how unfair it would be for Lysias, who had provided the exiles with three hundred mercenaries, two hundred shields, and two thousand drachmas, to be deprived of his property under the very democracy he had helped restore. The speaker suggested that the jurors should acquit Lysias because the demos owed him thanks for his assistance. If instead they decided in favor of the prosecutor, Lysias would be so unfortunate as to have his property taken away from him not only by force but also by the verdict of a democratic jury.[3] Unlike the speakers of Lysias 12 and 13, this speaker appealed to the jurors' sense of compassion and obligation to the defendant rather than to the city. Thus, details about his personal hardships and acts of loyalty were a necessary part of the defense.

Speakers who faced the men of Piraeus in the courts did not object to such appeals as inadmissible or irrelevant. Rather, they denied that their opponents were among the class of citizens who deserved to benefit from the high esteem in which the Athenians held the men of Piraeus. In Lysias

25, for example, the candidate declared that the jurors should trust those members of the Piraeus party who had acted bravely and encouraged the demos to abide by the oaths rather than those exiles who, although they owed their safety to others, returned to Athens only to act as sycophants. The latter considered the dangers the democratic exiles faced in Piraeus an excuse to do whatever they wanted (28–33).

The candidate implied that the prosecutor belonged to the latter category of exiles, but his accusations were so vague that it is impossible to determine what exactly he accused the prosecutor of doing. Rather than provide specifics, he left it up to the jurors to imagine for themselves what he meant by "exiles saved by others," "to act as sycophants" (29), and "believing that they could do whatever they wanted because of their dangers in Piraeus" (33).[4] His accusations could therefore appear more serious than what he actually said, and the prosecutor had no grounds for objection since none were directed specifically against him. Ambiguity also helped the candidate to separate the latter group of exiles, and by extension the prosecutor, from the men of Piraeus. He first called them "exiles saved by others," and then later mentioned Piraeus not to identify them but rather their dangers. Moreover, this reference was derogatory; these exiles exploited the civil war for their own personal gain, seeking to benefit from the perils the men of Piraeus faced. Thus, men like the prosecutor cheapened the title when they laid claim to it.

In other instances, speakers were more specific about the activities of the opposing litigants. The prosecutor of Lysias 28 said that he expected Ergocles to mention in his defense "that he returned from Phyle, that he is a democrat, and that he shared your dangers" (12). In response, he argued that Ergocles deserved the wrath of the Athenian people for the crimes he committed after the restoration of the democracy, but he was careful to distinguish him from the other members of the democratic army: "I do not say that they are wicked citizens who shared your dangers because they desired liberty and justice, wanted the laws to prevail, and hated the wrongdoers, nor do I say that it would be unfair for them to render their exile in their account. But they, who harm the people and enlarge their own households at your expense after they returned under the democracy, ought to anger you much more than the Thirty" (13). By conceding that the men of Piraeus deserved special recognition in the law courts, the prosecutor prevented himself from appearing hostile to the former exiles and made his attack on Ergocles more damning. He was not opposed to litigants who mentioned their exile in their defense; he considered this only fair. Instead, he objected to those who used their exile as an excuse for defrauding the demos. The prosecutor cleverly praised the men of Piraeus while he attacked Ergocles for using his service in the democratic army as a defense. This strategy allowed him to challenge the defendant's motives: Did he assist in the restoration of the democracy out of loyalty or so that he could later enrich himself at the expense of the demos?

In the case of Agoratus, on the other hand, it is difficult to believe that he intended to use Phyle as a defense. Even if most of the accusations against him were false, he was at best an informer who fled Athens only after the oligarchs no longer needed him. But this is probably the conclusion the prosecutor wanted the jury to reach. After he conceded that Agoratus had joined the democratic army at Phyle, the prosecutor said that this only further proved that he was a vile creature because he dared to approach those whom he had informed against (Lys. 13.77). Whether or not Agoratus intended to use Phyle as a defense, this claim provided the prosecutor an opportunity to juxtapose him with the men of Piraeus. Agoratus was responsible for the oligarchic coup, whereas the men of Piraeus were responsible for the restoration of the democracy. It would therefore be a travesty of justice if he were to defend his actions by presenting himself as a former member of the democratic resistance. Thus, speakers who faced the democratic exiles in court criticized the opposing speakers not by belittling the men of Piraeus but by extolling them.

Litigants who were unable to claim service in the democratic army used their exile to associate themselves with the men of Piraeus. For example, the invalid of Lysias 24 said, "I fled to Chalcis with your people, and although I could have participated in their government without fear, I preferred to leave and share in all your dangers" (24). This statement appears in what amounts to a list of commonly used rhetorical devices and strategies (23–27). Even if the speech was never delivered before the Council, this statement was probably a *topos* of early-fourth-century Athens.[5] But in the case of the invalid, such an appeal appears humorous. It is certainly ridiculous to believe that the Thirty would have allowed a poor invalid of low birth to participate in their rule. Hence Carey suggests that this argument was a parody of those typically advanced (1990: 48).

What the invalid did in exile remains unclear. If he had in fact been willing to share the dangers of the demos, then why was he in Chalcis? If he later joined the democrats, then why did he not explicitly say so? Perhaps he merely meant that, like the members of the Council, he suffered the dangers of exile. It is also possible that his claim of sharing in their dangers was part of the parody. Doubtless, he was intentionally misleading so that he could benefit from the praise the men of Piraeus received. In fact, such deception about a citizen's whereabouts during the civil war occurs in forensic speeches from as late as the 340s.[6] Certainly, litigants who had fought at Phyle and Munichia had greater proof of their bravery than those who could only point to their exile. But at the very least, those exiles who had failed to join the democrats could appeal to the jury's sympathy for the hardships they had suffered, and they could argue that, like the men of Piraeus, they were enemies of the oligarchs.

On the other hand, the statements of the opposing speakers reveal that exiles who did not assist the democrats were vulnerable to criticism. The speaker of Isocrates 18 stated that Callimachus would recount to the jury that he had lived in exile during the civil war.[7] As a preemptive strike, the speaker mentioned how Callimachus had fled to Boeotia only after the democrats had occupied Piraeus, and so he deserved to be called a deserter rather than an exile.[8] At the *dokimasia* of Philon, the prosecutor made a similar accusation against the candidate. He admitted that the Thirty had expelled Philon from Athens, but, unlike the rest of the exiles, Philon had not joined the democrats in Piraeus and shared their dangers. Instead he had fled to Oropus. Philon, so the prosecutor would have the Council believe, was unique among the exiles because he was willing neither to defend the oligarchy against the democratic rebels nor to expel the oligarchs and restore the democracy (Lys. 31.8–14, 34). His conduct therefore revealed both his disloyalty to the demos and his cowardice.

Likewise, the speaker of Lysias 30 dismissed Nicomachus's exile as proof of his loyalty since others who subverted the democracy were either put to death or banished from the city. In addition, he argued that Nicomachus owed his return to the people, and therefore it would be outrageous if the jury should take into account his involuntary exile only to acquit him of crimes he willingly committed (15–16). As in the case of Lysias 25, it is impossible to determine from the prosecutor's accusations what Nicomachus did during the civil war. Did he flee Athens as soon as the Thirty had seized power or after the democratic forces had defeated the oligarchs at Munichia? Did he join the exiles or did he return only once the democracy had been restored? The answer to any of these questions would have helped the prosecutor substantiate his charges, assuming that Nicomachus had not assisted the democrats. Perhaps he was vague because he had no proof of misconduct. But by denying that

Nicomachus had a part in the restoration of the democracy, the prosecutor undermined the use of exile as a defense. By using innuendo and ambiguous accusations to cast doubt and create smoke screens, he forced Nicomachus to apologize for his past rather than point to it as proof of his integrity.

Yet one should not conclude from such criticism that those former exiles who failed to join the democrats in Piraeus were unable to win the jury's sympathy by citing their exile. Even Andocides, although absent from Athens during the civil war of 404, attempted to use his self-imposed exile as proof of his loyalty. He asked the jurors to imagine what sentence the Thirty would have passed if he had been in Athens during their rule. Since he had not joined the Spartans in Decelea, demolished the walls of Athens, or subverted the democracy, the oligarchs would have put him to death for his loyalty to the demos (1.101–2). Neither complicit in the oligarchy nor a victim of the Thirty, he claimed he would have suffered the same harsh treatment at the hands of the oligarchs as did the supporters of the democracy.

One could, however, just as easily argue the opposite, that the only reason Andocides had not helped subvert the democracy was because he was in exile at the time of the civil war and did not return until after it had ended. Fear rather than loyalty had prevented him from returning. This attempt by Andocides to identify himself with the opponents of the Thirty is far-fetched, to say the least. But I would argue that the Athenians so firmly associated opposition to the Thirty with loyalty to the democracy that he needed only to compare himself to the democratic exiles to profess his loyalty. One was either an opponent or a supporter of the Thirty; there was no middle ground. Although his claims appear outrageous, Andocides had to present himself as a victim of the oligarchs to maintain that he had been and would continue to be loyal to the demos.

Those too young to have assisted the democrats during the civil war recalled the services of their relatives. A remarkable example of this type of appeal, in Lysias 18, is worth discussing in detail.[9] The speech concerns the property of Eucrates, brother of the famous general Nicias, and was written for one of his two sons. The prosecutor of a previous lawsuit had failed to obtain a verdict in favor of confiscation (14), but Poliochus brought a second suit against the sons of Eucrates. If successful, the sons would have lost their property as well as their civic rights (1, 13). The grounds for the suit remain unclear because, as Lamb (1930: 399) remarks, "The appeal throughout is to feeling rather than to reason." The defendant attempted to win an acquittal by recounting the suffering his family had endured in defense of the democracy; therefore, the speech provides excellent examples of the type of arguments explored in this chapter.

In addition to their uncle Nicias, who died in the disastrous Sicilian campaign before the oligarchic uprisings of 411 and 404, the sons of Eucrates lost their father and a cousin. After Aegospotami, Eucrates was elected general, and, although invited to participate in the oligarchy, he refused and later died while "trying to save the Athenians" (5). Once in power, the Thirty suspected that Niceratus, son of Nicias, would oppose them, so they had him killed. As far as the oligarchs were concerned, Niceratus was an irreconcilable enemy (6). Their other uncle, Diognetus, had more doubtful loyalties. Although Diognetus had returned to the city during the oligarchic rule, the defendant asserted that he had not held an office (9–10). Digonetus had been banished by the democracy, but the defendant was careful to point out that, unlike other exiles, he had not joined the Spartans at Decelea or marched against the city. This is the same litany of denials that Andocides used to prove his loyalty. If he had not been involved in the kinds of nefarious activities typical of oligarchs, then he must have remained an active supporter of the democracy.

The emotional appeal, which intensifies as the speaker describes his uncle's plea to Pausanias, deserves to be quoted in its entirety:

> As soon as the Lacedaemonians and Pausanias came to the Academy, Diognetus took the son of Niceratus and us who were children. Placing him on the knees of Pausanias and us beside, he told Pausanias and the rest who were present what we suffered and what our fate was. Because of their friendship and hospitality, he expected Pausanias to help, even to exact vengeance from those who had wronged us. Pausanias then began to be kindly disposed to the demos and presented our misfortunes to the rest of the Spartans as an example of the wickedness of the Thirty. It was clear to all the Peloponnesians who came that they were not killing the worst of the citizens, but those who, most of all, ought to be honored because of their birth, wealth, and other good qualities. We were so pitied and seemed by all to suffer such terrible things that Pausanias did not want to befriend the Thirty and received us instead. Therefore, it would indeed be terrible, men of the jury, for us as children to be pitied by the enemy when they came to defend the oligarchy, only to be deprived of our property by you, the men of the jury, although we have such qualities and after our fathers died on behalf of the democracy. (10–12)

This is an unusual explanation for the sudden reversal in Spartan policy, and not one shared by modern historians. Even if the jurors were also suspicious, it helped the defendant to dramatize the suffering of his family in a single, powerful image that united the victims and the perpetrator. In a sense, the orphans, bereft of their father, symbolically represented the demos, bereft of loyal supporters. Since even the enemy sympathized with the victims, it would be outrageous for a democratic jury to remain unmoved. Regardless of whether Pausanias reversed Spartan policy because of the plight of these children, the defendant used this story to pressure the jurors to vote in his favor. By addressing them twice as "men of the jury," he impressed upon them the inescapable irony should they vote to deprive his brother and him of their property under the very democracy they had helped restore.

Equally remarkable is the attempt of Alcibiades the younger to present his infamous father as an opponent of the Thirty, claiming that his father suffered the same misfortunes as the people.[10] His willingness to endure such hardships, although invited to participate in the oligarchy, proved, as his son maintained, that Alcibiades was a loyal supporter of democracy (36). In fact, once the Thirty had gained control of Athens, they immediately exiled him before anyone else (37). It was not enough for the Spartans to demolish the walls of Athens. They had also to exile the one man who was capable of rebuilding them (40). But one could just as easily conclude that the Spartans and the oligarchic conspirators distrusted Alcibiades as much as the democrats had. His personal ambition made him a threat to whichever faction was in power, and as a result he was banished by both the democracy and the oligarchy.[11] Regardless of the form of government, the Athenians could not tolerate his participation in politics.

Alcibiades the younger even defended his father by comparing his services on behalf of Sparta during the Peloponnesian War to the actions of the men of Piraeus. He pointed out that the democratic exiles had also sought help from every stranger and had even marched out against the city to secure their return.[12] Not surprisingly, he failed to mention that his father had helped the Spartans to defeat a democratic Athens, whereas the followers of Thrasybulus had fought against a murderous oligarchy. As in the case of Andocides, this defense is tendentious. But again, the Athenians so closely associated opposition to the Thirty with loyalty to the democracy that Alcibiades the younger needed to present his father as an opponent of the Thirty in order to prove that he was loyal to the demos. Litigants had to show that they and their family not only had been loyal before the civil war, but that they had remained so even after the Thirty seized power.

It is impossible to determine whether the jurors were ever moved to vote in favor of a litigant because of his services during the civil war. But at the very least, litigants considered it strategic to identify themselves with the men of Piraeus. Some admitted that the opposing speakers had joined the democrats in Piraeus, but only one speaker unambiguously claimed this honor for himself.[13] This is not surprising, given the number of speeches that have survived, and, in some cases, it might not have been useful for the litigant to provide such information. Moreover, few citizens fought on the side of the democrats at Phyle and Munichia. About seven hundred soldiers were with Thrasybulus at Phyle, but only one hundred were Athenian citizens. Others joined the band of exiles in Piraeus, but the democrats were still outnumbered by the oligarchic army, which was reinforced with troops sent by Sparta. Since the Athenians regarded the men of Piraeus as loyal democrats, more litigants appearing in court attempted to identify with them than could legitimately claim to have served in the democratic army.

The ambiguities of the civil war allowed speakers to represent themselves as democratic exiles and opposing speakers to challenge such representations. Few Athenians had rallied behind the democrats in the early stages of their campaign, so most were open to some form of reproach. Those who had remained in exile during the civil war were able to use their exile as proof of their hostility to the Thirty, but opposing litigants were able to respond by pointing out that they had failed to join the men of Piraeus. Whereas those who had fought with the democrats in Piraeus had substantial proof of their loyalty, their opponents could accuse them of joining the democrats only after they had gained the upper hand. Even those who had fought at Phyle were not beyond reproach. The prosecutor in Lysias 28, for instance, distinguished Ergocles from the rest of the democratic army by questioning his motives. Whether he was successful is another matter. But the fact that many Athenian citizens could not clearly be defined as members of the democratic army helped prevent recrimination from polarizing the community and insured that the demos rather than specific individuals received the credit for the restoration of the democracy.

In the end, only the role of the demos in its exile and in its return remain uncontested. It was, of course, to the advantage of those who claimed to be members of the resistance that the Athenians continued to admire the exiles. Their opponents, however, did not criticize the men of

Piraeus. Rather, they extolled them, because the more the men of Piraeus appeared exceptional, the easier it was to deny that the opposing speakers were of the same caliber. As litigants praised the democratic exiles, whether to win the sympathy of the jury or to undermine the arguments of the opposing speakers, they made it more difficult for any single citizen to appropriate this praise for himself. In a sense, they democratized the men of Piraeus. Only the demos could be identified as the men of Piraeus without challenge, since so few were beyond reproach, and since doubt could so easily be cast upon almost any individual who laid claim to this title. Hence, the demos became the focal point in the narratives of the period of civil unrest, and the Thirty was its foil.

Analyzing official narrative on "the Mexican Revolution of 1910–1917," Alonso (1988: 39–45) concluded that separate, regional uprisings in Mexico were unified and homogenized to depict "the Revolution" as a singular event in which all fought on the side of the "nation" and the "people." Through a process she calls departicularization, historical discourses and practices were emptied of local and concrete meaning to become "the property of all and no one." In Athens, a similar process occurred whereby the men of Piraeus were departicularized to include the demos collectively and to remove the foreigners and slaves, who were then remembered only as auxillary units, from their numbers. Of course, in Mexico this remapping of identity had a very different effect, namely to support the ideology of the emerging nation-state, whereas in Athens it reinvested the demos with its authority and gave legitimacy to the restored democracy.

In Chapter 4, we saw how the Athenians gained a sense of victory and continuity by representing the men of Piraeus as the demos in exile. Now it is possible to see that litigants, whether they had supported the democrats or remained in the city during the civil war, benefited from this image. It allowed the exiles to declare that they had defended the demos and the men of the city to show their approval for the restoration of the democracy without conceding that their opponents were praiseworthy for their assistance. Ironically, as the Athenians identified the demos as the men of Piraeus, those who had fought at Phyle and Munichia or presented themselves as such regained a claim to this title by asserting that they had been with the demos in exile. Hence, the invalid defended himself by saying, "I preferred to depart and share your dangers" (Lys. 24.25) and the speaker of *P. Oxy.* 1606 declared, "Lysias went into exile with you and returned with your people" (ll. 35–38).

THE MEN OF THE CITY

The men of the city established their loyalty by dissociating themselves from the Thirty and their crimes. Since they had not helped restore the democracy, they proved their loyalty by presenting themselves as innocent bystanders of the civil war. In some cases, their denials are difficult to believe. How had they avoided becoming involved? It was not as if they lived abroad, far from the confrontation. They were in Athens when Thrasybulus and his followers marched against the city and when the oligarchs led their troops against them. The men of the city denied any and all involvement in the crimes of the Thirty, even when such claims were difficult to maintain, in order to declare to the jury that they intended to adhere to the laws of the restored democracy regardless of the mistakes they might have made in the past. This fiction assured the jury that the men of the city would now be loyal citizens despite their past. It was also a tacit acknowledgment that there could be no defense for supporting the Thirty. So by professing their innocence, the men of the city deferred to a democratic version of the civil war.

At worst, the men of Piraeus did not benefit from recounting to the jury the dangers they had faced as exiles. The men of the city, however, had nothing to gain and much to lose if they were unable to justify why they had remained in the city during the civil war. The more they distanced themselves from the Thirty, the easier it was for them to assert that they had remained loyal to the democracy. The candidate in Lysias 25, for example, said that he behaved as the best men of Piraeus would have had they remained in the city (2). By comparing himself to them, he drew the attention of the jury away from himself and his own failings. This defense, however, was problematic, since the fact that the men of Piraeus went into exile was the very thing that set them apart from him. The moment the candidate identified himself with the exiles, locality betrayed his claim.

Mantitheus, on the other hand, stated that he was away from Athens at the outbreak of the civil war. Yet he admitted that he had returned to the city five days before the democrats seized Munichia (Lys. 16.4), which would place him in Athens during the rule of the Thirty. Although he denied that he had returned because of a desire to participate in their government (5), he explained neither his motives to return when the oligarchs still controlled Athens nor his failure to join the democrats at Phyle. Although he had lived abroad during the oligarchic revolution of

404, he was in the city when the oligarchs had most needed additional help to crush the democratic resistance.[14] No matter how much he emphasized his residence abroad, his opponents needed only to point out that he had chosen to return to Athens while the oligarchs still ruled. In contrast to the democratic exiles, litigants who remained in the city could not easily defend themselves against charges of oligarchic sympathies by mentioning where they had lived during the civil war, since location, even in the case of Mantitheus, created such suspicions.

The men of the city therefore distinguished themselves from the Thirty and their supporters by recounting not what they did but what they did not do.[15] Unable to claim that the oligarchs had driven them out of the city, they asserted that they had assisted in neither the maintenance nor the defense of the oligarchy. Some denied that they had sat on the oligarchic Council; others, that they had held offices or served in the cavalry.[16] In other words, although they had remained in Athens, they had been absent from places of power. By limiting the contaminated area of the city to specific strongholds of the oligarchy, they attempted to dispel suspicions and, like the democratic exiles, insisted that location was proof of loyalty. But absence from the oligarchic government did not prove that their conduct was beyond reproach. The oligarchy, as the Athenians believed, provided those who remained in the city an opportunity, if they so desired, both to enrich themselves and to exact vengeance on their enemies.

Not surprisingly, the men of the city denied that they committed any crimes during the civil war. Some defended their conduct in court by asserting that they had never arrested anyone, and others said that they had never sought arbitration against another nor placed anyone on "Lysander's list."[17] Such actions had grave consequences for the victim, including the loss of property, banishment, or execution. Nicias, for instance, after learning that his enemies had threatened to place his name on Lysander's list, immediately secured his property with friends and left the city (Isoc. 21.2). To avoid arousing the anger of the jury, the men of the city declared that they neither had participated in the oligarchy nor were responsible for the misfortunes many had suffered. But why, then, had they remained in Athens? The candidate of Lysias 25 said that some had stayed in the city to protect their property (18), but this defense only encouraged further inquiry. How had these individuals been able to avoid personal losses and escape from any involvement in the oligarchy when so many others had been unable to do so?

Suspect litigants recalled their prior conduct to make their denials of involvement in the oligarchy appear more convincing. Although they were unable to claim that they had assisted in the restoration of the democracy, they could at least cite examples of their previous generosity to the people. In Lysias 25, the candidate said that he had been trierarch five times, fought in four naval battles, paid the war tax, and performed other liturgies as well (12). The Thirty, so he would have the jury believe, did not trust him because of such services, and as a result, they had not allowed him to participate in the oligarchy (13). Oddly, he admitted that he had been intentionally generous in case he had to defend himself in court, which left him open to the accusation that his liturgical record proved that he cared only about his own self-preservation.[18]

If the candidate had lived in an Athens free from civil war, such an admission would have been unproblematic. By declaring that they generously performed their liturgies to win the goodwill of the people, litigants showed their deference to the legal and ideological power of the demos. But the candidate of Lysias 25 had lived in Athens under the oligarchy. His concern for his self-interest could be used to create suspicions against him concerning his conduct during the civil war. Perhaps he had been loyal before the overthrow of the democracy and intended to defer to the demos again because it was now useful for him to do so. But if self-interest motivated him, what had he done to protect himself and his property while the Thirty ruled Athens?

In Isocrates 18, the speaker stated that he was one of the few generals who returned with his trireme to Athens after Aegospotami, and, when Lysander blockaded Piraeus and threatened to execute anyone who violated the blockade, he nevertheless risked his life to supply the city with grain, for which he received a crown before the eponymous heroes (58–61). He then proceeded to argue: "Therefore you should not consider them loyal to the demos who were eager to be involved in public matters under the democracy, but those who willingly braved dangers for you when the city was in dire straits; you should thank not him who suffered misfortunes, but him who helped you; and pity not those who are poor because they lost their property, but those who are poor because they spent it on you" (62). The speaker attempted to convince the jurors that those who had supported the democracy in its time of need deserved their pity more than the victims of the civil war. But he failed to explain why he had not continued to aid the demos after the Thirty had seized power. Where was he in this time of crisis? Had the demos no longer needed his help?

The men of the city even attempted to use their remaining in Athens to their advantage, citing their conduct during the civil war as proof that they either did not or would not violate the laws of the restored democracy. In Lysias 7, the speaker defended himself against the charge of illegally removing an olive stump from his property by saying: "Was it easier for me, members of the Council, to violate the law under the democracy or the rule of the Thirty? I am not saying that I was powerful then or that I am discredited now, but rather that there was a greater opportunity then for one, if he so wanted, to commit a crime than now."[19] If he had refrained from misconduct even under the oligarchy, then surely, so the defendant maintained, he would not have waited until the democracy was restored to violate the laws. He was therefore a law-abiding citizen regardless of the city's constitution (41). In a like manner, the candidate of Lysias 25 declared that he would certainly be a good citizen under the restored democracy if he had refused to harm anyone under the oligarchy, when there had been ample opportunity for misconduct (17).

The speaker of Isocrates 18 also used this argument, but in his case it was more tenuous. Perhaps it is too strong to accuse him of lying outright; but surely he creatively interpreted the facts of the case. Since he had not wronged anyone during the civil war, it did not make sense for the jury to believe that he would have harmed Callimachus after the Thirty were expelled, the demos was in power, and the reconciliation was under discussion (17–18). Yet, as he indicated earlier in his speech, Callimachus accused him of stealing his money when the Ten were in power (5–8), which would place the alleged crime after the expulsion of the Thirty but before the restoration of the democracy. Moreover, the speaker brought a *paragraphe* against Callimachus on the grounds that he had violated the amnesty (2–3), a procedure that was useless if the alleged crime had been committed after the restoration of the democracy. He wanted to be protected by the amnesty without having to admit that he needed the amnesty.

Just as the men of the city denied that they had participated in the oligarchy, so their opponents insisted on their involvement in the crimes of the Thirty.[20] The very engagement of litigants in such contests seems to suggest that the amnesty was insufficient to protect the men of the city. Although some mentioned the amnesty in their defense, none relied solely on it. "To appeal to the amnesty," Lateiner (1981: 150) explains, "is to admit some measure of complicity." Mantitheus asserted that he had no reason to deny serving in the cavalry of the Thirty and even claimed that many of the former knights were now participating in politics. But he qualified this assertion by conceding that, if he had served in the cavalry, he would then need to show that no one had suffered any harm as a result of such service (Lys. 16.8). In other words, the knights were protected by the amnesty as long as they were innocent. But what use, then, was the amnesty if it protected only those who needed no protection? One does not find men of the city admitting that they participated in the oligarchy or committed crimes during the rule of the Thirty. No one says, "Yes, I supported the oligarchs and helped them harm the demos, but I cannot be punished since I am now protected by the amnesty."[21]

Even oligarchs had the audacity to deny involvement in the crimes of their regimes. For example, in a speech delivered before the oligarchic uprising of 404, the son of Polystratus portrayed his father, a former member of the Four Hundred, as a loyal democrat.[22] If we can believe Lysias, Eratosthenes had the audacity to deny participation in the crimes of the Thirty. Presenting himself as an ally of Theramenes, he hoped to persuade the jury that he was part of a faction within the Thirty which had acted in the best interest of the demos and which had opposed the extreme policies implemented by his fellow oligarchs.

Similarly, the men of the city, even when complicit, denied any and all involvement in the oligarchy. Once the democracy was restored, speakers proclaimed in public that they had been with the demos in exile, had suffered the same misfortunes, or had been innocent bystanders.[23] It was as if the oligarchic sympathizers had simply vanished or had not existed at all. As if unaided, the Thirty terrorized the Athenians, and once they were expelled, only the innocent remained. If even members of the Four Hundred and the Thirty could depict themselves and be depicted as loyal democrats, it is not surprising that former oligarchic sympathizers denied participation in the crimes of the Thirty. As members of the elite who had remained in Athens during the civil war, their loyalty was at best questionable. They belonged to that class of citizens with which the oligarchs had shared their power. Certainly, it was easier for them, and less risky, to profess innocence and to redirect the blame on someone else than to admit guilt.

As we saw in the previous chapter, litigants made such claims to assure the jury that the amnesty did not complicate Athenian law. Even without the amnesty, it was necessary for the jury to acquit the innocent. But did the jury really believe these claims of innocence? Ober's theory on the "suspension of disbelief" can help us better understand this fiction of innocence. Elite litigants sometimes presented themselves as average citizens, even though the jurors must have recognized such claims as patently false. But by lowering themselves to the level of average citizens, they declared to the jury that they approved of egalitarian principles. The jurors, as Ober further suggests, were willing to suspend disbelief and grant the litigants a sympathetic hearing because the litigants had humbled themselves.[24] So elite litigants who had remained in Athens during the civil war denied complicity not because they expected the jury to believe that they were completely innocent but to declare their intent to adhere to the laws of the restored democracy. Just as the wealthy presented themselves as if they were poor, so the men of the city presented themselves as if innocent.

The fiction of innocence assured the Athenians that former oligarchic sympathizers would now be loyal to the democracy despite whatever they might have done in the past. In a sense, the men of the city who were conspicuous in public, whether appearing in court or participating in politics, as they spoke before the jury, the Council, or the Assembly, were required to declare their allegiance to the restored democracy, thereby justifying their inclusion in the demos. By maintaining the fiction of innocence, they declared their disapproval of the Thirty and expressed their willingness to represent the reconciliation as a victory for the demos. As they insisted that they had been and would continue to be loyal to the people, they implicitly conceded that the reconciliation was not a compromise between oligarchs and democrats. By denying any involvement in the oligarchy, they not only presented the amnesty as unproblematic but also implicitly deferred to the democratic version of the civil war by acknowledging that the restored democracy had no place for oligarchic collaborators or even former collaborators.

Opposing speakers attempted to refute their claims of innocence and convince the jury that the Athenians ought not to allow them to participate in the affairs of the restored democracy. In Lysias 26, for example, the prosecutor claimed that Evander was able to subvert the democracy because the people trusted him on account of the liturgies that his father had performed. He conceded that Evander had not committed any crimes after the restoration of the democracy, but he suggested that this was only because others had prevented him from doing so.[25] In Isocrates 16, Alcibiades the younger declared how unfair it would be if he should lose his civic rights while Teisias, the prosecutor, should remain as powerful in the democracy as he himself had been in the oligarchy (49–50). Opposing speakers insisted that, no matter how much the men of the city voiced democratic principles, lavishly performed their liturgies, or behaved as outstanding citizens under the democracy, they had deceived the demos and could not be trusted to be loyal.

Whereas the men of the city implicitly conceded, the opposing speakers firmly insisted that the restored democracy had no place for oligarchic sympathizers. Inclusion within the demos therefore depended upon the jurors' willingness to suspend disbelief and maintain the fiction of innocence. They had powerful incentives to do so. If they refused, they would have had to recognize that reconciliation was not a victory but merely a compromise and that members of the demos had supported the oligarchy and continued to live in Athens even after the Thirty were driven out and the democracy was restored.

Moreover, defendants accused of oligarchic sympathies were able to discredit the prosecutors' accusations by responding with counteraccusations.[26] For example, Andocides said that his prosecutors would also be vulnerable to prosecution should the amnesty be violated. He claimed that Epichares had served on the Council of the Thirty and that Meletus had arrested Leon, and if it weren't for the amnesty the two could have been executed for their offenses (1.94–95). In Lysias 30, the prosecutor said that Nicomachus, unable to respond to his charges, would counter by accusing him of having been a member of the Four Hundred (7–9, 15–6). Finally, as discussed above, the speaker of Isocrates 18 called into question Callimachus's motives for fleeing Athens, and Alcibiades the younger defended himself by accusing Teisias of participating in the oligarchy. Although the men of the city, as well as such notorious individuals as Alcibiades the younger and Andocides, were vulnerable to accusations, they had ample ammunition to use against their opponents. Even if their counteraccusations were completely false, they at least cast doubt on the prosecutors' charges.

Ironically, the very same ambiguities that created areas of contention provided litigants a means of defense. In a sense, the weaknesses of the reconciliation were also its strengths. This does not mean that a renewal of civil turmoil was unlikely; rather, the Athenians were placed in a stalemate that could easily dissolve into *stasis*. Hence, the success of the reconciliation depended to a large degree on maintaining the fictions discussed in this and the previous chapter, namely that the men of Piraeus were the demos in exile returning in triumph and the men of the city remained, for the most part, uninvolved in the oligarchy. These fictions allowed the Athenians to believe that Athens was unified in spite of the civil war. Yet this blending of remembering and forgetting remained precarious because it depended upon the coexistence of competing and contradictory representations of the past. The Athenians could just as easily have used the past to construct division.

CONCLUSION

Disgruntled citizens were able both to profess principles of reconciliation and to recall in court the conduct of their enemies. Given that the civil war confounded the identity of the citizens and that so few were beyond reproach, litigants were easily able to manipulate the labels used to identify the factions. As they praised the men of Piraeus, whether to win for themselves the jury's sympathy or to discredit the opposing speakers, they made it difficult for anyone to lay claim to this title. In the end, only the demos could be identified as the men of Piraeus without question. The men of the city denied any involvement in the crimes of the oligarchy not only to profess their innocence but also to declare their intent to adhere to the laws of the restored democracy, regardless of their past conduct. Although their failure to leave Athens during the civil war compromised them, they could create suspicion against their opponents and cast doubt on the charges lodged against them.

Since so many were vulnerable to criticism, it was difficult for anyone to prevail in his recrimination of another. In this discourse between prosecutors and defendants, with some claiming to have helped restore the democracy and others professing innocence, the demos remained intact. Ironically, widespread complicity of the citizenry in the oligarchy helped prevent any serious challenges to these fictions, thus preventing the newly restored democracy from polarizing into two warring factions. The reconciliation was transformed into a victory, but only by narrowing the scope of blame to those excluded from the amnesty and by widening the scope of praise to include practically all who were allowed into the community.

6 ⊰ CONSTRUCTING A FUTURE

> Members of the jury, you ought to use the past as an example as you
> deliberate about the future, and to consider them the best democrats
> who, wanting you to live in harmony, adhere to their oaths and the
> agreement, considering this to be the most useful protection for the
> city and the greatest form of vengeance on your enemies.
>
> LYS. 25.23

As the Athenians assigned meaning to the civil war, they drew lessons from the past which had an impact not only on the success of the reconciliation but also on the future of the restored democracy. We have already seen that memory of the past could either promote peace or factionalize the community. We have explored how the exiles and the collaborators accounted for their actions, but we have not yet considered what the Athenians accused the oligarchs of doing. What was the legacy of the Thirty? The historical narratives of the civil war show that the defeat, surrender, and overthrow of the democracy were three separate events. And although there are similarities between the depiction of the Thirty in the historical narratives, especially in Xenophon, and that in the Attic orators, the effect is quite different.

Using the civil war as a litmus test to illustrate how the restored democracy should and should not operate, the Athenians distanced themselves from the civil war and rendered the Thirty and the democratic resistance as paradigms for the future. The rule of the Thirty became a mirror image of the restored democracy, serving to show Athenians what they must avoid if they did not want Athens to return to a state of civil unrest. As long as they recognized what was distinctive to oligarchy, and therefore despicable, they could construct a democracy devoid of these features. Only by doing the opposite of what the Thirty had done could they restore past greatness. But before exploring this mirror image, it is necessary first to discuss Athenian representations of the Thirty and the democratic resistance.

THE THIRTY

In the aftermath of the oligarchy, the Athenians explained to themselves how Sparta was able to defeat them and how fellow citizens could plot against the democracy and, after seizing control of the city, proceed to terrorize the community. But the Athenians did not come to terms with such troubling memories of weakness and division or acknowledge the complicity and passivity of many during the civil war. Rather, the Thirty—though certainly responsible for many atrocities—became a scapegoat for failures in which the entire community had a share. By locating the origins of defeat and civil war solely in the activities of the Thirty, the Athenians denied responsibility and convinced themselves that they did not need to fear further defeat from foreign armies or further uprisings from within the community. As speakers recalled what the Thirty had done, how they had victimized the entire community and how they were utterly unique in their villainy, they reassured the Athenians that Athens would not again experience civil war. Surely, the victims of the Thirty would hardly tolerate any future attempt by oligarchic conspirators to seize control of Athens, and, even if some wicked citizens were to follow in the path of the Thirty, it was unlikely that anyone could repeat their crimes.

Despite their insistence that the reconciliation was a victory for the returning demos and that the people were again in control of the city, the Athenians were daily exposed to visible reminders of their recent defeats: the destroyed fleet and the demolished Long Walls. They had to know that their city, which had once ruled over others, was now just as vulnerable to invasions by foreign armies and the conspiracies of fellow citizens as when Lysander had arrived with the Spartan fleet. It was not until 395/4, when Conon arrived in Piraeus as commander of the Persian fleet, that the walls were rebuilt. Until then, the landscape, showing the results of the recent wars, betrayed their claims of victory and denied them the security they so desperately sought to obtain. But by divorcing themselves from the ruins, rendering them a part of their past and associating them with the Thirty, the Athenians attempted to construct a future free of these horrors. Lévy (1976: 40–43) notes that speakers frequently described the naval defeat at Aegospotami and its consequences as "misfortunes" (*sumphorai*).[1] He argues that this imprecise term, which does not indicate duration, allowed the Athenians to place recent events safely in their past and to deny that these events had lasting repercussions. Buffering themselves from the shock of defeat, they spoke of their "misfortunes" instead of the dissolution of their empire, and thus transformed a perhaps irreparable loss that had crippled Athenian power into an event—or a series of interconnected events—of limited consequences. Moreover, by calling surrender to Sparta and the ensuing civil war "misfortunes," they implied that their sufferings were unavoidable accidents of chance and that, far from being responsible, they were themselves the victims.

At the same time, speakers often listed what defeat to Sparta had entailed: surrender of the fleet, destruction of the dockyard, demolition of the walls, enemy occupation of the Acropolis, enslavement to Sparta, rule of the Thirty, and slaughter of fellow citizens.[2] By listing Athenian losses, they were able to emphasize the magnitude of their suffering. Litigants, of course, stressed Athenian misfortune for rhetorical purposes, sometimes to incite the jurors' anger against the opposing speakers and sometimes to provoke the fear of further unrest should the jury violate the amnesty. But such lists also served to reduce Athenian responsibility. Each item became a stage in a chain reaction that had spun out of their control. Even if disaster had been initially avoidable, the series of misfortunes that followed became more difficult to stop as each additional misfortune rendered them more helpless.

Notwithstanding some minor variations, the surrender of the fleet, the demolition of the walls, and the rule of the Thirty were the misfortunes speakers most frequently listed. Strikingly, speakers did not refer more explicitly to the loss of empire, perhaps because the Athenians had so many other losses or so many more serious setbacks demanding their attention that the loss of empire seemed of minor importance. Or maybe they so closely equated loss of empire with the other misfortunes, such as the surrender of the fleet, that it was unnecessary to be more specific. The demolition of the Long Walls, the only item included in all lists, symbolized the full extent of Athenian defeat more than any other image.[3] Referring simultaneously to the surrender to Sparta and the overthrow of the democracy, this image conflated the two events. The enemy was able to defeat Athens because of the intrigues of citizens who were plotting within the very walls that protected them. Yet they succeeded only after the city had been defeated and lay exposed to the enemy. Inextricably bound, defeat pointed ahead to civil war and civil war back to defeat, and the two misfortunes were collapsed into one point of reference which referred only to itself, disconnected from Athenian past and future.

In the funeral oration of Lysias, the speaker declared that the restoration of the democracy, in spite of the presence of Spartan forces sent to preserve the oligarchy, proved that the Athenians would have defeated the enemy if only they had remained united (2.65). In what is considered a parody of this type of argument, Plato has Socrates recite a funeral oration in which the speaker makes an even more outrageous claim: the Athenians were actually victorious since they had been defeated not by Sparta but by themselves (*Mx.* 243d).[4] Using the civil war to justify the very defeat that had produced civil war, the speaker of the *epitaphios* turned defeat into an Athenian victory, but only by crediting the Athenians for their failure to remain united. It was indeed a strange victory, which instead of bringing the victors the spoils brought them only misery. But at least from this viewpoint they did not have to acknowledge the supremacy of Spartan military power.

In forensic oratory, speakers diminished the responsibility of the returning demos for the civil war by targeting Sparta, sycophants, or the Thirty. They disagreed not about the villainy of the Thirty but about whom the Athenians should hold ultimately responsible for the overthrow of the democracy. Andocides told the jury that, after the Athenians had made peace with Sparta and agreed to demolish their walls and restore the exiles, the Thirty came to power, Phyle and Munichia were seized, and other troubles occurred, which he did not need to recall (1.80). His narrative, brief because his main concern in this section was to prove that he was immune from prosecution (71–91), allows for alternative interpretations.[5] It was certainly in his interest to remain ambiguous. Rather than incur the animosity of the jurors by advancing an explanation that they opposed, Andocides constructed a narrative that gave them the leeway to reach disparate conclusions.

At the same time, however, he implicitly suggested to the jury one particular explanation. Using a list to narrate the events of the civil war, he implied that each additional event on the list was the consequence of the previous one, which thus made Sparta ultimately responsible.[6] The Thirty were only able to seize control of the city after the Athenians had destroyed their walls and restored the exiles, which were the terms of surrender that Sparta had forced them to accept. But why had the Spartans been able to defeat Athens? If the Spartans won the Peloponnesian War because of their military prowess, then the war was a victory for Sparta, and not Athens. If, on the other hand, the Athenians were responsible for the defeat, then they were ultimately to blame for the civil war. Sparta, although an easy target to blame for Athenian suffering, could not simultaneously satisfy their need both to deny their own responsibility for the civil war and to begrudge the enemy the credit for its victory.

Responding to accusations concerning his conduct during the rule of the Thirty, the candidate of Lysias 25 suggested that the civil war was the fault of sycophants who sought their own profit at the expense of the city: "For they persuaded you to condemn some to death without trial, to confiscate illegally the property of many, and to exile and disfranchise citizens. They were the sort to accept money and release the guilty or come before you and destroy the innocent. And they did not stop until they plunged the city into civil war and the greatest misfortunes while they themselves, previously poor, became rich" (26). The candidate further argued that many who had participated in the affairs of the city before the civil war robbed from the treasury and that some either accepted bribes at the expense of the demos or caused the allies to revolt by engaging in sycophancy (19). Critical of the fifth-century democracy, he maintained that the democratic leaders were responsible for defeat and civil war.[7] By alienating Athenian allies and by factionalizing the community through their sycophantic activities, they weakened Athenian military power and created the dissension the Thirty needed to seize control of the city. Yet the candidate was also careful to direct his criticism against corrupt democratic leaders, and not the demos.

Excluded from the amnesty, the Thirty were the most satisfying target of reproach. Unlike Sparta or corrupt democratic leaders, they could be blamed simultaneously for defeat and civil war without embarrassing the demos. Even their name, *triakonta*, served to reduce the size of the oligarchy and to separate them from the rest of the population. Limiting the oligarchic rulers to thirty, the Athenians could contain them. They could then recall the period of unrest without having to be reminded of the board of Ten which had replaced the Thirty or of those in the Three Thousand who had supported the oligarchic regime by holding offices and serving as knights and soldiers in the army. To refer to the oligarchy as the Thirty was to pass over in silence these other men. Thus, the Athenians neither acknowledged the nature of the civil war nor recognized the complicity of the demos in the rule of the Thirty. Just as they called defeat and civil war *sumphorai*, an imprecise term which buffered them from the actual events, so they referred to the oligarchy as the *triakonta*, an overly precise term that allowed them to limit the blame and confine it to a manageable number. It allowed them to overlook the many who either had been complicit in the crimes of the Thirty or had done nothing to stop them.

Given the reputation of the Thirty, a reputation that speaker after speaker helped perpetuate by recalling the crimes they had committed, the Athenians could link them to the defeat without difficulty. Void of all scruples, the Thirty and their supporters, as speakers maintained, were willing to serve as the slaves of the enemy. [8] Democracy was so despicable to them that they actually preferred to take the orders of the enemy rather than to obey the laws of the community and abide by the decisions of the demos. If they could stoop so low after the defeat, then perhaps even when the Athenians had still been capable of winning, when their fellow citizens had needed their help to avoid destruction, the Thirty had chosen instead to betray the walls and reap the rewards enslavement would bring them.

In response to those who claimed that Eratosthenes was different from the rest of the Thirty, Lysias reminded the jury that Eratosthenes had collaborated with the enemy. Rather than refute or concede the apologists' claims, Lysias maintained that they were irrelevant. As a member of the Thirty, Eratosthenes had harmed his fellow citizens more than all the other Greeks (89). He made the city his enemy and its enemies his friends (51). How, then, did it matter that he was less wicked than the rest of the Thirty? Unlike other defendants who say nothing about the charges but mention their many services in order to deceive the jury, Eratosthenes could not even resort to this strategy (38). With bitter irony, Lysias then suggested to the jury:

> But bid him show where they killed as many of the enemy as they did citizens, or where they captured as many ships as they surrendered, or what city they won over like yours which they enslaved. Did they strip the enemy of as many weapons as they took from you or capture hostile fortifications like the ones of their fatherland which they leveled? They are the men who tore down the forts around Attica and made it clear to you that they demolished Piraeus not because Sparta ordered them to, but because they thought it would make their rule more secure. (39–40)

Unable to recall any services from which his fellow citizens benefited, Eratosthenes could only show how he and his fellow oligarchs had been willing to betray Athens so that they could secure their regime. Thus, far from owing him gratitude, the jurors should feel anger for the plight they suffered because of his actions.

From such statements about the willingness of the Thirty to carry out the plans of the enemy, it was easy to take the next step and accuse them of helping Sparta defeat Athens. So in the same speech in which Andocides implied that Sparta caused the civil war, he also suggested that the oligarchs caused Athens to lose the Peloponnesian War. Again, he refused to be straightforward. He asked the jury to imagine what the Thirty would have done if they had captured him. Since he had participated in acts of treason at neither Decelea nor at sea (i.e., Aegospotami), and since he had neither destroyed the walls nor seized the city by force, they would have had him killed as an enemy of their regime (And. 1.101–102). In other words, the oligarchs and their supporters, seeking to overthrow the democracy, collaborated with Sparta even before Aegospotami, and after they had seized power they proceeded with a campaign of terror against all citizens who had failed to commit acts of treason against the democracy. Treason is what distinguished the oligarch from the democrat.

This explanation, far from incompatible with one focusing on Sparta, allowed the Athenians to deny responsibility for defeat without forcing them to acknowledge Spartan military power. By befriending the enemy, the Thirty became the enemy. Although they had once been citizens of a democratic Athens, the crimes they had committed against their fellow citizens turned them into outsiders. The Athenians could therefore convince themselves that any reproach they heaped onto the Thirty did not reflect back on the rest of the community. Moreover, they depicted the Thirty to be such villainous creatures, so greedy for power and money and so eager to satisfy their lawless passions, that the Athenians could easily deny the possibility that they could have prevented the Thirty from carrying out their plans.

Even though the Athenians could accuse oligarchic sympathizers of treason, Aegospotami remained a source of humiliation. But by denying that the destruction of the fleet had had to lead to the complete devastation of Athens and by maintaining that the terms of surrender Sparta imposed had been avoidable, they could convince themselves that Aegospotami did not reduce them to utter helplessness. For this reason, Lysias goes into great detail about oligarchic machinations after Aegospotami, which are absent from the narrative accounts of the civil war. Although we should not dismiss the evidence for such intrigue because it is mentioned only in Lysias, the omission of this information from the other accounts suggests that oligarchic conspiracies had minimal impact on the Athenian decision to surrender. But for our present discussion, it does not matter why the Athenians surrendered, but how such claims of intrigue functioned in postwar discourse. According to Lysias, the oligarchs prevented the Assembly from passing any useful measures after Aegospotami by setting up a board of five "ephors" and by instructing the phylarchs (calvary commanders furnished by the tribes) to tell the members of their faction how they should vote (12.43–44). Next, Theramenes became active, and, even though Lysander was clearly responsible for postponing negotiations (see Chapter 1), Lysias insists that it was Theramenes who delayed and that he did so in order to dissolve the democracy (13.10–11).

During Theramenes' absence, oligarchic conspirators paved the path for the surrender by placing Cleophon on trial for a capital offense. He was found guilty and executed (Lys. 13.12, 30.10–14). Then Theramenes returned, and some generals and commanders, including Dionysodorus and Strombichides, objected strongly to the treaty, believing that it would cause the overthrow of the democracy and that it was still possible to arrange better terms of surrender (Lys. 13.13–16). So the oligarchic conspirators slandered the generals to prevent them from being present at the Assembly when the surrender was to be discussed. They persuaded Agoratus to bring false accusation against the generals, and to make his accusations more believable they had him appear to give his testimony under compulsion. Theocritus reported to the Council that some men had information, and the Council (which was part of the conspiracy) passed a decree ordering Agoratus to testify. He then deposed the names of generals, commanders, and some other citizens, and once these men were arrested Lysander arrived with the Spartan fleet. The Athenians accepted the terms of surrender, and the democracy was overthrown (17–22, 34). Then, once the oligarchs were in power, they killed the generals (35–43). The speaker of Lysias 13, however, could maintain that the arrest and execution of the generals had led simultaneously to surrender and civil war only by collapsing the time between these two events.[9] As in Lysias 25, sycophancy played an important part in the defeat. But in Lysias 13, it was not democratic leaders that had caused the civil war but oligarchic conspirators who were using sycophants to carry out their plots (cf. Lys. 12.5).

After the oligarchs secured their control of Athens, they continued to wreak havoc, executing and exiling citizens and metics either to remove the opposition or to satisfy their greed. In attempts to win the sympathy of their respective juries, Lysias emphasized the greed of the Thirty and the nephew of Nicias recounted the oligarchs' campaign of terror against the democratic leaders.[10] The speaker of Lysias 34, on the other hand, recalled the suffering of those with property to persuade the jury to vote against the proposal of Phormisius to reduce the citizen class.[11] Collectively, these references helped create the impression that the entire population of Athens was victimized. Even the speaker of Lysias 25, who dared to say that the Athenians would have regarded the Thirty as good men (*andres agathoi*) if they had punished only the few who deserved it, conceded that they had oppressed the entire community.[12] Thus, as speaker after speaker claimed victim status or pointed to particular groups that had suffered, they rendered the Thirty the enemy of everyone, thereby reassuring the Athenians that no one still living in Athens would want to see oligarchs take control of the city again.

Speakers also created this impression by depicting the Thirty as utterly unique in their villainy, which was easy to do because they needed only to mention that the oligarchs had murdered 1,500 citizens. Again, Lysias 12 and 13 provide the most detailed accounts of the rule of the Thirty. Emphasizing their cruelty, the speaker of Lysias 13 described the deaths of their victims as most shameful and ignominious. Some victims left behind parents who had expected to be buried by their children, and others left behind sisters unwed or children who still needed their support (45). In his speech against Eratosthenes, Lysias gave an even more graphic description. Dragging their victims from their parents, children, and wives, the Thirty compelled them to kill themselves and then refused them the customary burial (12.96). Lysias even said that many were deprived of burial altogether, many were excluded from citizenship, and many were prohibited from giving their daughters in marriage (21).

By prohibiting the customary burial, the Thirty denied their opponents a site to challenge their authority. The funeral could not become an occasion for the opposition to assemble and to protest the actions of their oppressors.[13] But the violation of traditional norms was not simply a byproduct of the regime. As has been shown in Chapter 1, violence was the means by which the oligarchs established their authority. It was not enough to execute or disfranchise those whom they excluded from their ranks. By condemning them to a death "without *kleos*" (glory), by depriving them of the customary burial, and by forbidding their daughters the right to marry, the oligarchs marked themselves as the only Athenians who possessed *kleos* and, therefore, the only ones who were worthy to rule. In a perverse way, lawlessness legitimized their regime. It gave them their authority. But for the Athenians, this was not the lesson to be learned, and this was not why speakers recalled the atrocities of the Thirty. The behavior of the oligarchs proved only that they were willing to violate every and all established norms and that oligarchy, by extension, was an entirely unacceptable form of rule.

When the oligarchs found Lysias at home entertaining, they did not hesitate to drive out his guests and hand him over to Peison. He offered Peison one talent to let him go, and although he knew that Peison had respect for neither gods nor men, he still had him swear an oath. He then went into the bedroom to get the money from a chest. But Peison, once he saw what was inside, decided to seize all of the contents: three talents of silver, four hundred cyzicenes, one hundred darics, and four silver cups. Lysias pleaded with Peison to leave him some money for his journey, to which Peison replied that he should be happy to be alive (Lys. 12.8–11).

As the two left the house, Melobius and Mnesitheides saw Lysias and instructed Peison to deliver his prisoner to them. They then took Lysias to Damnippus's house and handed him over to Theognis. Realizing that he would still be put to death if he were to bribe Theognis, Lysias attempted an escape. Successful, he set sail only after he found out that Eratosthenes had placed his brother, Polemarchus, in prison. Then, without putting him on trial or even telling him why he was to be executed, the Thirty ordered Polemarchus to drink hemlock. They prohibited his family from using any of their three houses or any of Polemarchus's own cloaks for the funeral, so the family was forced to pay for a small hut for him to be laid in and to use a cloak and pillow that their friends could provide (12–18).

Lysias then disrupted the chronological sequence of his narrative to conclude with the description of one minor incident when the oligarchs seized his family's property: "Although they had 700 of our shields, so much gold and silver, bronze and jewelry, furniture and women's clothing, more than they ever thought that they would take, and 120 slaves (of which they kept the best and delivered the rest to the treasury), yet they came to such a state of greed and sordid desire of gain and displayed their character that golden earrings, which the wife of Polemarchus happened to be wearing, were ripped out from her ears by Melobius as soon as he entered the house."[14] Wooten (1988/89: 29–31) notes how the subordinate clauses, creating suspense, highlighted the completion of the thought, which was delayed until the very end of the sentence. By contrasting the total amount of confiscated property, which he listed at length, with the seizing of the earrings, which he described in drawnout detail, Lysias was able to emphasize the depravity of the Thirty. Despite all that they already had, a pair of earrings, obtained only by laying their hands on a married woman, was too much of a temptation for them to resist.

For the Athenians who had suffered at the hands of the oligarchs, the lesson to be learned was that law had become a farce under the oligarchy. The Thirty dragged citizens away by force from the *agora* and the temples

(Lys. 12.96) and violated the sanctity of the home by searching inside houses for wanted individuals (30). They compelled others to commit wrongs (Isoc. 18.17), and they created such a state of lawlessness that even individuals with private disputes were unable to go to court to settle them (Isoc. 21.3).[15] As the speaker of Isocrates 21 said, it was a time when those who had borrowed money in the presence of witnesses dared to deny it (7). The laws were no longer valid, and now greed determined the behavior of all: "So that Nicias, even if he used to engage in sycophancy, would then have stopped, and Euthynus, even if he had never before thought of committing crimes, would have been tempted then since he was being honored for his wrong while Nicias was the objects of plots because of his possessions. You all know that it was worse at that time to be wealthy than to harm others for the latter were taking the property of others while the former were deprived of their own possessions" (11–12). Using irony to show how completely the Thirty transformed Athenian society, the speaker suggested that Athens had been in a state of anarchy where greed was the rule. Under such circumstances, the wealthy became an enticing target, and only those who yielded to temptation prospered.

Perhaps such depictions of the Thirty provided the Athenians a safe outlet for their anger. When speakers recalled what had happened during the civil war, accusing the oligarchs of despicable acts of violence, maybe the jurors were able to vent their anger against the Thirty without transferring it to the defendants on trial. Perhaps just hearing speakers publicly denounce the oligarchs provided some form of satisfaction. But it is also possible that recounting the crimes of the Thirty only intensified animosities and encouraged others to demand retribution. But as speakers depicted the oligarchs as utterly depraved, they appeared unique in their villainy, thereby reassuring the Athenians that it was unlikely for others ever to repeat their crimes. The more despicable they were, the more unlikely that anyone would match them in the future. Thus, intentionally or not, speakers assured the Athenians that their community would not experience further oligarchic sedition. By relegating the Thirty to the past, by distancing themselves from defeat and civil war, and by denying that the period of civil unrest had any lasting repercussions, they attempted to free themselves from the anger and fear that the civil war had produced.

THE DEMOCRATIC RESISTANCE

Unlike the oligarchs, who were objects of disdain and reproach, those who resisted their tyranny became paradigms of excellence. We have already seen that speakers praised the men of Piraeus, either claiming this title for themselves to win the jury's admiration or denying their opponents credit for the restoration of the democracy. Speakers also depicted the democratic resistance as a foil to the Thirty and their supporters. Using what was traditionally aristocratic language to praise those who had fought against the oligarchs, they rendered elite values serviceable to democratic ideals. This coopting of aristocratic language does not suggest that the Athenians accepted aristocratic pretensions at face value or that they were attempting to elevate the democratic resistance by portraying it as if all of its members were part of the political and social elite. Rather, the use of this language shows how memory of the civil war enabled the Athenians to democratize elite values. Perhaps the democrats would have continued to appropriate aristocratic language even if they had not had the rule of the Thirty as a pretext. Indeed, this process was already under way in the fifth century.[16] But by casting reproach on the Thirty, they were more easily able to encroach further on aristocratic ideals and claim them for the demos, further invalidating aristocratic pretensions.

Still, this appropriation remained a difficult task because the elite accommodated themselves to democracy. As Adkins has shown, those traditionally called *agathoi* earned this praise because of their services (*agatha*) to society. In democratic Athens, any citizen who performed valuable services for the polis could possess arete. But since men of substance provided for the city's most pressing needs, they had a greater claim to arete than ordinary citizens. They fitted the triremes, paid the war tax, and financed choruses for the festivals. Incorporated within the framework of the democracy, the traditional *agathoi* maintained their privileged status by presenting themselves as the most valuable citizens of the polis. They continued to possess the same claims to arete that they always had, but now they were *agathoi politai* (Adkins 1960: 207–8).

Although ordinary citizens did not have the resources to compete with an elite that justified its prestige through magnificent displays of public generosity, they certainly provided other important services for the community. Citizens of modest wealth made up, after all, the bulk of the soldiers who fought on the battlefield and manned the triremes. Certainly, the Athenians recognized the importance of their contribution. Thus, typically in funeral orations, speakers described the dead as *agathoi*.[17] Honoring the soldiers who had died in the Corinthian War, the speaker of Lysias 2 said, "These men are enviable both in their life and after their death since they were reared in the good deeds of their ancestors, and then in manhood, they preserved their ancestors' reputation and displayed their own excellence" (69). Yet if ordinary citizens became *agathoi* only by dying or were addressed as *agathoi* only after they were dead, then men of substance remained the exclusive holders of this privilege while alive.[18]

Provided that the Athenians agreed about what was good for their city, the traditional elite could maintain their privileged status without much controversy and ordinary citizens could gain recognition only through extraordinary actions on the battlefield. But after *stasis* had divided the community and the elite had fought on opposing sides, aristocratic pretensions were particularly vulnerable. The traditional *agathoi* who supported the democratic cause gained further proof of their merit, whereas those who participated in the oligarchy lost credibility. Since in the past they had earned the gratitude of their fellow citizens for their services to community, they now by the same logic deserved to suffer infamy for the harm they had inflicted on the city. In the *dokimasia* of Evander, for example, the prosecutor told the members of the Council that they should be more mindful of the candidate's offenses than his family's generosity.[19]

Just as the civil war undermined the credibility of some aristocrats, so it gave the Athenians the impetus to rethink what they regarded as valuable services. Of course, those in the liturgical class still benefited from their public munificence. Now, however, the Athenians considered other services valuable which ordinary citizens could also perform. Loyalty to the democracy was now a sufficient reason for an individual to earn arete. In Lysias 13, for example, the speaker called the citizens whom the Thirty had killed "good men [*andres agathoi*] with regard to the demos" (2). Refusing to tolerate a peace that would cause the overthrow of the democracy, these good citizens believed that they could arrange favorable terms of surrender, and so they opposed the agreement that Theramenes had arranged with Sparta (13–17). Some were even willing to help Agoratus escape from Athens to prevent him from testifying against the many *andres agathoi* whom the conspirators wanted to kill (27). But Agoratus refused, and, as a result, they were executed (47–48, 61).

It was not displays of courage on the battlefield that earned them this title but rather their opposition to the plans of the oligarchic conspirators. In other words, they did not become *agathoi* by dying; the oligarchs decided to kill them because they were *agathoi* to the demos. Although the speaker said that some had been generals and commanders, men who therefore had already earned their claim to arete, he described the others as merely citizens who had later shown themselves to be well disposed to the demos (13). It was their refusal to submit to the demands of Sparta and to endure the overthrow of the democracy which made them conspicuous and earned them the right to be called *agathoi*. By conferring aristocratic praise on those who had died while opposing the Thirty, the speaker of Lysias 13 made loyalty to the democracy a virtue. As Adkins (1960: 211) remarks, "It is now *agathos* to be a democrat *per se.*"

Such praise was extended even to members of the democratic resistance who had survived the civil war. The men of Piraeus, as has been shown, had displayed conduct to which all were to aspire. Preferring to die as free men rather than live in slavery (Lys. 2.62), they were diametrically opposed to the Thirty in every way: "But nevertheless, unafraid of the mass of their opponents, risking their own lives, they set up a trophy over their enemy, and they rendered the tombs of the Spartans which are near this monument as proof of their arete (63). Depicting the men of Piraeus as ideal democrats, the speaker of Lysias 2 said that they possessed what were traditionally aristocratic virtues: bravery, wisdom, and moderation. He implicitly suggested that the oligarchs could claim none of these. They had weakened the city, created *stasis*, and destroyed the walls.

Loraux (1986: 201) believes that the speaker undermined democratic values by treating the men of Piraeus as *agathoi* "in the social and political sense." I argue that the speaker was doing exactly the opposite. He was not calling them the social and political elite; rather, he was rendering aristocratic language serviceable to democratic ideals. Denying the oligarchs their claim to privilege, he suggested that the men of Piraeus performed the most valuable services for the city, whereas the oligarchs caused the most harm: oligarchs destroy walls and democrats rebuild them. Democrats were now the *agathoi* and oligarchs the *kakoi*. Partly in response to the excesses of the Thirty, democrats—regardless of class, position, or status—could now be said to possess virtues that before aristocrats had kept for themselves.[20] Therefore, far from undermining democratic values, the speaker of Lysias 2 declared the men of Piraeus to be paramount democrats and democracy to be the paramount form of government.

Still, this example is from an *epitaphios,* so perhaps one might argue that it was only a minor extension of the type of praise that was already customary in funeral oratory. Yet in the conclusion of his speech against Eratosthenes, Lysias made similar remarks as he addressed separately the members of the jury who had joined the democrats in Piraeus. Reminding them of their suffering in exile, how they freed some and restored others to their fatherland, he called them *andres agathoi* (Lys. 12.97). Not surprisingly, he failed to mention the intervention of Pausanias, since it would only have undermined his praise of the democratic resistance.[21] By passing over in silence the role of Sparta in the restoration of the democracy, the Athenians could remember the reconciliation as victory for the men of Piraeus and bestow such praise on them for their success. They denied that the demos was responsible for defeat and civil war, and they maintained that only the men of Piraeus deserved the credit for the restoration of the democracy. Whether or not this mindful forgetfulness helped the Athenians reconcile, it allowed them to divorce themselves from the period of civil unrest. Previously subject to the commands of Sparta, Athens was again autonomous thanks to the men of Piraeus.

Equally remarkable is the claim that even citizens who failed to intervene when the Thirty seized control of Athens were also worthy of praise. According to Lysias, the Athenians first reacted to the proposed terms of surrender with an uproar and refused to do as Theramenes ordered. Lysander then warned them that he would consider them in violation of the truce if they did not approve the proposal. A few wicked men (*poneroi*) voted in favor of the order, whereas good men (*andres agathoi*) either remained silent or left the Assembly (Lys. 12. 71–75). But who were these good men? If only a few consented, then the rest must have refused to ratify the oligarchy, and that group would therefore include the demos.

From the outset of the civil war, the lines were clearly drawn. Those who were willing to assist the oligarchs were blameworthy (*kakoi*), and those who opposed them were *agathoi*. In a sense, Lysias suggested that the period of exile began immediately with this initial silencing of the demos. Rather than consent to the relinquishing of its authority and bestow on the oligarchs the legitimacy they were seeking, the demos preferred to remove itself altogether from civic discourse. This passivity was at best a feeble form of resistance. But at least then Lysias could maintain that the demos had no part in the oligarchy, thereby preserving its integrity in spite of civil war, which in turn made it easier to declare the demos *agathos*. The democratic resistance became a paradigm of excellence so long as democrats remained untainted by acts of complicity. Otherwise, they could be blamed for the ease with which the oligarchs overthrew the democracy, and then doubt could be placed on their eagerness to restore the democracy.

THE MIRROR IMAGE

Depicting the rule of the Thirty as the mirror image of the restored democracy, speakers suggested the reconciliation would succeed only if the Athenians acted differently from the Thirty. As soon as the restored democracy appeared similar to the rule of the Thirty, Athens might again be in danger of suffering civil unrest. In Lysias 18, for example, the nephew of Nicias told the jurors that it was unfair for him to suffer under both the democracy and the oligarchy (22). If his family had remained loyal to the democracy when the Thirty were wreaking havoc, then surely he deserved the gratitude of his fellow citizens after the democracy was restored (25, 27). Only by avoiding what the Thirty had done could the Athenians now prevent *stasis*. Thus, if they wanted harmony, they had to forbid the unjust confiscations of property (17). Alcibiades the younger was equally blunt, declaring it unfair that the actions of the Athenians should be the opposite of the Thirty in all other matters except with regard to him. Since he was forced to live in exile during the civil war, a democratic jury should not inflict on him the same punishment as the oligarchs had (Isoc. 16.50).

The Athenians learned from the civil war that Athens had suffered the greatest harm after it lost its autonomy. Now that the democracy was restored, the Athenians could begin the process of repairing the damages that the oligarchs had inflicted on the community, but only if they first removed all traces of the oligarchy. They needed to rebuild the walls (And. 3.10–12, 36–37), and they had to adhere to their oaths. Until the Athenians regained their autonomy and eliminated the source of dissension, their city would remain vulnerable to invasions by foreign armies and uprising from within the community. The solution was to avoid the crimes the Thirty had committed (Lys. 25.20). But speakers could use this same logic to justify circumvention of the amnesty. Under oligarchic rule, the guilty were permitted to harm others without suffering the consequences. So it was now the responsibility of the democrats to deter others from crime by convicting all who had violated the laws during the civil war.

Yet whether appealing to the amnesty or to the desire for satisfaction, litigants agreed that the rule of law, antithetical to oligarchy, was manifested in its fullest form under democracy. They insisted that the oligarchs had destroyed the laws in order to overthrow the democracy and that the democrats could prevent further sedition only if they now restored the rule of law. Declaring Lochites to have emulated the behavior of the oligarchs, the speaker of Isocrates 20 remarked: "If anyone now dares to break the law when it is not permitted, what would he have done when those ruling even rewarded individuals for committing such crimes?" (4). The prosecutor did not accuse Lochites of participating in an oligarchic conspiracy or even of membership in an aristocratic club. He charged the defendant with only battery. Although he acknowledged that some might consider the case unimportant (5), he replied that Lochites had proved himself to be of the same disposition as the oligarchs by committing *hybris* and by disregarding the laws (10–11). The jury should therefore take the accusations seriously (7). Moreover, if they wanted to prevent criminals from bringing Athens into the same condition as when the Thirty ruled, they must immediately punish the guilty rather than give them the opportunity to commit even more crimes (12).[22]

By contrasting the rule of the Thirty with the restored democracy, speakers discredited oligarchy and validated democratic rule. The more they appeared to be polar opposites, the more democracy was vindicated, the consequences of which spread even beyond civic discourse to elite writing. So in the *Areopagiticus,* Isocrates conceded praise for the democracy to dispel any suspicion that he favored oligarchy (7.70). After comparing the Thirty to the men of Piraeus (64–68), he summarized by saying that the oligarchs preferred to rule over their fellow citizens and to be the slaves of the enemy, whereas the democrats chose to rule over other cities and to be on equal terms with their fellow citizens (69). Essentially, he accepted the "mirror image" we have seen promoted in civic discourse.

But after making this concession, Isocrates then denied the comparison its ideological sting: "For I do not believe that we ought to be proud and content if we are more lawful than madmen, possessed by evil spirits, but rather we ought to be more vexed and more upset if we are worse than our ancestors; for we must compare ourselves to their excellence than to the wickedness of the Thirty, especially since we should be the best among all mankind" (73). As long as his contemporaries compared their present circumstances to the state of affairs under the Thirty, they could be satisfied and even proud of their democracy. Isocrates, however, cleverly undermined democratic complacency by displacing the point of reference from the Thirty to the democracy of Solon and Cleisthenes. In an Athens that had attempted to rebuild its empire and had experienced devastating setbacks, reminders about past greatness were troubling. But in the Athens of Lysias, which had just ended the civil war and where the Athenians imagined the restored democracy to be a continuation of the democracy of the fifth century, reminders about their glorious past were a source of hope. Contrasting the rule of the Thirty with the restored democracy, they reinforced this sense of continuity with the fifth century, and they reassured themselves that Athens would be great again. If their present situation was different from that under the Thirty, they could repair the damage the oligarchs had inflicted.

CONCLUSION

By casting reproach on the Thirty and their supporters, speakers assured the Athenians that no one would ever be able to rival the oligarchs in their villainy. Their crimes were so terrible that it was nearly impossible for anyone to repeat them. But even if someone should attempt to emulate their behavior, the rest of the community, having suffered at the hands of the Thirty, knew the dangers, and they would do their best to stop that individual. As the oligarchs appeared more detestable, the democratic resistance became even more deserving of praise. The Thirty were responsible for defeat and civil war, whereas the democratic resistance alone deserved the credit for the restoration of the democracy.[23] Serving as paradigms to illustrate how the Athenians should and should not act, these complementary images gave them the pretext to appropriate aristocratic praise and to bestow it on the democrats.

This "paradigm-making" also helped them bracket the period of civil unrest from their past and future. Since those responsible for Athenian misfortunes were no longer a part of the community, the Athenians no longer needed to fear future invasions by foreign armies or future uprisings from within the community. Yet they could believe that those responsible for the civil war were no longer living in Athens only by overlooking that the Thirty had needed help to carry out their crimes and that few had actually opposed the oligarchs. Heaping blame on the Thirty for all that had happened through this blending of remembering and forgetting, they constructed a future that, while a break from the recent events, was a continuation of their remote past. As long as they did the opposite of the Thirty, they could repair the damages. They convinced themselves that Athens would be great yet again, but only by denying that the divisions that had surfaced during the civil war had lasting repercussions.

CONCLUSION

Was it [not] because of the madness of the Thirty that we have become
more eager supporters of democracy than those who seized Phyle?

(ISOC. 8.108)

The events of 403 bear directly on the debate about the nature of the Athenian democracy. Most historians conclude either that the democracy continued where it had left off before the Thirty seized power or that the Athenians retreated from popular rule. Central to the debate is the creation of boards of *nomothetai*. But, by drawing this reform into the larger discussion on the democracy and by looking at it in isolation from the history of postwar Athens, we run the risk of missing its significance for the Athenians living under the restored democracy. Perhaps structurally the democracy continued in much the same way as it had in the fifth century, but the city was not the same culturally.

Law was a great concern for the Athenians, as the law reforms amply show. The Athenians also attempted to protect the community from lawlessness by placing on trial individuals who transgressed Athenian norms. Socrates is the most notorious victim of this renewed concern for the rule of law. The civil war had taught the Athenians that democracy ultimately depended upon law and that law was possible only under democracy. Implicitly responding to the elite critics who insisted that democracy led to lawlessness (see especially Ober 1998), the Athenians found in their recent history proof of just the opposite, that oligarchy led to lawlessness and that only democrats respected the laws. *Nomothesia* was merely one of the ways that they reclaimed law for democracy. In the end, 403 was a watershed year not because of institutional changes but because the Athenians redefined the community from their experiences during the civil war and because memory of the civil war remained the focus of their attention.

The fact that Athens did not suffer from further oligarchic revolution until the Macedonian conquest provides perhaps the greatest proof of the success of the reconciliation. One could easily conclude that oligarchy was no longer a viable option because of the Thirty. But oligarchs did not simply disappear from the Athenian scene. Depicting the rule of the Thirty as the antithesis of democracy and the rule of law, the democrats regained control of civic discourse by actively discrediting oligarchy and by forcefully asserting democratic values. They concluded from the past that the oligarchs were the cause of their misery and that it was the democracy that provided them with the greatest benefits. This may seem to us an obvious conclusion to reach after what they had suffered at the hands of the Thirty. But unless the democrats succeeded in promoting their version of the past, the Athenians could just as easily have concluded that their own recklessness, cowardice, and foolishness had allowed the oligarchs to seize control of the city. By actively and forcefully constructing an image of the past which preserved the integrity of the demos and which the men of the city could tolerate and even advocate, they prevented the opposition from effectively voicing such forceful criticisms of democracy within civic discourse.

Instead of asking why the reconciliation agreement was a success, we have considered how the Athenians were able to tolerate, accommodate themselves to, and conceptualize reconciliation. Certainly the political condition of the Greek world, the social and economic problems of Athens, and the very terms of the agreement constrained them. Revenge and retribution were not realistic options. But the Athenians could have just as easily dismissed pragmatic considerations to seek satisfaction for past grievances. The terms of the agreement were open to conflicting interpretations, and even they were a source of conflict. Unless the jurors who heard these disputes and the litigants who pursued their grievances espoused the principles of reconciliation, the agreement could never have succeeded, regardless of how well its terms were drafted. Reconciliation cannot be reduced to a system of imposed rules, regulations, and procedures. And whatever the reasons for its success, the Athenians had to justify to themselves not only the abandoning of revenge but also the erasure of memory. They needed to construct a culture that promoted amnesty. Reconciliation was first and foremost a cultural construct, which the Athenians were responsible for maintaining and promoting. It was highly elastic, subject to conflicting and competing interpretations. Peace was therefore never final; rather, it was reinvented and renegotiated every time a conflict erupted between members of the former factions and every time a citizen recalled the period of civil unrest in order to justify a particular policy, law, or action under discussion by the Athenian people. No matter how much the Athenians attempted to relegate the civil war to their past, it continued to surface in civic discourse and continued to shape Athens.

From speeches delivered at civic settings, whether in the Assembly, Council, and law courts or at the public burial of soldiers, we have seen how the Athenians collectively remembered the period of civil unrest. Since the speakers did not know beforehand the composition of their audience, they needed to express values and beliefs shared by a broad range of the citizenry. Far from professing views that only a narrow section of the population supported, they were more likely to appeal to a common culture or, at least, what they believed to be a commonly shared culture. There are few extant speeches for this time period, but those that have survived provide significant and meaningful statements about the civil war and reconciliation. Even when the actions of the Thirty did not pertain to the particular disputes, litigants still found it useful to mention them. Rather than dismiss their remarks as empty rhetoric, this study takes them seriously. Perhaps the speakers were exploiting the anger and fear in the community, but this does not mean that they were inventing these emotions. Anger and fear were normal reactions to a trauma on the scale of the civil war, and although the Athenians wanted consensus now more than ever, they had legitimate disagreements about the reconciliation which were not easy to resolve. To put it simply, they had to decide whether it was better to remember the past or to pass over it in silence.

The most disturbing aspect of the reconciliation is that it required compromise. After the brutality of the Thirty, the Athenians agreed—or were forced by Sparta—to accept an amnesty that allowed oligarchic sympathizers to live in Athens and to participate in the restored democracy. It denied the democratic resistance the opportunity to punish many of their former enemies. By depicting the men of Piraeus as the demos in exile, which returned in triumph to rule the city once again, the Athenians transformed the reconciliation into victory. Ironically, this victory was only possible if they then reincorporated the men of the city into the demos so that they no longer existed as a separate faction. Otherwise, these men would serve as a reminder that the restored democracy was vulnerable to oligarchic conspiracies and that the reconciliation was a compromise between democrats and oligarchs. Forgetting that the men of the city had supported the Thirty and remembering how they had opposed the Thirty once the reign of terror began, the Athenians maintained that opposition from within and without made it possible for the democratic exiles to return. Thus, they could insist that the demos had remained unified in spite of civil war and that the restored democracy was now composed of the opponents of the Thirty, their victims, and innocent bystanders. Even former exiles who prosecuted former oligarchs and oligarchic sympathizers advanced favorable depictions of the men of the city, in part to make those jurors who had remained in Athens more receptive to their arguments. The Athenians had their victory, but only by foregoing revenge and by denying that the factionalism of the past carried over into the present. But at least this victory did not force them to acknowledge the complicity of the demos.

Although Athenian memory of the civil war promoted reconciliation at the representational level, litigants still recalled the past in order to harm their opponents. Insisting that most who were living in the restored democracy were victims of the Thirty, prosecutors claimed that the Athenians could punish the few who had committed crimes during the civil war without disrupting the reconciliation. But, given that so few were beyond reproach, defendants were able to raise doubts about the charges by responding with counteraccusations. More importantly, they declared to the jury that they had been and would continue to be loyal to the democracy, thereby reassuring them that Athens would not again suffer civil unrest.

These same ambiguities in turn created obstacles for any individual who attempted to benefit from the praise bestowed on the men of Piraeus for their success. As speakers extolled them, whether to benefit from their reputation or to deny that their opponents deserved to be included within their ranks, the men of Piraeus appeared even more exceptional. In the end, only the demos had unquestionable claim to this title. Law provided the Athenians with further reassurance that they could put an end to the cycle of bloodshed. As long as they observed, promoted, and protected the laws, the democracy would remain intact. Although the reconciliation in fact complicated the legal process and created competing and conflicting claims to justice, Athenians preferred to deny these negative consequences so they could pass over the unsettling problems of reconciliation. Perhaps the Athenians sometimes interpreted the laws in ways that promoted reconciliation. But as the trial of Socrates reveals, fear of unrest could justify intrusive prosecutions, which could in turn factionalize the community. This effort to reaffirm the value of justice was unable to guarantee the stability of the restored democracy.

But somehow, as the Athenians remembered the civil war and assigned it meaning, the reconciliation lasted. Doubtless, the blending of remembering and forgetting—although a strategy of avoidance and denial—gave them time to heal. Constructing competing and conflicting representations of the past, they created a reconciliation that was always renegotiable and required their vigilance. Its success was not a given, nor was it decided by one momentous event; rather, it was part of a process by which a peaceful solution to the civil war was reconstructed in daily practice.

In comparison to that of the fifth century, Athens of the fourth century may seem a disappointment. Frequently, historians refer to this period as a time of decline. Once great, Athens would soon be eclipsed by other powers. But the Athenians of the restored democracy did not know that they would fail to rebuild the empire. For them, the recent past gave the democracy a new legitimacy. Distancing themselves from these horrors and denying that the Thirty had lasting repercussions, they attempted to escape from the anger and fear that the civil war had produced. They convinced themselves that, as long as they avoided what the Thirty had done and as long as they preserved the democracy, they could again restore its greatness. And it would not be too great of an exaggeration to conclude that the ability of the Athenians to continue on after the civil war was as great an achievement as anything that they had done in the fifth century.

ABBREVIATIONS

Aesch.	Aeschines	Lys.	Lysias
Aeschy.	Aeschylus	Nep.	Nepos
Eum.	*Eumenides*	Paus.	Pausanias
And.	Andocides	Pl.	Plato
Arist.	Aristotle	*Ap.*	*Apology*
Ath. Pol.	*Athenaion Politeia*	*Ep.*	*Epistles*
Pol.	*Politics*	*Mx.*	*Menexenus*
Rhet.	*Rhetoric*	Plut.	Plutarch
Dem.	Demosthenes	*Alc.*	*Alcibiades*
Din.	Dinarchus	*Lys.*	*Lysander*
D.H.	Dionysius of Halicar-nassus	*Mor.*	*Moralia*
		Sol.	*Solon*
Lys.	*Lysias*	*Them.*	*Themistocles*
D.L.	Diogenes Laertius	*X Orat.*	*Vitae Decem Oratorum* (in *Moralia*)
D.S.	Diodorus Siculus		
Front.	Frontinus	Thuc.	Thucydides
Her.	Herodotus	Xen.	Xenophon
Hyp.	Hyperides	*Mem.*	*Memorabilia*
Is.	Isaeus	*Hell.*	*Hellenica*
Isoc.	Isocrates	[Xen.]	"The Old Oligarch"
Just.	Justin the Martyr		
Lyc.	Lycurgus		

AO	R. Develin, *Athenian Officials, 684–321 B.C.* (Cambridge 1989)
APF	J. K. Davies, *Athenian Propertied Families, 600–300 B.C.* (Oxford 1971)
DK	H. Diels and W. Kranz, eds., *Die Fragmente der Vorsokratiker,* 6th ed. (Berlin 1951–52)
FGH	F. Jacoby, ed., *Die Fragmente der griechischen Historiker* (Berlin 1923–58)
IG	*Inscriptiones Graecae*
ML	R. Meiggs and D. M. Lewis, eds., *A Selection of Greek Historical Inscriptions to the End of the Fifth Century B.C.,* rev. ed. (Oxford 1988)
PA	J. Kirchner, *Prosopographia Attica* (Berlin 1901–3)
P. Hib.	*Hibeh Papyri*
P. Mich.	*Michigan Papyri*
P. Oxy.	*Oxyrhynchus Papyri*

P. Ryl.	*Catalogue of the Greek Papyri in the John Rylands Library*
SEG	*Supplementum Epigraphicum Graecum*
W	M. L. West, *Iambi et Elegi Graeci,* 2d ed. (Oxford 1989–92)

JOURNALS

AC	*L'Antiquité classique*
AHB	*Ancient History Bulletin*
AHR	*American Historical Review*
AJAH	*American Journal of Ancient History*
AJP	*American Journal of Philology*
BICS	*Bulletin of the Institute of Classical Studies*
BSA	*Annual of the British School at Athens*
CA	*Classical Antiquity*
CJ	*Classical Journal*
C&M	*Classica et Mediaevalia*
CP	*Classical Philology*
CQ	*Classical Quarterly*
CR	*Classical Review*
CSCA	*California Studies in Classical Antiquity*
CW	*Classical World*
EMC / CV	*Échos du monde classique / Classical Views*
G&R	*Greece and Rome*
GRBS	*Greek, Roman, and Byzantine Studies*
HSCP	*Harvard Studies in Classical Philology*
JHS	*Journal of Hellenic Studies*
LCM	*Liverpool Classical Monthly*
PCPS	*Proceedings of the Cambridge Philological Society*
PQ	*Philological Quarterly*
QUCC	*Quaderni urbinati di cultura classica*
REG	*Revue des études grecques*
RhM	*Rheinisches Museum für Philologie*
RP	*Revue de philologie*
RSA	*Rivista storica dell' antichità*
TAPA	*Transactions of the American Philological Association*
WS	*Wiener Studien*
YCS	*Yale Classical Studies*
ZPE	*Zeitschrift für Papyrologie und Epigraphik*

NOTES

INTRODUCTION

1. For a late composition of Thucydides' *History,* see Munn (2000: 303–27). Gomme (1945–81: iii. 498), however, argues that the passages on Corcyra were written before the Athenian reconciliation; cf. Hornblower (1987: 154).
2. D.S. 13.52.2; Arist. *Ath.* Pol. 34.1.
2. For *stasis* in Greek political theory, see Cohen (1995: 25–57); Ober (1998).
3. For the terms of the reconciliation agreement, see Dorjahn (1946: 53); Ostwald (1986: 497); Loening (1987: 149); for the political condition of the Greek world, see Funke (1980: 12–17); for the social and economic problems of Athens, see Cloché (1915: 476); Mossé (1973: 12–20, 30); Strauss (1986: 3–6, 114, 173).
4. The danger of history is that it can reduce what happened to a chain of events leading to one inevitable outcome. Compare the remarks of Bernstein (1994: 29): "The Roman Empire ultimately collapsed, but does its downfall make what happened during its lengthy existence meaningless or count only as a step toward the sacking of Rome by barbarians?"
5. Aesch. 1.39, 173, 2.77–78, 147–48, 176, 3.187–95, 208, 235; Dem. 19.196, 277, 280, 20.11–12, 22.52, 24.57–58, 90, 164, 40.46, 58.67; Din. 1.25; Hyp. 2.8; Lyc. 1.61, 124. For the use of the civil war as a historical *exemplum* by late-fourth-century orators, see Nouhaud (1982: 301–16). Mathieu (1914) suggests that the orators obtained their information about the Thirty from pamphlets on the *patrios politeia.* But it is also possible that they were drawing from an oral tradition, which would explain why their references are little more than the "simple commonplaces" that Nouhaud (1982: 316) finds objectionable. The speakers were not delving into the civil war so they could use "historical facts" from the past to validate their arguments; rather, the memory of the Thirty had become part of the polis tradition in which they and their listeners were engaging. The civil war, although a historical event, was still a living memory, shaping and shaped by the outlook of the Athenians who were living in late-fourth-century Athens. See Thomas (1989: esp. 196–237), who offers an innovative approach to the study of Athenian oral tradition; also more generally Hutton (1993), who collapses the distinction between memory and history.
6. For the composition of Athenian political institutions, see Rhodes (1972: 3–6); Markle (1985; 1990); Ober (1989a: 127–48); Todd (1990a); Hansen (1991: 125–27, 182–86, 248–49). Despite disagreement over the extent to which the wealthy were over-represented, the poorer citizens had to attend in large numbers in order to meet the requisite quorum, and they were probably the majority in each of these institutions.
7. Dover (1974: 5–8); Ober (1989a: 43–49). It is possible that the published version of a speech could vary greatly from that delivered in public; see Worthington (1991). This makes it even more difficult to reconstruct a trial or to determine its

outcome from a speech in the corpus of Attic orators; see further Todd (1990c). But, assuming that an orator would not render the published version less persuasive, revisions are actually useful for this study. Besides improving his style, the orator might strengthen his arguments or reply to objections raised by the opposing speaker. He might also improve upon his appeals to the jury, thus making it easier for us to uncover common opinions from the Attic orators.

8. Adkins (1978: 144–47). Yet it is also worth noting that speakers sometimes avoided appearing intellectual; see Pearson (1941); Perlman (1961); Dover (1974: 10–13); Ober (1989a: 177–82).

9. Adkins (1960: 197–214; 1972: 117–26); Loraux (1986: 180–202, 217–20, 334–35); Roberts (1986).

10. For the reapplying of aristocratic language and values, see North (1966: 116–17, 135–42); Seager (1973: 20–26); Donlan (1978: 101–2; 1980: 168–80); Whitehead (1983; 1993); Bleicken (1985: 193–95); Ober (1989a: 289–92 with n. 74, 336–39); Thomas (1989: 213–21); Raaflaub (1994: 126–30).

11. See especially Todd (1990c). Questions concerning the logographer's own attitudes are nearly impossible to answer. Hence Dover (1968: 56) asserts, "We have *no* political or ideological grounds for denying the ascription to Lysias of *any* extant or lost speech in the corpus" (italics in the original).

12. Halbwachs (1941: 7). For further discussion of Halbwachs's theories on collective memory, see Schwartz (1982: 374–77; 1991: 221–22). For criticism of the term, see Gedi and Elam (1996).

13. E.g., Nora (1984–97); Gregory and Lewis (1988); Wagner-Pacifici and Schwartz (1991); Young (1993); Gillis (1994); Berdahl (1994); Zerubarel (1995).

14. Although I find more convincing the arguments in favor of attributing the *Athenaion Politeia* to Aristotle, it does not affect my findings whether Aristotle was the author; cf. Ostwald (1986: xx–xxi n. 1). On the authorship of the *Athenaion Politeia* see Rhodes (1981: 58–63); Chambers (1990: 77–82); Keaney (1992: 3–19).

15. Dover (1974: 30); Ober (1989a: 36–38); Hunter (1994: 6–7); Christ (1998: 6); Johnstone (1999: 19). See also Loraux (1986); Cohen (1991; 1995). Ober and Strauss (1990: 243, 269–70) argue for continuity in Athenian political culture from the second quarter of the fifth century to the third quarter of the fourth.

16. See Morris (1992: 10–12). For a response to such criticism, see Golden (1992); Hunter (1994: 6–7). Winkler (1990: 43) remarks, "Our modern impetus to locate changes, to write all kinds of history as a story of development and transition, has probably led to deep falsifications at least in the study of Mediterranean cultural patterns." While it is true that there were few technological or scientific advances in the ancient world compared to the modern world, we run the risk of overlooking changes in antiquity if we look for them where they are found most today. For Athens, it is in the political arena where we are more likely to observe change. In stark contrast to our own polity, in which political participation for most citizens is reduced to the private and impersonal act of voting (see the remarks of Barber [1984: 188]), the Athenians were actively engaged in decision-making. To say that the Athenians deliberated in the same way at the meetings of the Assembly when they decided to fight Sparta in the fifth century

and Macedon in the fourth or that litigants used the same rhetorical strategies in the courts from 420 to 320 is to dismiss that Athenian concerns and fears had changed. As the Athenians responded to new foreign threats and to new domestic problems, their political culture invariably underwent significant change, regardless of how stable society, political institutions, or methods of public speaking may have been.

17. As Ober (1993: 224) explains, "Although such comparisons are supplementary, and not evidentiary in a formal sense, they are useful if they expand common assumptions about the limits of the possible." Cf. Cartledge (1985: 20–22).

1 CIVIL WAR

EPIGRAPH: Usher (1968) argues in favor of the authenticity of Critias's speech; contra: Gray (1989: 183–84).

1. Cf. Adeleye (1976: 9).
2. D.S. 13.52.2; Arist. *Ath. Pol.* 34.1
3. For an overview of the Ionian War, see Kagan (1987).
4. Xen. *Hell.* 2.1.20–21; D.S. 13.105.1. For the topography of the battle, see Lotze (1964: 32); Bommelaer (1981: 111–13); Strauss (1987).
5. Xen. *Hell.* 2.1.25–27; D.S. 13.105.2. See Ehrhardt (1970: 227); Kagan (1987: 386–88).
6. Some accounts are derived from Xenophon: Plut. *Lys.* 9–11, Frontin. 2.1.18; Polyaenus 1.45.2; Paus. 9.32.9. Others combine elements from both Xenophon and Diodorus: Plut. *Alc.* 36–37; Nep. *Alc.* 8.
7. For a biography of Alcibiades, see Hatzfeld (1951); Ellis (1989); Romilly (1995); Gribble (1999).
8. Various explanations for this maneuver have been suggested. Lotze (1964: 34) raises the possibility of a retreat to Sestos; others think Philocles sent out a squadron to lure Lysander into battle; see Ehrhardt (1970: 227); Bommelaer (1981: 110). Kagan (1987: 391–92) suggests the Athenians only feigned a retreat, whereas Wylie (1986: 134 35) believes that Lysander was setting a trap for Philocles.
9. Xenophon's version is more favorable to Lysander than Diodorus's since in Xenophon he received the decisive information on his own initiative rather than by chance. Elsewhere he displays a similar bias in favor of Lysander; see Krentz (1989: 178).
10. Ehrhardt (1970); Bommelaer (1981: 103–15); Wylie (1986); Kagan (1987: 391 with n. 52); Ellis (1989: 94–95, 131 with n. 147).
11. Ehrhardt (1970: 225–26); Wylie (1986: 133–34).
12. Accusations that the Thirty and their supporters were responsible for the defeat also had this effect; see Chapter 6.
13. E.g., Lys. 21.10.
14. Cf. Aesch.1.173. Although his prosecution of Timarchus took place in 346 / 45, Aeschines addressed the jurors as if they had been members of the jury that had convicted Socrates in 399. Since the minimum age for serving on the jury was thirty, they would have had to have been at least eighty-four when Timarchus was prosecuted. Clearly, few if any of them could have been present at both trials.

15. Of course, in the case of Aegospotami, it becomes problematic to associate the jurors with the defeat without also making them responsible for it; litigants, however, solved this problem by accusing oligarchic conspirators of helping the enemy. Holding out as long as possible, the sailors were doomed to defeat because their leaders had betrayed them. Speakers were thus able to promote the fiction of continuity while simultaneously distancing the jury from past failures; see Chapter 6.

16. Cf. Lotze (1964: 31–37); Strauss (1983: 25–27); Krentz (1989: 177–78).

17. The sources disagree about the number of ships that escaped. None: Frontin. 2.1.18. One: Polyaenus 1.45.2. Nine: Xen. *Hell.* 2.1.29 (Conon with eight to Cyprus, the *Paralus* to Athens); cf. Plut. *Alc.* 37.4, *Lys.* 11.5–6. Ten: D.S. 13.106.6 (Conon with one to Cyprus, the other nine to Athens); Paus. 3.11.5 (all ten to Cyprus). Twelve: Lys. 21.11. Few: Isoc. 18.59.

18. Xen. *Hell.* 2.1.31–32; cf. Plutarch, who mentions the execution of three thousand Athenian prisoners (*Lys.* 13.1, *Alc.* 37.4). Pausanias states that four thousand were killed (9.32.9), and Diodorus mentions only the execution of Philocles (13.106.7). Wylie (1986: 139–41) doubts the mass execution; contra: Strauss (1983: 32–34).

19. Xen. *Hell.* 2.2.6–7; D.S. 13.106.8; *IG* I³ 127 = ML 94. For the fall of Samos, see Hignett (1952: 381–82); Lotze (1964: 87–98); Bommelaer (1981: 138–41); Hamilton (1979: 55–64); Green (1991: 13–15).

20. Xen. *Hell.* 2.2.5, 9; Plut. *Lys.* 13.2–5, 14.2–3; cf. D.S. 14.13.1.

21. Xen. *Hell.* 2.2.7–8; D.S. 13.107.2; Plut. *Lys.* 14.1; see Lotze (1964: 40–41).

22. Hamilton (1979: 44–46); Kagan (1987: 399).

23. The withdrawal of Lysander: Plut. *Lys.*14.1; the withdrawal of Pausanias (and not Agis): Xen. *Hell.* 2.2.11, 2.3.3; D.S. 13.107.2–3; see Bommelaer (1981: 142 n. 169); Green (1991: 7 n. 34).

24. Xen. *Hell.* 2.2.10–13. For the date of negotiations, see Lotze (1964: 42).

25. Xenophon mentions only the Spartan demand for the destruction of the Long Walls (*Hell.* 2.2.15; cf. Lys. 13.8), but Krentz (1982: 33) plausibly suggests that the two concessions mentioned by Aeschines (2.76)—internal autonomy and retention of Lemnos, Imbros, and Scyros—were part of this same proposal. Yet Aeschines could also be referring to the Spartan overtures after Arginusae (Arist. *Ath. Pol.* 34.1); see Munro (1938: 19–20 n. 7); Kagan (1987: 401 n. 97). To further complicate this question, Andocides includes these islands as a clause in the final terms of surrender (3.12); see Table 1.

26. For the Arginusae Affair, see Perrin (1904: 657–63); Cloché (1919); Andrewes (1974); Adeleye (1977 / 78); Kagan (1987: 354–75); Buck (1995: 18–20).

27. Cf. Engels (1993: 128–29). Tuplin (1993: 44) suggests that hostile statements earlier in the *Hellenica* do not detract from the positive sentiment expressed in 2.3.56 (tr. R. Warner): "Of course, I realize that these remarks are not really worth mentioning; but I do think it admirable in the man that, with death hanging over him, his spirit never lost either the ability to think or the taste for making a joke." Even though Xenophon expresses his admiration for Theramenes' composure at the moment of death, he falls short of praising Theramenes for his politics.

28. Cf. Harding (1974: 104–5).

29. Hignett (1952: 290); Buck (1995).

30. Perrin (1904); Krentz (1982: 36–37); Kagan (1987: 154–56).

31. Xen. *Hell.*2.2.16. Ostwald (1986: 451) suggests that Theramenes made this motion at the same meeting at which the ambassadors reported the Spartan response to their peace proposal.

32. Lys. 12.68–69; cf. *P. Mich.* 5982. For the similarities between Lys.12.69 and the Theramenes papyrus, see Merkelbach and Youtie (1968); Henrichs (1968). Andrewes (1970) suggests that the papyrus was probably a polemical pamphlet written in defense of Theramenes and in response to the charges made by Lysias. If so, the myth of Theramenes may have become a way to rehabilitate the men of the city. See Lehmann (1976: 282–83). Sealey (1975: 281–82) suggests that the papyrus is from an independent account of the fateful meeting of the Athenian Assembly, and thus corroborates Lysias. The papyrus has also been ascribed to various historians, including the Oxyrhynchhus Historian and Ephorus. Most recently Pesely (1989) has suggested that it comes from a rhetorical treatise. But given the fragmentary nature of the papyrus, the author and his political viewpoints must remain elusive. For further discussion, see Harding (1974: 108–9); Engels (1993).

33. Merkelbach (1977: 113–14); Pesely (1989: 31–32).

34. Xen. *Hell.* 2.2.16–17, 19. Not even an envoy *autokrator* had full power in negotiations. In 392 / 1, the Athenian embassy to Sparta held such a title; yet when the ambassadors returned the Athenians rejected the settlement and indicted them (And. 3.33). *Autokrator* was more likely a title bestowed on an envoy to honor the state to which he was sent. So in the case of surrender, the defeated city sent *presbeis autokratores* to hear the demands of the victorious city and report back to their fellow citizens, who would then decide whether to accept or reject them. See Mosley (1973: 30–38); Missiou-Ladi (1987).

35. In contrast to Xenophon, who reports that the Assembly met two separate times to appoint Theramenes to lead two separate embassies (first to Lysander and then to Sparta), Lysias mentions only one meeting and only his mission to Sparta (13.9–11). Most historians believe that Lysias collapses the two missions. See Munro (1938: 20–21); Krentz (1982: 34–35 with n. 17); Ostwald (1986: 452); contra: Sealey (1975: 286–87).

36. Lehmann (1972: 206–7); McCoy (1975: 135); Adeleye (1976: 10); Krentz (1982: 35–36); Kagan (1987: 402–409); Buck (1995: 21).

37. Cf. Perrin (1904: 666–67).

38. Paus. 3.8.6; Polyaenus 1.45.5; see Hamilton (1979: 50–54), who suggests that Theramenes persuaded Lysander that Spartan interests were best served by sparing Athens; cf. Kagan (1987: 405–7). McCoy (1975: 137–39) argues that Lysander accepted Theramenes' demand for *patrios politeia* because he was eager to end the war quickly. Munro (1938: 21–23) believes that Theramenes persuaded the ephors to grant Athens internal autonomy after he failed to gain this concession from Lysander.

39. Xen. *Hell.* 2.2.19; cf. Plut. *Lys.* 15.2.

40. See Cloché (1918); Hamilton (1979: 53–54); Kagan (1987: 405).

41. See Fuks (1953a: 52–57).

42. As a subordinate member of the Peloponnesian League, the Athenians were required to have the same friends and enemies as Sparta and to assist in military expeditions.

43. Land on these islands was to remain in possession of the current occupants. Andocides (3.12) is the only source to list them, but this is an insufficient reason to dismiss him; cf. Krentz (1982: 42); contra: Kagan (1987: 410 n. 133). His speech dates to 391, placing it much closer to the surrender than the other two sources, which discuss Condition 5: Diodorus and Plutarch. Moreover, Andocides indicates that he obtained this information from the stele recording the conditions of surrender (pace Fuks 1953a: 53). And although elsewhere in the speech he inaccurately recounts fifth-century events, he recalls the terms of surrender in order to make the peace proposal of 392/1 (which he was speaking in favor of) look that much better. He therefore had greater incentive to pass over these exceptions rather than invent them.

44. For the debate over the ancestral constitution, see Fuks (1953a); Ruschenbusch (1958); Finley (1975: 34–59); Lévy (1976: 193–97); Walters (1976); Harding (1978); Mossé (1978); Hansen (1989b).

45. McCoy (1975); Cartledge (1987: 280–81).

46. Munro (1938: 19); Hignett (1952: 285); Fuks (1953a: 57–63); Adeleye (1976: 10–11); Rhodes (1981: 427); Green (1991: 6 n. 21).

47. Cf. McCoy (1975: 136–37); contra: Fuks (1953a: 57–58); Adeleye (1976: 10).

48. Xen. *Hell.* 2.2.23 (tr. P. Krentz); cf. Plut. *Lys.* 15.3–5. For the chronology of the surrender and civil war, see Colin (1933: 31–34, 65–66); Munro (1937); Hignett (1952: 378–83); Lotze (1967); Badian and Buckler (1975); Rhodes (1981: 436–37, 462–63); Krentz (1982: 131–52); Loening (1987: 21–22); Green (1991); Munn (2000: 340–44). Although Plutarch (*Lys.* 15.1) dates the surrender to 16 Munychion (April), the mistakes, repetitions, and inconsistencies in *Lys.* 15 make this date untrustworthy. Rather than attempt to reconcile Plutarch with Thucydides (5.26.3) or explain away the contradictions between the two, it is preferable to follow Thucydides and reject Plutarch's date.

49. Rhodes (1981: 419) concludes from the "differences in content and arrangement" of the four narrative accounts that they are independent from one another: Arist., *Ath. Pol.* 34.2–40; D.S. 14.3–5, 32–33; Just. 5.8–10; Xen. *Hell.* 2.3.11–4.43. I focus on Xenophon and Aristotle because Diodorus and Justin do not deviate significantly from Xenophon's sequence.

50. Favor Xenophon: Cloché (1915: 4–7); Hignett (1952: 384–89); Adeleye (1976: 16–18); Rhodes (1981: 422); Buck (1995: 24 n. 58); Munn (2000: 225, 413 n. 15). Favor Aristotle: Colin (1933: 41–45, 57–61); Krentz (1982: 131–47), Ostwald (1986: 481–90).

51. Xen. *Hell.* 2.3.2, 11. This is an exaggeration since there was a delay of a few months between the surrender (late spring) and the overthrow of the democracy (late summer/early fall); see note 48. In *Hell.* 2.3.2, Xenophon lists the members of the Thirty: Polychares, Critias, Melobius, Hippolochus, Eucleides, Hieron, Mnesilochus, Chremon, Theramenes, Aresias, Diocles, Phaedrias, Chaereleos, Anaetius, Peison, Sophocles, Eratosthenes, Charicles, Onomacles, Theognis, Aeschines, Theogenes, Cleomedes, Erasistratus, Pheidon, Dracon-

tides, Eumathes, Aristoteles, Hippomachus, and Mnesitheides. For a discussion on their selection and identity, see Whitehead (1980); Krentz (1982: 51–56).

52. *Kaloikagothoi* literally means "the beautiful and good." It was a term that Athenian aristocrats used to refer to themselves.

53. Xen. Hell. 2.3.15–22. Lysias (12.7) mentions only ten, whereas Diodorus (14.5.6) reports that they killed sixty. It is possible that the Thirty also sold the dockyards as scrap for three talents (Isoc. 7.66) and melted down two gold-plated statues (*SEG* 21.80) to pay for the guards; see Krentz (1982: 87–88).

54. Xen. *Hell.* 2.4.1; Diodorus (14.5.7) states that half the Athenians fled, whereas Isocrates (7.67) reports that five thousand Athenians retreated to Piraeus. These numbers are conservative, assuming that the Thirty fully carried out their mandate (which would have been difficult given the size of the population prohibited from Athens).

55. Although Xenophon neglects to mention Lysander's involvement in the establishment of the Thirty and Sparta's decree against harboring democratic exiles, his account is not pro-Spartan. He neither conceals the Thirty's admiration for Sparta nor the help they received from the Spartan garrison; see Tuplin (1993: 45–46); Dillery (1995: 159–60).

56. Adeleye (1976: 19); Tuplin (1993: 44); Buck (1995: 23); contra: Ostwald (1986: 481).

57. Lys 12.43–47, 75–76. See Rhodes (1981: 428).

58. Todd (1985: 175); cf. Keaney (1992: 140–44) who shows how Aristotle describes Theramenes in nonfactional language.

59. For a summary of their political careers, see Rhodes (1981: 431–33).

60. Arist. *Ath. Pol.* 34.3. According to Lysias, Theramenes waited to call a meeting of the Assembly until Lysander arrived from Samos. Then at the meeting he spoke in favor of Dracontides' proposal, and, when the Athenians objected, Lysander forced them to accept the motion by accusing them of violating the treaty and by threatening them with death (12.71–76). According to Diodorus, when Lysander appeared before the Assembly to demand that the Athenians install the Thirty, Theramenes spoke out against him. He invoked the terms of the treaty, which permitted Athens to live under its *patrios politeia*, but his argument was to no avail. Lysander told the Athenians that they had violated the peace by failing to dismantle the walls, and he threatened Theramenes until finally the Athenians voted the Thirty into power (14.3.4–7). Salmon (1969: 497–500) reconciles Lysias's account with Diodorus's by suggesting that Theramenes first spoke against the proposal and then, after Lysander threatened him, he spoke in favor of it. Cf. McCoy (1975: 142–44); Krentz (1982: 48–50). Many, however, find Diodorus unreliable and accept Lysias's account of the meeting: Adeleye (1976: 13); Rhodes (1981: 433–34); Buck (1995: 21–22).

61. D.S. 14.4.1. Hignett (1952: 287, 383); Adeleye (1976: 13–16); Rhodes (1981: 434–35). Contra: Fuks (1953a: 75).

62. Presumably this is a reference to the task of drafting laws as specified in Xen. *Hell.* 2.3.11 and D.S. 14.4.1; see Fuks (1953a: 74).

63. Arist. *Ath. Pol.* 35.1. For Aristotle's statement that the magistrates were chosen from one thousand previously selected individuals; see Rhodes (1981: 438).

64. Arist. *Ath. Pol.* 35.2. Some believe that the Thirty repealed the laws of Ephialtes

and Archestratus in order to restore the traditional powers of the Areopagus: Cloché (1915: 416–18); Lévy (1976: 195 with n. 4); Krentz (1982: 61). Others doubt that the repeals happened because there is no proof that the Thirty made any use of the Areopagus: Day and Chambers (1962: 129 n. 108); Ruschenbusch (1966). But it is more likely that the repeals were either a mere pretense in order to justify the overthrow of the democracy or that the Thirty failed to restore the powers of the Areopagus after it refused to cooperate with them; see Hignett (1952: 288); Wallace (1989: 140–44). Hall (1990: 321–26) suggests instead that the Thirty set out to restrict the Areopagus.

65. Hignett (1952: 387); Rhodes (1981: 422). Adeleye (1976: 17) believes, "Aristotle's pro-Theramenean bias prompted him to reverse Xenophon's sequence of events." Contra: Krentz (1982: 144–45); Ostwald (1986: 483–84).

66. For the repression of opposition under hegemonic regimes, see Dahl (1973: 11–13). Studies on Argentina's Dirty War are particularly helpful in showing how terror can isolate and silence the subject population, and in the case of the Dirty War, the language of terror was as important as the acts that the regime carried out to accomplish this goal. See Corradi (1982); O'Donnell (1986: 249–68); Perelli (1994: 42–45); Feitlowitz (1998: esp. 63–109).

67. 1,500: Isoc. 7.67; 20.11. Over 1,500: Aesch. 3.235; Arist. *Ath. Pol.* 35.4. According to the Scholion of Aeschines (1.39), Lysias stated in a (lost) speech that 2,500 were killed, whereas others mentioned 1,500. In Xenophon, Thrasybulus tells his soldiers before their last battle against the Thirty that they had killed more Athenians in eight months than the Peloponnesians had in ten years of the war (*Hell.* 2.4.21). Making an even more remarkable claim, Isocrates asserts that the Thirty executed more men without trial in three months than the Athenians tried during the entire period of the empire (4.113). Christ (1992: 343–46; 1998: 72) hypothesizes that those executed by the Thirty were routinely accused of sycophancy.

68. For most of the fourth century, the citizen population of Athens ranged from 20,000 to 30,000; see Ober (1989a: 127–29). Hansen (1985b) estimates the citizen population after the Thirty to be about 25,000. Strauss (1986: 70–86) suggests it may have been even as low as 14,000–16,250.

69. The Thirty may even have been responsible for erasing laws inscribed on a wall adjacent to the Royal Stoa; see Fingarette (1971); Ostawald (1986: 479–80). Others suggest the erasure occurred after the restoration of the democracy in order to make room for a new sacrificial calendar: Clinton (1982: 32, 35); cf. Robertson (1990: 65–75); Rhodes (1991: 94–95).

70. *Proxenoi* looked after the interests of a foreign city while residing in the city of which they were citizens.

71. Plut. *Them.*19.6; see Hansen (1987: 13).

72. Dorjahn (1932: 63–64); Ollier (1933–43: i. 167); Krentz (1982: 64–68); Whitehead (1982/83); Ostwald (1986: 485–87); Buck (1998: 63–64). Contra: Lévy (1976: 197–203); Cartledge (1987: 282).

73. Xen. *Hell.* 2.3.51 (cf. Arist. *Ath. Pol.* 37.1); Xen. *Mem.* 1.2.31; see Ruschenbusch (1956: 124–25); Fingarette (1971: 332–33); Krentz (1982: 61 with n. 23).

74. D.S. 14.6.1; Plut. *Lys.* 27.2.

75. See Hamilton (1979: 78); Cartledge (1987: 282–83); Harding (1988: 191); Buck (1998: 66–69).

76. Xen. *Hell.* 2.4.1; Dem. 15.22; D.S. 14.6.2–3; Plut. *Lys.* 27.3.

77. Chalcis: Lys. 24.25; Elis: Plut. *Mor.* 835F; Oropus: Lys. 31.9, 17.

78. For a biography of Thrasybulus, see Buck (1998).

79. For the knights as members of the Three Thousand, see Cloché (1915: 7–9); Rhodes (1981: 458); contra: Bugh (1988: 123–25). It remains undisputed that the cavalry overwhelmingly supported oligarchic rule, under both the Thirty and the Ten. See Bugh (1988: 126–27).

80. Xen. *Hell.* 2.4.2–4; D.S. 14.32.1–3.

81. Xen. *Hell.* 2.4.5–7. Diodorus places this battle after the execution of the Eleusinians and Salaminians (14.32.6–33.1). Hignett (1952: 291) and Buck (1998: 75–76) prefer Xenophon's sequence, whereas Krentz (1982: 85–90) and Ostwald (1986: 489–90) prefer Diodorus's.

82. For Xenophon's participation in the rule of the Thirty and the possibility that he personally observed the massacre, see Schwartz (1889: 165); Delebecque (1957: 61–62); Higgins (1977: 22–24); Rahn (1981: 103–4); Bugh (1988: 123 n. 10, 128–29, 151); Green (1994: 221–22).

83. Xen. *Hell.* 2.4.10; Diodorus reports that the democratic resistance now consisted of 1,200 (14.33.1).

84. Xen. *Hell.* 2.4.10–22; D.S. 14.33.2–3.

85. Arist. Ath. Pol. 38.3, 40.2; D.S. 14.33.4; Xen. *Hell.* 2.4.25; IG II² 10.

86. P. *Oxy.* 1606 Fr. 6. i = Lys. Fr. I.6.i. (Gernet and Bizos 1924–26); Plut. *Mor.* 835F.

87. Cloché (1915: 61–76; 1916: 17–18); Krentz (1982: 93); Buck (1998: 80 n. 44).

88. Aristotle wrongly reports that the Ten were replaced by a second board of Ten (*Ath. Pol.* 38.3). See Cloché (1915: 170–85); Fuks (1953b: 198–99); Rhodes (1981: 459–60); contra: Dorjahn (1944); Kühn (1967: 38–39); Krentz (1982: 96–97); Ostwald (1986: 492–93).

89. Xen *Hell.* 2.4.28–39; Arist. *Ath. Pol.* 38.1; D.S. 14.33.5–6; Plut. *Lys.* 21.3, *Mor.* 349F. For the democratic procession, see Strauss (1992: 69–72).

90. Cf. Todd (1985: 165–83); Harding (1988: 192–93). For the internal politics of Sparta and the conflict between Pausanias and Lysander, see Hamilton (1970; 1979: 82–98); Ste. Croix (1972: 144–46); Cartledge (1987: 283–86).

2 RESTORATION OF THE DEMOCRACY

1. Cloché (1915: 251–59); Kühn (1967: 39–41); Rhodes (1981: 462–67); Loening (1987: 30–38).

2. And.1.90; Isoc. 18.2–4, 20; Lys. 13.88; Arist. *Ath. Pol.* 39.4. See Dorjahn (1946: 20–21); Loening (1987: 28–30).

3. Xen. *Hell.* 2.4.43; Arist. *Ath. Pol.* 40.4. Xenophon erroneously implies that the amnesty was implemented only after the expulsion of the oligarchs from Eleusis in 401 / 0; see Dorjahn (1946: 19–23); Krentz (1982: 104); Loening (1987: 23–38). For the arguments in favor of a reconciliation agreement separate from the peace treaty, see Cloché (1915: 239–44).

4. For the appointment of ten governors to oversee Piraeus, known as the Ten of Piraeus and not to be confused with the Ten (who ruled the city), see page 20.

5. Arist. *Ath. Pol.* 39.5–6. Xenophon neglects to mention the exclusion of the Ten from the amnesty (*Hell.* 2.4.38). Andocides omits both the Ten and the governors of Piraeus (1.90). See Cloché (1915: 273–74); MacDowell (1962: 130–31); Rhodes (1981: 469); Krentz (1982: 104–5); Loening (1987: 41–46).

6. Hansen (1981: 14–15); for *traumatos ek pronoias,* see Lipsius (1905–15: 605–8); Todd (1993: 271–73).

7. *P. Oxy.* 1606 ll. 38–48. The original owner may have had to pay some form of compensation to recover immovable property; see Gernet and Bizos (1924–26: ii. 253); Krentz (1982: 105–6); Loening (1987: 51–52); Todd (1993: 233–36).

8. Arist. *Ath. Pol.* 39.6. For the composition of the courts, see Cloché (1915: 268–72); Rhodes (1981: 470–71); Loening (1987: 47–49).

9. Cf. Cloché (1915: 312–13).

10. Arist. *Ath. Pol.* 38.4; Lys. 10.31; see MacDowell (1963: 66–67); Krentz (1982: 122–23); pace Todd (2000: 110 n. 14).

11. Carawan (1998: 125–33). A person who either intentionally or unintentionally provided assistance in a plan or participated in an act that resulted in the death of another could be charged with *bouleusis phonou.* Historians traditionally believed that *bouleusis phonou* was tried in the Palladion under a separate procedure; see MacDowell (1963: 60–69). Gagarin (1990: 81–99), however, argues that *bouleusis* was tried under the regular homicide procedure (*dike phonou*) and that the person accused of planning murder was charged with *phonos;* cf. Lipsius (1905–15: 125–27). This suggestion explains why the provision on *autocheiria* was included in the amnesty. If *bouleusis phonou* was tried under a separate procedure, it would have been unnecessary to add *autocheiria,* since the amnesty was for all wrongs except those that fell under the procedure of *dike phonou.* But if, on the other hand, planning murder was tried under the procedure of *dike phonou,* as Gagarin argues, then *autocheiria* was added to prohibit prosecution for planning murder.

12. And. 1.94; Lys. 6.45, 12.48, 13.1–61; Xen. *Hell.* 2.3.50–56, 4.8–10; Pl. *Ap.* 32c4–7.

13. Cf. Cloché (1915: 261); Bonner (1924: 176); Ostwald (1986: 503); Loening (1987: 40); Chambers (1990: 318).

14. Dem. 24.42. Andocides gives a different version (1.87: "to apply the laws from the archonship of Eucleides") that implies that crimes committed prior to 403 / 2 were not prosecutable; see MacDowell (1962: 128–29); Rhodes (1991: 97); Sickinger (1999: 100–101). If Andocides were correct, the Athenians passed a law that invalidated the clause in the amnesty that permitted prosecution for murder and attempted murder (*autocheiria*). A comparison of the two versions, however, reveals his selective quotation to be misleading; see Todd (1996: 127).

15. Isoc. 18.2–3. For further discussion on *paragraphe,* see Kühn (1967); Isager and Hansen (1975: 123–31); Todd (1993: 136–38).

16. Although Thucydides rightly emphasizes the intrigue of the conspirators (8.45–69), one should not dismiss their legal maneuvering, discussed in Aristotle (*Ath. Pol.* 29.1–4). For the differences between their accounts, see Gomme (1945–81: v. 240–256); Rhodes (1981: 362–69, 379–81).

17. Arist. *Ath. Pol.* 29.1–2; cf. Thuc. 8.67.1. This is possibly the same Pythodorus who

became the eponymous archon of the Thirty; see Gomme (1945–81: v. 213); Rhodes (1981: 370–71).

18. Arist. *Ath. Pol.* 29.3. This passage implies that the original motion included a clause calling for an investigation into the laws of Solon; see Sartori (1951: 27); Walters (1976: 136–37); Lévy (1976: 192); Ostwald (1986: 370); Hansen (1989b: 88–89). Contra: Jacoby (1949: 384 n. 30); Day and Chambers (1962: 102); Mossé (1978: 83).

19. Hignett (1952: 130, 273) believes that Cleitophon never intended to restore the Cleisthenic constitution, whereas Fuks (1953a: 1–32) argues that he was sincere. Finley (1975: 38) suggests that the amendment was intended to win over moderates who were opposed to oligarchy but were eager for reforms.

20. Thuc. 8.67.2. Kagan (1987: 147); Munn (2000: 140).

21. Thuc. 8.67.3–69; cf. Arist. *Ath. Pol.* 29.4.

22. Finley (1975: 37); Hansen (1989b: 86–87 n. 70); Munn (2000: 136–37).

23. Sickinger (1999: 73–92) suggests that during the fifth century the Council maintained an archive of laws and decrees passed by the Assembly. If so, it would be difficult to understand why it took the Athenians over a decade to complete the law reforms.

24. Traditionally, scholars date the central archive to 403; see Kahrstedt (1938: 25–32); Harrison (1955: 27–29). Interpreting *en toi demosioi* in the decree of Patrocleides (And.1.79) and in the decree of 405 honoring the Samians (*IG* I³ 127) as references to a central archive, Boegehold (1972) has moved the date back several years; cf. Thomas (1989: 38–40); Sickinger (1999: 105–13). Others deny that *en toi demosioi* has a technical meaning in these decrees: MacDowell (1962: 119); Andrewes (1976: 24 n. 5); Rhodes (1980: 308 with n. 26).

25. Rhodes (1981: 375–76). Hansen (1989b: 83–87) suggests that the Athenians would have relied extensively on oral tradition to complete this investigation.

26. Lys. 30.2–5. For the chronology, see Dow (1960: 271–72); Robertson (1990: 52 with n. 25); Rhodes (1991: 88–89). Ostwald (1986: 407–11 with n. 249, 414–20) believes the *anagrapheis* began their work in 411/10 under the intermediate regime of the Five Thousand and continued it when the democracy was restored; cf. Munn (2000: 148–49, 392 n. 46). For the meaning of *anagrapheis,* see Robertson (1990: 45, 52–56); Todd (1996: 108–9).

27. See Robertson (1990: 56–60); Rhodes (1991: 89–90).

28. It is likely that the *anagrapheis* completed their work on the secular laws by 403 and that their second term was devoted to sacred laws; see Harrison (1955: 31); Clinton (1982: 34–35); Hansen (1990a: 65). For the erasure of the sacrificial calendar, see note 69 of Chapter 1.

29. Harrison (1955: 30); Ostwald (1986: 415–17); Sickinger (1999: 98–100); cf. Rhodes (1991: 90–93), who argues that originally the *anagrapheis* were instructed to republish the laws of Solon, and later this was understood to mean all currently valid laws that applied to the whole community. Clinton (1982: 28–35) suggests that the *anagrapheis* published the laws of Draco and Solon which were still in force and any subsequent revisions and/or additions to the Solonian code, but they ignored any post-Solonian legislation that did not affect the Solonian code

(cf. Oliver [1935: 6]). Hansen (1990a: 64–68) agrees with Clinton that the *anagrapheis* prepared the Solonian code for the Stoa Basileios, but he believes that they were also responsible for examining regulations that were not included on the wall and that they determined which of these other regulations would be allowed to stand.

30. Pearson (1941: 221–24); Hansen (1989b: 78–79, 97–99); Rhodes (1991: 90; 1993: 60–63); Thomas (1994: 121–24).

31. And. 1.83: "On the motion of Teisamenus, the people resolved that the Athenians are to live according to their ancestral customs [*patria*], use the laws of Solon, his weights and measures, and the ordinances of Draco, as we had before."

32. Fuks (1953a: 39); Finley (1975: 39). Ostwald (1986: 415) suggests that subsequent legislation was considered Solonian because it perpetuated "the *patrios politeia* Solon had founded."

33. The law of Diocles did differ from the decree of Teisamenus, but by making explicitly clear that the actions of the Thirty were invalid and that laws enacted after the restoration of the democracy were valid. And while the primary aim of the decree of Teisamenus was to establish procedures for implementing new laws, the law of Diocles reinforced their validity.

34. For the myth of autochthony, see Loraux (1986: esp. 143–53, 192–98; 1993; 2000: esp. 13–38); Rosavich (1987); Connor (1994: 35–38); Dougherty (1996: 254–56); Shapiro (1998).

35. Studies of other cultures show that it is quite common for people to remember the past to fit present needs and concerns, even in modern societies, which have increased archival capacities, more sophisticated ways of storing and retrieving information, and a greater variety of media. See Halbwachs (1941; 1992); Schwartz (1982; 1987); Hobsbawm and Ranger (1983); Lowenthal (1985); Fentress and Wickham (1992); Ben-Yehuda (1995); Zerubavel (1995).

36. For the use of dramatic fictions in civic discourse to resolve social tensions, see Ober (1989a: 152–55, 190–91, 306–9).

37. This, of course, is not the end of the story. Both Aristotle in the *Politics* and Isocrates in the *Areopagiticus* provide a more conservative image of Solon than that found in forensic oratory; see Finley (1975: 55–56); Hansen (1989b: 93–97).

38. Oliver (1935: 7–8); Ferguson (1936: 144–48); Hignett (1952: 302–3); Fingarette (1971: 333–34); MacDowell (1978: 46–48). Contra: Atkinson (1939: 144), who suggested that the *anagrapheis* were instructed merely to make copies of the laws of Draco and Solon and place them in the Stoa Basileios since the original inscriptions were no longer legible.

39. Ferguson (1936: 146); Harrison (1955: 33); Robertson (1990: 63); Rhodes (1991: 97).

40. And. 1.82. Andocides also states that a board of twenty served as a transitional government before the restoration of the democracy until the laws were passed (1.81). He is probably distorting the decree of Teisamenus, which calls for the appointment of *nomothetai* (1.83); see Robertson (1990: 60 n. 60).

41. E.g., Ferguson (1936: 145–47). MacDowell (1962: 196) suggests Andocides was speaking loosely when he mentioned a review of all laws. He did not mean that

all the existing laws had to be formally ratified; rather, the *nomothetai* would investigate the laws to determine which needed to be revised.

42. Robertson (1990: 53–55).

43. See Rhodes (1991: 91–93).

44. See n. 24.

45. Cf. Todd (1996: 128).

46. See MacDowell (1975); Hansen (1978b; 1979; 1980; 1985a; 1991: 161–77); Rhodes (1984).

47. Atkinson (1939: 113–14, 133–34); Harrison (1955: 35); MacDowell (1978: 49); Sinclair (1988: 84).

48. Mossé (1973: 22); Rhodes (1980: 320); Bleicken (1985: 289–90; 1987: 270, 280–81); Sinclair (1988: 84); Ober (1989a: 96–97; 1989b: 330–33).

49. Hansen (1987: 94–107, 129; 1989a; 1990b: 239–43; 1991: 150–60, 303–4).

50. Hansen (1991: 151); cf. his earlier remarks (1987: 94), which are less critical of Athenian leaders.

51. Ober (1989b: 327). Hansen (1990c: 351–52) points out that the *nomothetai* had to be at least thirty, and therefore one third of the population was excluded from service. But we cannot conclude that older Athenians were necessarily more conservative than younger Athenians; see Millett (2000: 339–40).

52. See Harrison (1955: 35); MacDowell (1978: 48); Bauman (1990: 77); Christ (1998: 22).

53. Approximately 900 to 1,200 foreigners served in the democratic resistance; see Osborne (1981–83: ii. 42); Krentz (1980: 305–6).

54. Funke (1980: 17–18) suggests Archinus was a moderate; Strauss (1986: 96–98) believes that he was more closely aligned to the "few."

55. Dem. 57.30–32; schol. Aesch. 1.39; see Ostwald (1986: 507–8), Munn (2000: 259–60). For Pericles' citizenship law, see Patterson (1981); Walters (1983); Boegehold (1994).

56. Cf. Todd (1985: 197). Millett (2000) argues that the modern practice of labeling the fifth-century democracy as "radical" and that of the fourth century as "moderate" has caused historians wrongly to cast a modern debate on popular rule onto fourth-century Athens and has led to serious distortions about Athenian political activity.

57. But no matter how much the Athenians may have wanted to preserve their link with the past, recent events had caused such serious disruptions that the community was irrevocably changed. Pace Bleicken (1985: 289).

58. The recipients and the nature of their honors remain disputed because of the fragmentary condition of *IG* II² 10; Hereward (1952). Whitehead (1984) believes that the decree granted citizenship to all foreigners who fought with the democrats. Osborne (1981–83: i. 37–41; ii. 26–43) suggests that the seventy to ninety foreigners who joined Thrasybulus at Phyle received citizenship whereas those who joined later received only *isoteleia*. Krentz (1980; 1986) doubts that the decree granted any citizenship. He suggests that it awarded the foreigners who joined the democrats at Piraeus with *isoteleia* and those who joined at Phyle with additional honors, but not citizenship. Harding (1987a) questions the as-

sumption that the recipients of these honors were metics and foreigners. He argues that they might have been slaves who were granted their freedom and varying degrees of privileges, including *isoteleia*.

59. Harding (1987a: 177 n. 8); contra: Whitehead (1984: 9).

60. Aesch. 3.187, 190. Raubitschek (1941: 294) believes that the first list included the names of fifty-eight citizens who seized Phyle and the second the names of more than forty noncitizens who accompanied them. Aeschines, however, states that those who were besieged at Phyle by the Thirty and the Spartans were awarded. Krentz (1982: 83–84 n. 54), therefore, suggests that the first list included the names of the citizens who set out from Thebes with Thrasybulus and the second list those citizens who later joined the force at Phyle.

61. *P. Hib.* 1.14 Fr. a-b = Lysias Fr. VI. 1–2 (Gernet and Bizos 1924–26); Stroud (1971).

62. See especially Hedrick (1994); Morris (1996: 21–24).

63. Cf. Roy (1998). For further discussion on Piraeus, see Amit (1965); Garland (1987); von Reden (1998: 185–86).

64. For class tensions in postwar Athens, see especially Strauss (1986: 55–59).

65. *P. Hib.* 1. 14 Fr. c = Lysias Fr. VI. 3 (Gernet and Bizos 1924–26).

66. Cloché (1915: 373, 396–97); Stroud (1971: 298–99); Krentz (1982: 116–17); Ostwald (1986: 506); Bugh (1988: 129–43); Spence (1993: 217–18).

67. Cited by Strauss (1986: 124 with n. 12); Bugh (1988: 138–39). Morris (1992: 128–55; 1994b: 81–82) suggests that the extravagant cenotaph of Dexileus was part of a new trend in burials among wealthy Greeks which began in the 420s. The wealthy set up lavish funerary monuments, using state imagery to declare that the dead had been extraordinary individuals as well as loyal citizens of the polis. Meyer (1993: 112–20) argues that the increase in the number of Athenian epitaphs with demotics at the beginning of the fourth century reflects a new emphasis on citizenship.

68. Mossé (1973: 16, 30) and Strauss (1986: 55–63, 104, 173) are notable exceptions. But, while they stress the internal divisions between the rich and poor of postwar Athens, both conclude that these divisions never seriously disrupted Athenian unity. For the fourth-century crisis, see Eder (1995b); Davies (1995).

69. As Millett (2000: 340–42, 53–54) notes, it is remarkable how the Athenians allocated their resources to bolster the democracy despite their postimperial economic problems.

70. See for example Eder (1998: 114–21).

71. Arist. *Ath. Pol.* 41.2: "The eleventh change of the constitution occurred after the return of the exiles from Phyle and Piraeus, and it continued uninterrupted until the present, always increasing the power of the people. The people made itself masters of everything, managing everything by decrees and by the law courts where it held the power."

3   RECRIMINATION

EPIGRAPH: *Mnesikakein* literally means "to remember wrongs," the significance of which is explored at length in Chapter 4. But in this passage, Aristotle must be referring narrowly to the amnesty, and he must mean that no one was convicted of a crime for which the amnesty granted him immunity; cf. Rhodes (1981: 478).

Otherwise, his statement that the Athenians never again "recalled wrongs" would be so patently false that it would be difficult to understand how he could make such a claim.

1. And. 1, 3; Lys. [6], 12, 13, 16, 18, 25, 26, 30, 31, 34; Isoc. 16, 18, 20, 21. This list does not include the numerous passing references in the Attic orators.

2. And. 1.140; Lys. 2.61–66; Isoc. 7.62–70, 18.44, 46, *Ep.* .3; Xen. *Hell.* 2.4.43; Pl. *Ep.* 325b, *Mx.* 243e–244b; Dem. 40.32; Plut. *Mor.* 814B. Ober (1998: 281) suggests that elite writers praised the restored democracy so that they could voice their criticism of democracy without appearing treasonous.

3. For a comprehensive study of civil war during the classical period, see Gehrke (1985).

4. General: *Ath. Pol.* 38.4; Isoc. 18.6, 8; treasurer: *IG* II² 1371 ll. 2–4. See *PA* 12532; *APF* 67; *AO* 2692.

5. Dem. 24.138; D.S. 15.20.1. See *PA* 5267 = 5271; *APF* 187–88; *AO* 1092; Blass (1887–98: i. 476–77); Cloché (1915: 398–99); Loening (1987: 113); Weissenberger (1987: 207).

6. Secretary of the Council: *IG* II² 1 ll. 1–2, 56; *epistates:* Raubitschek (1941: 295); treasurer: *IG* II² 1388 l. 4. See *PA* 8400 = 8415 = 8416; *APF* 148; *AO* 1613; Krentz (1982: 118).

7. Evander could also have passed his scrutiny, because the jury found the complaints to be groundless. At the very least, the accusation that Evander had served on the Council and in the cavalry of the Thirty was ambiguously worded (Lys. 26.10), and therefore suggests a degree of uncertainty. See Usher (1999: 111); cf. Todd (2000: 276 n. 11); contra: Weissenberger (1987: 223 n. 561).

8. Lys. 13.56–57. Menestratus was probably prosecuted by the procedure of *apagoge:* MacDowell (1963: 137–38); Hansen (1976: 104; 1981: 21–22); Loening (1987: 79–81).

9. Lys. 26.13–15; Arist. *Rhet.* 1400a32–36.

10. Pace Todd (1993: 288–89).

11. That is, if he was summarily arrested by the procedure of *apagoge* for having illegally entered prohibited places.

12. For the difficulties in using the Attic orators as historical sources, see especially Todd (1990c); also Harding (1987b); Ober (1989a: 43–50); Hunter (1994: 5–8).

13. The trial of Andocides for impiety (And. 1 and Lys. 6) would be the one exception if Lysias 6 is an authentic speech, as Dover (1968: 78–83, 193–94) argues with some reservations. For the reasons its authenticity has been doubted, see Blass (1897–98: i. 562, 568); Gernet and Bizos (1924–26: i. 91–93).

14. Cf. Todd (1990c: 171–73; 1993: 37–38).

15. For a critique of formalist and instrumentalist approaches to law, see Bourdieu (1986 / 87).

16. E.g., Nader and Todd (1978); Moore (1978). Comaroff and Roberts (1981) depart from the processual paradigm, which they accuse of leading to a crude form of instrumentalism, and they move instead to a theory that recognizes the dialectical relationship between rules and processes. See also Bourdieu (1977: 1–95); Giddens (1984).

17. E.g., Baumgartner (1988); Ellickson (1991); Miller (1993); Sayer (1997).

18. Humphreys (1985a; 1985b); Osborne (1985b); Cohen (1991; 1995); Cartledge, Millett, Todd (1990); Todd (1993); Hunter (1994); Johnstone (1999).

19. For gossip in Athens, see Hunter (1990); contra: Harding (1991). For gossip more generally, see Lincoln (1994).

20. For the failure to codify Athenian laws, see Todd (1996: 128–31).

21. For the amateur quality of Greek law in general, see Finley (1975: 142–44); for Athenian law in particular, see MacDowell (1978: 250–53); Hansen (1991: 180). Harris (1994b: 136) believes, "There appears to have grown up an 'oral tradition' of jurisprudence." While I agree that the dicasts acquired considerable knowledge of Athenian law by virtue of their experience on the courts, they did not receive formal training and they were not formally required to take into account previous decisions of the court when giving their verdict. Although litigants appealed to precedent (see, for example, Carey and Reid [1985: 10–11]), its effect was primarily rhetorical (Todd [1993: 60–61]). Moreover, the Athenians did not set up barriers to separate the courts from the rest of the citizen's life; see Carey (1994b). The jurors therefore rendered their verdict as ordinary citizens rather than as experts in law.

22. Todd (1993: 54–62). The use of witnesses in Athenian courts reveals that other modern assumptions about evidence are misleading when applied to Athens: Humphreys (1985b); Todd (1990b); pace Carey (1994b: 183–184). For the rhetorical deployment of witness testimony, see Carey (1994a: 97–105).

23. Lys. 13.88–90; cf. [Lys.] 6.37–39.

24. Loening (1987: 100–101) and Todd (2000: 158 n. 57) find the argument to be specious, whereas Carawan (1998: 367–69) and Usher (1999: 67–68) believe it cannot be dismissed out of hand.

25. Arist. *Rhet.* 1356a, 1377b. For the use of ethical arguments, see Carey (1994c: 34–43).

26. On appeals to liturgies in the Attic orators: Adkins (1960: 195–219; 1972: 119–25); Davies (1981: 92–97); Roberts (1986); Ober (1989a: 226–36); Missiou (1992: 32–40); Johnstone (1999: 93–108).

27. Osborne (1985b); also Humphreys (1985a); Cohen (1995: esp. 18–24, 117–18, 121–22).

28. For a summary of their quarrel, see MacDowell (1990: 1–16). In the extended dispute between Lysitheus and Theomnestus (Lys. 10), the following legal procedures were used: *epangelia, dike pseudomarturion,* and twice *dike kakegorias.* See Todd (1993: 258–62).

29. In his study of Tswana disputes, Roberts (1983: 19–23) found a disparity between court records and the view that the parties expressed outside of court about the causes of their dispute. For further discussion on law and narrative, see Brooks and Gewirtz (1996).

30. Most recently by Carawan (1998: 376–77 with n. 8).

31. Lipsius (1905–15: 106 n. 209); Cloché (1915: 310–12, 447–48); Gernet and Bizos (1924–26: i. 157 with n. 2); Loening (1981: 289–91); Edwards (1999: 86–87); Todd (2000: 114).

32. See Todd (2000: 113–14). Loening (1981; 1987: 69–71) has most recently argued that Lysias 12 is a *dike phonou.*

33. *APF* 184–85; Kapparis (1993); contra: *PA* 5035; Avery (1991).

34. Blass (1887–98: i. 555); Cloché (1915: 331–32); Gernet and Bizos (1924–26: i. 186 n. 1); Todd (1996: 118–19). Contra: Loening (1987: 74) who dates the trial before 401 / 0.

35. See Todd (1993: 275).

36. MacDowell (1963: 130–40); Hansen (1976: 99–108). Gagarin (1979: 313–19), however, divides *apagoge* for homicide into two basic categories.

37. *Apagoge phonou:* MacDowell (1963: 131–36); Gagarin (1979: 319–21); Loening (1987: 73 with n. 42); Carawan (1998: 336). *Apagoge kakourgon:* Hansen (1976: 101–2; 1981: 21–30).

38. Hansen (1976: 103–7); Carawan (1998: 333–50).

39. Harrison (1968–71: ii. 227); cf. Gagarin (1979: 321).

40. Loening (1987: 77–79) suggests that the Eleven added *ep' autophoroi* to prevent the suit from violating the amnesty. But if that were their intent, they should have added *autocheiria.*

41. See MacDowell (1963: 132–33); Hansen (1976: 48–53; 1981: 27–29); Krentz (1982: 116 with n. 17); Harris (1994a).

42. D.L. 2.40; cf. Pl. *Ap.* 24b8–c1; Xen. *Mem.* 1.1.1. See Brickhouse and Smith (1989: 30–37).

43. Aesch. 1.173. For the date of Aeschines 1, see Harris (1985); Wankel (1988).

44. Although Aeschines does not explicitly state that Socrates deserved to be executed, the effectiveness of this comparison depended upon the jurors believing that Socrates was guilty. Otherwise, he would have called to their attention an example of a citizen who was wrongly convicted. And then there was the danger that the jurors could reach a rather different conclusion from that which Aeschines intended, namely that, like Socrates, Demosthenes was innocent and that they should not make the same mistake twice.

45. D.S. 14.37.7; D.L. 2.43. Cf. Mossé (1987: 130–31); Stone (1988: 176–78). On the other hand, if Anytus was later exiled for his part in the prosecution of Socrates, this would explain why the historical sources make no mention of him after 395; see Strauss (1986: 95–96).

46. While Dodds (1951: 179–95) suggests that there was a "witch-hunt" against intellectuals in the late fifth century, others argue convincingly that the evidence is unreliable: Dover (1976); Cohen (1991: 212–13); Wallace (1994).

47. Vlastos (1983: 496); cf. Mossé (1987: 99); Hansen (1995: 30).

48. Chroust (1957: 69–75); Allen (1980: 19); Brickhouse and Smith (1989: 82–87) Irwin (1989: 186–87).

49. See Hansen (1995: 7–15).

50. E.g., Lys. 12.43, 55, 13.55.

51. For a prosopography of Socrates' associates, see Hansen (1995: 27–29).

52. Dover (1976: 50); Stone (1988: 154–55); Bauman (1990: 114–15).

53. Garner (1987: 48–51); Wallach (1988: 397–98); Irwin (1989: 188–91); Connor (1991); Garland (1992: 142–51).

54. Thuc. 6.27–29, 60–61; And. 1.11–70; Plut. *Alc.* 18–21. For the mutilation of the herms and the profanation of the mysteries, see Aurenche (1974); Powell (1979); Osborne (1985a); Ostwald, (1986: 323–33, 537–50); Furley (1996).

55. And. 2.22; Lys. 6.9, 24. MacDowell (1962: 3–4).

56. For the date of the trial, see MacDowell (1962: 204–5).

57. Lys. 30.9–14; cf. Lys. 13.12–13.

58. Arist. *Ath. Pol.* 45.3, 55.2; Dem. 20.90. See Lipsius (1905–15: 269–85); Harrison (1968–71: ii. 200–207); MacDowell (1978: 167–69); Rhodes (1981: 615–17); Weissenberger (1987: 14–23).

59. Arist. *Ath. Pol.* 55.3–4; Din. 2.17–18.

60. Headlam (1933: 96–102); Hignett (1952: 205, 232); Harrison (1968–71: ii. 201).

61. Adeleye (1983); Hunter (1990: 311–12); Winkler (1990: 55); Weissenberger (1987: 16–17).

62. Lys. 16, 25, 26, 31; *P. Ryl.* 489.

63. See Dover (1978: esp. 19–39); Halperin (1990: 88–112); Winkler (1990: 45–70); Cohen (1991: 171–202).

64. Blass (1887–98: i. 510–11); Adams (1905: 253 n. 1); Cloché (1915: 387–88); Gernet and Bizos (1924–26 ii. 111); Lamb (1930: 534–35); Dover (1968: 7); Loening (1987: 103); Weissenberger (1987: 84).

65. See Dover (1968: 5); Loening (1987: 106–7 with n. 19). Compare *P. Ryl.* 489 ll. 68–76 with Lys. 25.13; *P. Ry.* 489 ll. 76–81 with Lys. 25.5; and *P. Ryl.* 489 ll. 108–18 with Lys. 25.14–16.

66. Hansen (1978b: 319; 1979: 36–37); MacDowell (1978: 168); Adeleye (1983: 303–5); cf. Bugh (1988: 141–43).

67. See Weissenberger (1987: 14 n. 39, 225–26 with n. 570).

68. Lys. 31.7–13, 17. The candidate defended himself against this charge by arguing that he had not violated Athenian laws by remaining neutral. In response, the prosecutor said that the Athenians never created a law forbidding neutrality because they did not believe a citizen would commit such an offense (27). This passage led Hignett (1952: 26–27) to challenge the authenticity of Solon's law forbidding neutrality in times of civil war (see Arist. *Ath. Pol.* 8.5; Plut. *Sol.* 20.1). Others, however, maintain that Solon's law is authentic. Goldstein (1972: 542) believes that the prosecutor of Lysias 31 did not cite the law because Philon could then accuse him of violating the amnesty. Yet such restraint on the part of the prosecutor is doubtful, given the arguments we have already seen speakers use. As an alternative solution, Carey (1989: 199) suggests, "Solon's law had fallen into disuse and had long been forgotten by the end of the fifth century," whereas Rhodes (1981: 157) believes that it was not included in the revised law code. But surely it would have helped the prosecutor's case to cite the law, even if it were no longer in use. Still, this is an argument of silence, so I agree with Bers (1975: 493–95) that Lysias 31 cannot be used to determine whether Solon's law against neutrality is authentic.

4 REMEMBERING AMNESTY

1. Loraux (1988: 26–27), translated in Loraux (1998: 86–87). See also Carawan (1998: 128–30).

2. Arist. *Ath. Pol.* 39.6: *medeni pros medena mnesikakein exeinai.*

3. Aeschy. *Eum.* 382–83: *kakon te mnemones;* see Loraux (1980: 237). A revised version of her article is in Loraux (1997: 11–40).

4. For the sake of comparison, *Le Monde* characterized the Barbie trial as forcing the French to choose between forgetting and justice (see Yerushalmi [1989: 117]). And, although the Athenians viewed reconciliation as contingent on forgetting, South Africans have recently sought a more ambitious solution to their past through the Truth and Reconciliation Commission, by which offenders were granted immunity should they divulge accurately their knowledge of atrocities. See Minow (1998).

5. Morris (1996; 2000: 109–54). On the rise of the polis, see Morris (1987).

6. See also Lévêque and Vidal-Naquet (1964); Jameson (1990); Hedrick (1994: 289–93).

7. On hoplite warfare: Vernant (1968); Hanson (1983; 1989); Connor (1988); Rich and Shipley (1993).

8. See Loraux (1991; 1997: esp. 41–84, 146–72).

9. For sake of convenience, I translate *philia* between citizens as "friendship." Konstan (1997: 55–56, 67–72) suggests that *philia* has a wider range of meaning than the corresponding substantive, *philos,* and prefers to translate only *philia* between *philoi* as "friendship."

10. Loraux (1980: 221–23; 1991: 38–39); Vernant (1980: 25); Meier (1990: 116–18).

11. Cf. Meier (1990: 114, 132).

12. Isoc. 18.44; cf. And. 1.140; Lys. 25.27, 33.

13. For the *Historikerstreit* and its aftermath, see Habermas (1988a; 1988b); Maier (1988); Friedlander (1992).

14. Israel: Appelfeld (1994); Gouri (1994); Zerubavel (1994: 78–89); Germany: Buruma (1994: esp. 54–60, 262–75); Geyer and Hansen (1994); Krondorfer (1995: 98–103).

15. Schwartz, Zerubavel, Barnett (1986); Paine (1994); Ben-Yahuda (1995); Zerubavel (1995: 60–76, 192–213); Vidal-Naquet (1996: 20–36).

16. Compare the remarks of Buruma in Chapter 3. For a discussion of French collaboration and accommodation under German occupation, see Burrin (1996).

17. Rousso (1991: 60–97). Other studies of twentieth-century Europe draw similar conclusions. For Europe in general, see Judt (1992). For the Netherlands, see de Keizer (1996). For Eastern Europe after the fall of communism, see Esbenshade (1995: esp. 78–84); Rosenberg (1995). For the United States after the Civil War, see Handlin (1961); Stark (1975); Blight (1989); Savage (1994).

18. Lys. 12.87, 95, 96, 13.48, 52, 95, 26.4; cf. Isoc. 20.12; Lys. 34.1–2.

19. Cf. Arist. *Rhet.* 1420a.

20. Cf. Seager (1967: 112–13).

21. Isoc. 18.31, 45–46; Lys. 18.18–19, 25.34–35; cf. Lys. 26.16.

22. And. 1.103–4; Isoc. 18.42–44; Lys. 26.16

23. And. 1.92–95; Isoc. 16.42–45, 18.47–50; Lys. 30.7. See Lévy (1976: 215).

24. Nagy (1990: 58); see Detienne (1967: esp. 51–80).

25. For inscriptions as commemorative monuments, see Thomas (1989: 45–60; 1992: 85–88, 137–40).

26. Paus. 1.29.3. Meyer (1993: 118) suggests, "Pausanias's description implies that this arrangement directed a traveller's attention to the savior, rather than to one of the original exponents, of the Athenian democracy. It was also an arrangement

    designed more to impress Athenians as they left their city than foreigners as they entered, giving prominence to those involved in the troubles of 403 and to the re-established democracy."

27. Philochorus *FGH* 328 F 40; see Osborne (1985a: 60).

28. And. 1.81; Isoc. 16.12–14, 50, 18.2, 48–49; Lys. 10.4, 12.57–58, 13.47–48, 14.32–33, 16.6, 18.18, 24.25, 25.18, 20–22, 26.2; *P. Oxy.* 1606 ll. 34–38, 113–18. Cf. Gribble (1999: 118–19).

29. Murphy (1989: 48) believes that Lysias addressed the men of the city separately from the men of Piraeus "to exploit class-prejudice."

30. Lys. 13.47–48; cf. Isoc. 18.48; Lys. 26.2.

31. E.g., And. 1.81; Isoc. 18.2; Lys. 25.18, 20–22.

32. Ober (1989a: 144–46; 1989b: 329–30); cf. MacDowell (1962: 66). Contra: Hansen (1978a: 135–36; 1989a: 103–6; 1990b: 220–21).

33. Cloché (1916: 20); cf. Mossé (1973: 6).

34. Blass (1887–98: i. 597–98); Gernet and Bizos (1924–26: i. 133); Lamb (1930: 182–83).

35. Lys. 25.35; cf. Lys. 26.20.

5   LOYALTY TO THE DEMOS

1. Lys. 12.1–2, 26, 82, 88, 90–91, 99; Lys. 13.1–3, 33–34, 43, 48, 69, 91–97.

2. So Usher (1965: 114) accounts for the minimal self-characterization in Lysias 12. Murphy (1989) argues that lack of evidence forced Lysias to attack Eratosthenes as an oligarchic type rather than as an individual. For arguments of generalization in forensic oratory, see Lavency (1964: 171–74); for the use of antithesis in Lysias, see Bateman (1962).

3. *P. Oxy.* 1606 ll. 135–67. This section is remarkable for its intense emotion and serves as a reminder that only a few of the conflicts that occurred after the reconciliation are represented in the extant orations (see Chapter 3). The fragment unfortunately provides little information about the legal proceeding and the nature of the dispute; see Loening (1987: 89–93) and Todd (1993: 234–35) for a recent discussion of these issues.

4. The charge of acting as sycophants would have triggered a whole set of other associations; see Harvey (1990: 107–12); Christ (1998: esp. 48–71). It is possible that the other charges were also catchwords.

5. Some believe that the speech is too unimportant and too comical to have been delivered to the Council. Others argue that the speaker was comical because that was his best defense; see Adams (1905: 231–35); Dover (1968: 189); Carey (1990: 49–50 with n. 19); Todd (1990c: 166–67). It is more difficult to explain why the invalid would have bothered contesting a dole that amounted to only an obol per day if he could afford to pay Lysias to write the speech (pace Dillon [1995: 39]). If the speech is authentic, are we to conclude that Lysias wrote the speech free of charge or that the invalid preferred to pay a logographer rather than be deprived of his dole? Moreover, even if he won the case, he had no guarantee that he would continue to receive the dole uninterrupted.

6. Aeschines' claim that his father, Atrometus, restored the demos while serving as

a soldier in Asia (2.78, 147) led the *scholion* to conclude that Atrometus returned to Athens with Conon (2.78); see Mathieu (1914: 197–98). Similarly, in Dem. 58.67 the speaker said incorrectly that his ancestor, Aristocrates, participated in the razing of Eëtioneia during the rule of the Thirty, an event that actually occurred under the Four Hundred (Thuc. 8.89–92). This was not merely a chronological confusion. By making the error, the speaker was able to depict Aristocrates as a member of the Piraeus party. See Thomas (1989: 132–38).

7. Isoc. 18.35–36; cf. Lys. 30.15: "I would not have mentioned this, but I have learned that he will attempt to save himself and defy justice by claiming to be a democrat and that he will use his exile as proof of his loyalty."

8. Isoc. 18.48–50; cf. Isoc. 16.14.

9. Cf. Lys. 10.26–28.

10. Isoc. 16.41; cf. 12–14. Gribble (1999: 128) suggests, "He does not actually compare Alcibiades' exile to that of the jurors: he merely encourages them to think of Alcibiades' experience in terms of their own." But clearly the purpose of such statements was to compare as well as to conflate Alcibiades' exile with that of the men of Piraeus. Otherwise, the speaker would not have mentioned how Alcibiades suffered the "same misfortunes" as the democratic resistance (12) or how his sufferings were "at the hands of the same people" (41).

11. In response to such attempts to rehabilitate Alcibiades, the speaker of Lysias 14 insisted that Alcibiades' motives were disloyalty and immorality. See Gribble (1999: 131, 134–35).

12. Isoc. 16.13–15; cf. Lys. 14.32–33.

13. Lys. 13.90. In contrast, four speeches and one fragment survive delivered by men who had remained in Athens during the oligarchic rule (Lys. 7.27, 41; 16; 25; Isoc. 18; *P. Ryl.* 489).

14. Adams (1905: 138) argues, "The fact that Mantitheus chose this time to return to the city, and that he was admitted by the administration, looks as though he was avowedly on their side."

15. So Murphy (1992: 547–48) observes in the case of Lysias 25. For an analysis of the political defense speeches in Lysias, see Lateiner (1981).

16. Council: Lys. 25.14; *P. Ryl.* 489 ll. 111–12; offices: Lys. 25.14; *P. Ryl.* 489 ll. 112–13; cavalry: Lys. 16.3. These are also the typical charges lodged against the men of the city.

17. Arrests: Lys. 25.15; cf. Pl. *Ap.* 32c4–d8; arbitration: Lys 25.16; *P. Ryl.* 489 ll.113–16; Lysander's list: Lys. 25.16; Isoc. 18.16; *P. Ryl.* 489 ll. 116–18. The "list," although referred to differently in these passages, probably contained the names of those Athenians who were removed from the citizen roll and forced to serve in Lysander's army; see Roberts (1938: iii. 109); Krentz (1982: 78). Loening (1987: 104 n. 15) suggests that they were sent to Lysander as hostages.

18. Lys. 25.13; so also Lys. 20.31; *P. Ryl.* 489 ll.93–99. Cf. Murphy (1992: 555–56).

19. Lys. 7.27; cf. Isoc. 15.27; Lys. 26.17.

20. Membership on the Council: And. 1.95; Isoc. 16.43; service in the cavalry: Lys. 26.10; arrests: And. 1.94; Lys. 26.18; executions: Lys. 26.18, 30.14.

21. Besides the five speeches delivered by speakers who had remained in the city

during the rule of Thirty and insisted that they had no part in the oligarchy, speakers in four other speeches denied accusations of oligarchic activities (And. 1; Lys. 20, 30; Isoc. 16).

22. Lys. 20.5, 13–14; see Lateiner (1981: 150).

23. This same phenomenon occurred after the overthrow of the Peisistratids. Rather than acknowledge that the tyrants had received extensive support from fellow citizens, the Athenians insisted that they had opposed the regime; see Lavelle (1993: esp. 79–85, 106–25).

24. Ober (1989a: 153–55, 189–91, 222–24, 306–7).

25. Lys. 26.3–5; cf. Lys. 12.38–40, 14.24, 31.

26. Cf. Voeglin (1943: 143).

6 CONSTRUCTING A FUTURE

1. Isoc. 16.14, 20.10; Lys. 2.62, 6.41, 7.6, 12.92, 13.44, 14.16, 35, 16.10, 18.18, 25, 21.18, 25.15, 16, 25, 26, 30.3, 31.17, 34.1; *P. Oxy.* 1606 ll. 120–21, 198–200; cf. And. 3.31.

2. And. 1.80, 101, 3.31; Isoc. 20.11; Lys. 13.34, 46, 14.39, 18.5; cf. And. 3.10–11; Isoc. 15.319; Lys. 2.63, 28.11, 34.3.

3. As Seager (1967: 112) remarks, "The fleet, together with the walls, was the great symbol of empire, and its loss in 404 was synonymous with the loss of the empire. So, when the charges are repeated [i.e., Lys. 28.11], the conduct of Ergocles is openly equated with the surrender to the enemy not only of the fleet but of the walls."

4. See Lévy (1976: 39); Loraux (1986: 138–41); Thomas (1989: 210–11, 230).

5. See MacDowell (1962: 200–203).

6. Cf. And. 3.10–11.

7. Cf. Murphy (1992: 557).

8. Lys. 2.64; cf. Isoc. 4.111, 7.69.

9. Cf. Lys. 12.68–76, where the meeting of the Assembly to approve the terms of surrender is conflated with the meeting of the Assembly at which the Thirty were appointed. See Lehmann (1972: 208–12); Bommelaer (1981:144). Contra: Krentz (1982: 43 with n. 35). Attempts to reconcile Lysias's chronology with Xenophon's only further show how Lysias compresses the sequence of events.

10. Greed: Lys. 12.6–8. Murder of democratic leaders: Lys. 18.11; cf. 16.5, 25.13.

11. Lysias 34.4; cf. Isoc. 21.12.

12. Lys. 25.19; cf. Arist. *Ath. Pol.* 35.3.

13. For the authorizing of places, see Lincoln (1994: esp. 8–9, 143–44).

14. Lysias 12.19; see Wooten (1988 / 89); Bons (1993); Borthwick (1990 / 91: 44–45).

15. Loening (1987: 120) suggests that the speaker cannot be referring to the entire period of civil war since he would then be contradicting Dem. 24.56. But this would not be the only time when the statements of one speaker contradict those of another (e.g., Lys 16.8, 26.9–10).

16. Pace Donlan (1980: 147–53).

17. Loraux (1986: 98–100); Thomas (1989: 217–20).

18. Cf. Whitehead (1993: 45–46).

19. Lys. 26.4; cf. Xen. *Hell.* 2.4.39–43. Even if Thrasybulus's speech to the men of the

city is fictive, it shows us how democrats could use the rule of the Thirty to challenge aristocratic pretensions.

20. North (1966: 135–37); Donlan (1980: 174–76).
21. Cf. Nouhaud (1982: 310).
22. See Garner (1987: 133–34); Cohen (1991: 228–31).
23. Speakers who asserted that the democratic army was successful because of dissent from within the city were not denying the men of Piraeus their victory; rather, they were claiming that these dissidents deserved to be recognized as part of the resistance.

BIBLIOGRAPHY

Adams, C. D. 1905. *Lysias: Selected Speeches*. New York.

Adeleye, G. 1976. "Theramenes: The End of a Controversial Career." *Museum Africum* 5: 9–22.

———. 1977 / 78. "The Arginusae Affair and Theramenes' Rejection at the *Dokimasia* of 405 / 4 B.C." *Museum Africum* 6: 94–99.

———. 1983. "The Purpose of the *Dokimasia*." *GRBS* 24: 295–306.

Adkins, A. W. H. 1960. *Merit and Responsibility: A Study in Greek Values*. Oxford.

———. 1972. *Moral Values and Political Behaviour in Ancient Greece from Homer to the End of the Fifth Century*. London.

———. 1978. "Problems in Greek Popular Morality." *CP* 73: 143–58.

Allen, D. 2000. *The World of Prometheus: The Politics of Punishing in Democratic Athens*. Princeton.

Allen, R. E. 1980. *Socrates and Legal Obligation*. Minneapolis.

Alonso, A. 1988. "The Effects of Truth: Re-Presentations of the Past and the Imagining of Community." *Journal of Historical Sociology* 1: 33–57.

Amit, M. 1965. *Athens and the Sea: A Study in Athenian Seapower*. Brussels.

Andrewes, A. 1970. "Lysias and the Theramenes Papyrus." *ZPE* 6: 35–38.

———. 1974. "The Arginousai Trial." *Phoenix* 28: 112–22.

———. 1976. "Androtion and the Four Hundred." *PCPS* 22: 14–25.

Appelfeld, A. 1994. "The Awakening." In Hartman, ed.: 149–52.

Atkinson, K. M. T. 1939. "Athenian Legislative Procedure and Revision of Laws." *Bulletin of the John Rylands Library* 23: 107–50.

Aurenche, O. 1974. *Les groupes d'Alcibiade, de Léogoras et de Teucros*. Paris.

Avery, H. 1991. "Was Eratosthenes the Oligarch Eratosthenes the Adulterer?" *Hermes* 119: 380–84.

Badian, E., and Buckler, J. 1975. "The Wrong Salamis?" *RhM* 118: 226–39.

Barber, B. 1984. *Strong Democracy: Participatory Politics for a New Age*. Berkeley.

Bateman, J. 1958. "Lysias and the Law." *TAPA* 89: 276–85.

———. 1962. "Some Aspects of Lysias' Argumentation." *Phoenix* 16: 157–77.

Bauman, R. 1990. *Political Trials in Ancient Greece*. London.

Baumgartner, M. 1988. *The Moral Order of a Suburb*. New York.

Ben-Yehuda, N. 1995. *The Masada Myth: Collective Memory and Mythmaking in Israel*. Madison, Wis.

Berdahl, D. 1994. "Voices at the Wall: Discourses of Self, History and National Identity at the Vietnam Veterans Memorial." *History and Memory* 6: 88–124.

Bernstein, M. 1994. *Foregone Conclusions: Against Apocalyptic History*. Berkeley.

Bers, V. 1975. "Solon's Law Forbidding Neutrality and Lysias 31." *Historia* 24: 493–98.

Blass, F. 1887–98. *Die attische Beredsamkeit*. 3 vols. 2d ed. Leipzig.

Bleicken, J. 1985. *Die athenische Demokratie*. Paderborn.

———. 1987. "Die Einheit der athenischen Demokratie in klassischer Zeit." *Hermes* 115: 257–83.

Blight, D. 1989. "For Something beyond the Battlefield: Frederick Douglass and the Struggle for the Memory of the Civil War." *Journal of American History* 75: 1156–78.

Boedeker, D., and Raaflaub, K. A., eds. 1998. *Democracy, Empire, and the Arts in Fifth-Century Athens*. Cambridge, Mass.

Boegehold, A. 1972. "The Establishment of a Central Archive at Athens." *AJA* 76: 23–30.

———. 1994. "Perikles' Citizenship Law of 451 / 0 B.C." In Boegehold and Scafuro, eds.: 57–66.

Boegehold, A., and Scafuro, A., eds. 1994. *Athenian Identity and Civic Ideology*. Baltimore.

Bommelaer, J.-F. 1981. *Lysander de Sparte: Histoire et traditions*. Paris.

Bonner, R. 1924. "Note on Aristotle *Constitution of Athens* XXXIX. 5." *CP* 19: 175–76.

Bons, J. A. E. 1993. "Lysias 12,19: The Earrings Again." *Hermes* 121: 365–67.

Borthwick, E. 1990 / 91. "Two Emotional Climaxes in Lysias' *Against Eratosthenes*." *CW* 84: 44–46.

Bourdieu, P. 1977. *Outline of a Theory of Practice*. Trans. R. Nice. Cambridge.

———. 1986 / 87. "The Force of Law: Toward a Sociology of the Juridical Field." *Hastings Law Journal* 38: 814–53.

Boyarin, J., ed. 1994. *Remapping Memory: The Politics of TimeSpace*. Minneapolis.

Brickhouse, T., and Smith, N. 1989. *Socrates on Trial*. Princeton.

Brooks, P., and Gewirtz, P., eds. 1996. *Law's Stories: Narrative and Rhetoric in the Law*. New Haven.

Buck, R. 1995. "The Character of Theramenes." *AHB* 9: 14–23.

———. 1998. *Thrasybulus and the Athenian Democracy: The Life of an Athenian Statesman*. *Historia* Einzelshriften 120. Stuttgart.

Bugh, G. 1988. *The Horsemen of Athens*. Princeton.

Burrin, P. 1996. *France under the Germans: Collaboration and Compromise*. Trans. J. Lloyd. New York.

Buruma, I. 1994. *Wages of Guilt: Memories of War in Germany and Japan*. New York.

Carawan, E. 1998. *Rhetoric and the Law of Draco*. Oxford.

Carey, C. 1989. *Lysias: Selected Speeches*. Cambridge.

———. 1990. "Structure and Strategy in Lysias XXIV." *G&R* 37: 44–51.

———. 1994a. " 'Artless' Proofs in Aristotle and the Orators." *BICS* 39: 95–106.

———. 1994b. "Legal Space in Classical Athens." *G&R* 41: 172–86.

———. 1994c. "Rhetorical Means of Persuasion." In Worthington, ed.: 26–45.

Carey, C., and Reid, R. 1985. *Demosthenes: Selected Private Speeches*. Cambridge.

Cartledge, P. 1985. "Rebels and Sambos in Classical Greece: A Comparative View." In Cartledge and Harvey, eds.: 16–46.

———. 1987. *Agesilaos and the Crisis of Sparta.* Baltimore.

Cartledge, P., and Harvey, F. D., eds. 1985. *Crux: Essays in Greek History Presented to G.E.M. de Ste. Croix on His Seventy-fifth Birthday.* London.

Cartledge, P., Millett, P., and Todd, S., eds. 1990. *Nomos: Essays in Athenian Law, Politics and Society.* Cambridge.

Cartledge, P., Millett, P., and von Reden, S., eds. 1998. *Kosmos: Essays in Order, Conflict and Community in Classical Athens.* Cambridge.

Chambers, M. 1990. *Aristoteles Staat der Athener.* Berlin.

Christ, M. 1992. "Ostracism, Sycophancy, and the Deception of the Demos: [Arist.] *Ath. Pol.* 43.5." *CQ* 42: 336–46.

———. 1998. *The Litigious Athenian.* Baltimore.

Chroust, A.-H. 1957. *Socrates, Man and Myth: The Two Socratic Apologies of Xenophon.* London.

Clairmont, C. 1983. *Patrios Nomos: Public Burial in Athens during the Fifth and Fourth Centuries B.C.* 2 vols. Oxford.

Clinton, K. 1982. "The Nature of the Late-Fifth-Century Revision of the Athenian Law Code." In *Studies in Attic Epigraphy, History and Topography Presented to Eugene Vanderpool. Hesperia,* supplement 19: 27–37. Princeton.

Cloché, P. 1915. *La restauration démocratique à Athènes en 403 avant J.-C.* Paris.

———. 1916. "Les Trois-mille et la restauration démocratique à Athènes en 403." *REG* 29: 14–28.

———. 1918. "La politique thébaine de 404 à 396 avant J.-C." *REG* 31: 315–43.

———. 1919. "L'affaire des Arginuses (406 avant J.-C.)." *Revue historique* 130: 5–68.

Cohen, D. 1991. *Law, Sexuality, and Society: Enforcement of Morals in Classical Athens.* Cambridge.

———. 1995. *Law, Violence, and Community in Classical Athens.* Cambridge.

Colin, G. 1933. *Xénophon historien d'après le livre II des Helléniques (hiver 406/5 à 401/0).* Paris.

Comaroff, J., and Roberts, S. 1981. *Rules and Processes: The Cultural Logic of Dispute in an African Context.* Chicago.

Connor, W. R. 1988. "Early Greek Land Warfare As Symbolic Expression." *Past and Present* 119: 3–29.

———. 1991. "The Other 399: Religion and the Trial of Socrates." In M. Flower and M. Toher, eds., *Georgica: Greek Studies in Honour of George Cawkwell. Institute of Classical Studies,* supplement 58: 49–56. London.

———. 1994. "The Problem of Civic Identity." In Boegehold and Scafuro, eds.: 34–44.

Corradi, J. 1982. "The Mode of Destruction: Terror in Argentina." *Telos* 54: 61–76.

Dahl, R., ed. 1973. *Regimes and Oppositions.* New Haven.

Davies, J. K. 1981. *Wealth and the Power of Wealth in Classical Athens.* New York.

———. 1995. "The Fourth-Century Crisis: What Crisis?" In Eder, ed.: 29–39.

Day, J., and Chambers, M. 1962. *Aristotle's History of Athenian Democracy. University of California Publications in History,* vol. 73. Berkeley.

Delebecque, É. 1957. *Essai sur la vie de Xénophon.* Paris.

Detienne, M. 1967. *Les maîtres de vérité dans la grèce archaïque.* Paris.

Dillery, J. 1995. *Xenophon and the History of His Times.* London.

Dillon, M. 1995. "Payments to the Disabled at Athens: Social Justice or Fear of Aristocratic Patronage?" *Ancient Society* 26: 27–57.

Dodds, E. R. 1951. *The Greeks and the Irrational.* Berkeley.

Donlan, W. 1978. "Social Vocabulary and Its Relationship to Political Propaganda in Fifth-Century Athens." *QUCC* 27: 95–111.

———. 1980. *The Aristocratic Ideal in Ancient Greece: Attitudes of Superiority from Homer to the End of the Fifth Century B.C.* Lawrence, Kans.

Dorjahn, A. 1932. "The Athenian Senate and the Oligarchy of 404/3 B.C." *PQ* 11: 57–64.

———. 1944. "On Aristotle, *Ath. Pol.,* XXXVIII, 3." *PQ* 23: 289–96.

———. 1946. *Political Forgiveness in Old Athens: The Amnesty of 403 B.C.* Evanston, Ill.

Dougherty, C. 1996. "Democratic Contradictions and the Synoptic Illusion of Euripides' *Ion.*" In Ober and Hedrick, eds.: 249–70.

Dougherty, C., and Kurke, L., eds. 1993. *Cultural Poetics in Archaic Greece: Cult, Performance, Politics.* Cambridge.

Dover, K. J. 1968. *Lysias and the Corpus Lysiacum.* Berkeley.

———. 1974. *Greek Popular Morality in the Time of Plato and Aristotle.* Berkeley.

———. 1976. "The Freedom of the Intellectual in Greek Society." *Talanta* 7: 24–54.

———. 1978. *Greek Homosexuality.* Cambridge, Mass.

Dow, S. 1960. "The Athenian Calendar of Sacrifices: The Chronology of Nikomakhos' Second Term." *Historia* 9: 270–93.

Eder, W., ed. 1995a. *Die athenische Demokratie im 4. Jahrhundert v. Chr.: Vollendung oder Verfall einer Verfassungsform?* Stuttgart.

———. 1995b. "Die athenische Demokratie im 4. Jahrhundert v. Chr.: Krise oder Vollendung?" In Eder, ed.: 11–28.

———. 1998. "Aristocrats and the Coming of Athenian Democracy." In Morris and Raaflaub, eds.: 105–40.

Edwards, M. J. 1999. *Lysias: Five Speeches.* London.

Ehrhardt, C. 1970. "Xenophon and Diodorus on Aegospotami." *Phoenix* 24: 225–28.

Ellickson. 1991. *Order without Law: How Neighbors Settle Disputes.* Cambridge, Mass.

Ellis, W. M. 1989. *Alcibiades.* London.

Engels, J. 1993. "Der Michigan-Papyrus über Theramenes und die Ausbildung des 'Theramenes-Mythos.'" *ZPE* 99: 125–55.

Esbenshade, R. 1995. "Remembering to Forget: Memory, History, National Identity in Postwar East-Central Europe." *Representations* 49: 72–96.

Euben, P., Wallach, J., and Ober, J., eds. 1994. *Athenian Political Thought and the Reconstruction of American Democracy.* Ithaca, N.Y.

Feitlowitz, M. 1998. *A Lexicon of Terror: Argentina and the Legacies of Torture.* New York.

Fentress, J., and Wickham, C. 1992. *Social Memory.* Oxford.

Ferguson, W. S. 1936. "The Athenian Law Code and the Old Attic Trittyes." In *Classical Studies Presented to Edward Capps:* 144–58. Princeton.

Fingarette, A. 1971. "A New Look at the Wall of Nikomakhos." *Hesperia* 40: 330–35.

Finley, M. I. 1962. "Athenian Demagogues." *Past and Present* 21: 3–24.

———. 1975. *The Use and Abuse of History.* London.

———. 1988. *Democracy Ancient and Modern.* Rev. ed. New Brunswick, N.J.

Foxhall, L., and Lewis, A. D. E., eds. 1996. *Greek Law in Its Political Setting: Justifications Not Justice.* Oxford.

Friedlander, S., ed. 1992. *Probing the Limits of Representation: Nazism and the 'Final Solution.'* Cambridge, Mass.

Fritz, K. von, and Kapp, E. 1950. *Aristotle's Constitution of Athens and Related Texts.* New York.

Fuks, A. 1953a. *The Ancestral Constitution.* London.

———. 1953b. "Notes on the Rule of the Ten at Athens in 403 B.C." *Mnemosyne* 6: 198–207.

Funke, P. 1980. *Homónoia und Arché. Athen und die griechische Staatenwelt vom Ende des peloponnesischen Krieges bis zum Königsfreiden. Historia* Einzelschriften 37. Wiesbaden.

Furley, W. D. 1996. *Andokides and the Herms: A Study of Crisis in Fifth-Century Athenian Religion. Institute of Classical Studies,* supplement 65. London.

Gagarin, M. 1979. "The Prosecution of Homicide in Athens." *GRBS* 20: 301–23.

———. 1986. *Early Greek Law.* Berkeley.

———. 1990. "*Bouleusis* in Athenian Homicide Law." In G. Nenci and G. Thür, eds., *Symposion 1988: Vorträge zur griechischen und hellenistischen Rechtsgeschichte:* 81–99. Cologne.

Garland, R. 1987. *The Piraeus from the Fifth to the First Century B.C.* Ithaca.

———. 1992. *Introducing New Gods: The Politics of Athenian Religion.* Ithaca.

Garner, R. 1987. *Law and Society in Classical Athens.* London.

Gedi, N., and Elam, Y. 1996. "Collective Memory—What Is It?" *History and Memory* 8: 30–50.

Gehrke, H.-J. 1985. *Stasis. Untersuchungen zu den inneren Kriegen in den griechischen Staaten des 5. und 4. Jahrhunderts v. Chr. Vestigia* 35. Munich.

Gernet, L., and Bizos, M. 1924–26. *Lysias: Discours.* 2 vols. Paris.

Geyer, M., and Hansen, M. 1994. "German-Jewish Memory and National Consciousness." In Hartman, ed.: 175–90.

Giddens, A. 1984. *The Constitution of Society: Outline of the Theory of Structuration.* Berkeley.

Gillis, J., ed. 1994. *Commemorations: The Politics of National Identity.* Princeton.

Golden, M. 1992. "Continuity, Change and the Study of Ancient Childhood." *EMC* 36: 7–18.

Goldstein, J. 1972. "Solon's Law for an Activist Citizenry." *Historia* 21: 538–45.

Gomme, A. W., with A. Andrewes and K. J. Dover. 1945–81. *A Historical Commentary on Thucydides*. 5 vols. Oxford.

Gouri, H. 1994. "Facing the Glass Booth." In Hartman, ed.: 153–60.

Gray, V. 1989. *The Character of Xenophon's Hellenica*. Baltimore.

Green, P. 1991. "Rebooking the Flute-girls." *AHB* 5: 1–16.

———. 1994. "Text and Context in the Matter of Xenophon's Exile." In I. Worthington, ed., *Ventures into Greek History*: 215–27. Oxford.

Gregory, S., and Lewis, J. 1988. "Symbols of Collective Memory: The Social Process of Memorializing May 4, 1970, at Kent State University." *Symbolic Interaction* 11: 213–33.

Grenfell, B. P., and Hunt, A. S. 1906. *The Hibeh Papyri: Part I*. London.

Gribble, D. 1999. *Alcibiades and Athens: A Study in Literary Presentation*. Oxford.

Habermas, J. 1988a. "Concerning the Public Use of History." *New German Critique* 44: 40–50.

———. 1988b. "A Kind of Settlement of Damages (Apologetic Tendencies)." *New German Critique* 44: 25–39.

Halbwachs, M. 1941. *La topographie légendaire des évangiles en terre sainte: Etude de mémoire collective*. Paris.

———. 1992. *On Collective Memory*. Trans. L. Coser. Chicago.

Hall, L. G. H. 1990. "Ephialtes, the Areopagus and the Thirty." *CQ* 40: 319–28.

Halperin, D. 1990. *One Hundred Years of Homosexuality and Other Essays on Greek Love*. New York.

Hamilton, C.D. 1970. "Spartan Politics and Policy, 405–401 B.C." *AJP* 91: 294–314.

———. 1979. *Sparta's Bitter Victories: Politics and Diplomacy in the Corinthian War*. Ithaca and London.

Handlin, O. 1961. "The Civil War As Symbol and As Actuality." *Massachusetts Review* 3: 133–43.

Hansen, M. H. 1975. *Eisangelia: The Sovereignty of the People's Court in Athens in the Fourth Century B.C. and the Impeachment of Generals and Politicians*. Odense.

———. 1976. *Apagoge, Endeixis and Ephegesis against Kakourgoi, Atimoi and Pheugontes: A Study in the Athenian Administration of Justice in the Fourth Century B.C.* Odense.

———. 1978a. "*Demos, Ecclesia* and *Dicasterion* in Classical Athens." *GRBS* 19: 127–46.

———. 1978b. "*Nomos* and *Psephisma* in Fourth-Century Athens." *GRBS* 19: 315–30.

———. 1979. "Did the Athenian *Ecclesia* Legislate after 403 / 2 B.C.?" *GRBS* 20: 27–53.

———. 1980. "Athenian *Nomothesia* in the Fourth Century B.C. and Demosthenes' Speech against Leptines." *C&M* 32: 87–104.

———. 1981. "The Prosecution of Homicide in Athens: A Reply." *GRBS* 22: 11–30.

———. 1985a. "Athenian *Nomothesia*." *GRBS* 26: 345–71.

———. 1985b. *Demography and Democracy: The Number of Athenian Citizens in the Fourth Century B.C.* Herning, Denmark.

———. 1987. *The Athenian Assembly in the Age of Demosthenes.* Oxford.

———. 1989a. "*Demos, Ekklesia* and *Dikasterion:* A Reply to Martin Ostwald and Josiah Ober." *C&M* 40: 101–6.

———. 1989b. "Solonian Democracy in Fourth-Century Athens." *C&M* 40: 71–99.

———. 1990a. "Diokles' Law (Dem. 24.42) and the Revision of the Athenian Corpus of Laws in the Archonship of Eukleides." *C&M* 41: 63–71.

———. 1990b. "The Political Powers of the People's Court in Fourth-Century Athens." In Murray and Price, eds.: 215–43.

———. 1990c. Review of Ober (1989a). *CR* 40: 348–56.

———. 1991. *The Athenian Democracy in the Age of Demosthenes.* Oxford.

———. 1995. *The Trial of Sokrates from the Athenian Point of View.* Copenhagen.

Hanson, V. D. 1983. *Warfare and Agriculture in Classical Greece. Biblioteca di Studi Antichi* 40. Pisa.

———. 1989. *The Western Way of War: Infantry Battle in Classical Greece.* New York.

Harding, P. 1974. "The Theramenes Myth." *Phoenix* 28: 101–11.

———. 1978. "O Androtion, You Fool!" *AJAH* 3: 179–83.

———. 1987a. "Metics, Foreigners or Slaves? The Recipients of Honours in *IG* II^2 10." *ZPE* 67: 176–82.

———. 1987b. "Rhetoric and Politics in Fourth-Century Athens." *Phoenix* 41: 25–39.

———. 1988. "King Pausanias and the Restoration of Democracy at Athens." *Hermes* 116: 86–193.

———. 1991. "All Pigs Are Animals, but Are All Animals Pigs?" *AHB* 5: 145–48.

Harris, E. 1985. "The Date of the Trial of Timarchus." *Hermes* 113: 376–80.

———. 1994a. " 'In the Act' or 'Red-Handed'? *Apagoge* to the Eleven and *Furtum Manifestum.*" In G. Thür, ed., *Symposion 1993: Vorträge zur griechischen und hellenistischen Rechtsgeschichte*: 169–84. Cologne.

———. 1994b. "Law and Oratory." In Worthington, ed.: 130–50.

Harrison, A. R. W. 1955. "Law-Making at Athens at the End of the Fifth Century B.C." *JHS* 75: 26–35.

———. 1968–71. *The Law of Athens.* 2 vols. Oxford.

Hartman, G., ed. 1994a. *Holocaust Remembrance: The Shapes of Memory.* Oxford.

———. 1994b. "Introduction: Darkness Visible." In Hartman, ed.: 1–22.

Harvey, F. D. 1985. "*Dona Ferentes:* Some Aspects of Bribery in Greek Politics." In Cartledge and Harvey, eds.: 76–117.

———. 1990. "The Sykophant and Sykophancy: Vexatious Redefinition?" In Cartledge, Millett, and Todd, eds.: 103–21.

Hatzfeld, J. 1951. *Alcibiade, étude sur l'histoire d'Athènes à la fin du Ve siècle.* Paris.

Headlam, J. W. 1933. *Election by Lot at Athens.* 2d ed. Cambridge.

Hedrick, C. 1994. "The Zero Degree of Society: Aristotle and the Athenian Citizen." In Euben, Wallach, and Ober, eds.: 289–318.

Henrichs, A. 1968. "Zur Interpretation des Michigan-Papyrus über Theramenes." *ZPE* 3: 101–8.

Hereward, D. 1952. "New Fragments of *IG* II² 10." *BSA* 47: 102–17.

Higgins, W. E. 1977. *Xenophon the Athenian: The Problem of the Individual and the Society of the Polis.* Albany.

Hignett, C. 1952. *A History of the Athenian Constitution to the End of the Fifth Century B.C.* Oxford.

Hobsbawm, E., and Ranger, T., eds. 1983. *The Invention of Tradition.* Cambridge.

Hornblower, S. 1987. *Thucydides.* Baltimore.

Humphreys, S. 1985a. "Law As Discourse." *History and Anthropology* 1: 241–64.

———. 1985b. "Social Relations on Stage: Witnesses in Classical Athens." *History and Anthropology* 1: 313–69.

Hunter, V. 1990. "Gossip and the Politics of Reputation in Classical Athens." *Phoenix* 44: 299–325.

———. 1994. *Policing Athens: Social Control in the Attic Lawsuits, 420–320 B.C.* Princeton.

Hutton, P. 1993. *History As an Art of Memory.* Hanover, N.H.

Irwin, T. 1989. "Socrates and Athenian Democracy." *Philosophy and Public Affairs* 18: 184–205.

Isager, S., and Hansen, M. H. 1975. *Aspects of Athenian Society in the Fourth Century B.C.: A Historical Introduction to and Commentary on the Paragraphe-Speeches and the Speech against Dionysodorus in the Corpus Demosthenicum (XXXII–XXXVIII and LVI).* Odense.

Jacoby, F. 1949. *Atthis: The Local Chronicles of Ancient Athens.* Oxford.

Jameson, M. 1990. "Private Space and the Greek City." In Murray and Price, eds.: 171–95.

Johnstone, S. 1999. *Disputes and Democracy: The Consequences of Litigation in Ancient Athens.* Austin.

Judt, T. 1992. "The Past Is Another Country: Myth and Memory in Postwar Europe." *Daedalus* 121: 83–118.

Kagan, D. 1987. *The Fall of the Athenian Empire.* Ithaca, N.Y.

Kahrstedt, U. 1938. "Untersuchungen zu athenischen Behörden." *Klio* 32: 1–32.

Kapparis, K. 1993. "Is Eratosthenes in Lys. 1 the Same Person As Eratosthenes in Lys. 12?" *Hermes* 121: 364–65.

Keaney, J. J. 1992. *The Composition of Aristotle's Athenaion Politeia: Observation and Explanation.* New York and Oxford.

Keizer, M. de. 1996. "The Skeleton in the Closet: The Memory of Putten, 1/2 October 1944." *History and Memory* 7: 70–99.

Konstan, D. 1997. *Friendship in the Classical World.* Cambridge.

Krentz, P. 1980. "Foreigners against the Thirty: *IG* 2² 10 Again." *Phoenix* 34: 298–306.

———. 1982. *The Thirty at Athens.* Ithaca, N.Y.

———. 1986. "The Rewards for Thrasyboulos' Supporters." *ZPE* 62: 201–204.

———. 1989. *Xenophon: Hellenika I–II.3.10.* Warminster.

———. 1995. *Xenophon: Hellenika II.3.11–IV.2.8.* Warminster.

Krondorfer, B. 1995. *Remembrance and Reconciliation: Encounters between Young Jews and Germans.* New Haven, Conn.

Kühn, J.-H. 1967. "Die Amnestie von 403 v. Chr. im Reflex der 18. Isokrates-Rede." *WS* 80: 31–73.

Lamb, W. R. M. 1930. *Lysias.* Cambridge, Mass.

Lateiner, D. 1981. "An Analysis of Lysias' Political Defense Speeches." *RSA* 11: 147–60.

Lavelle, B. 1993. *The Sorrow and the Pity: A Prolegomenon to a History of Athens under the Peisistratids, c. 560–510 B.C. Historia* Einzelschriften 80. Stuttgart.

Lavency, M. 1964. *Aspects de la logographie judiciaire attique.* Louvain.

Lehmann, G. 1972. "Die revolutionäre Machtergreifung der 'Dreissig' und die staatliche Teilung Attikas (404–401/0 v. Chr.)." In *Antike und Universalgeschichte:* 201–33. Münster.

———. 1976. "Ein Historiker Namens Kratippos." *ZPE* 23: 265–88.

———. 1995. "Überlegungen zu den oligarchischen Machtergreifungen im Athen des 4. Jahrhunderts v. Chr." In Eder, ed.: 139–50.

Lévêque, P., and Vidal-Naquet, P. 1964. *Clisthène l'Athénien: Essai sur la représentation de l'espace et du temps dans la pensée politique grecque de la fin du VIe siècle à la mort de Plato.* Paris.

Lévy, E. 1976. *Athènes devant la défait de 404: Histoire d'une crise idéologique.* Paris.

Lincoln, B. 1994. *Authority: Construction and Corrosion.* Chicago.

Lipsius, J. H. 1905–15. *Das attische Recht und Rechtsverfahren.* 3 vols. Leipzig.

Loening, T. 1981. "The Autobiographical Speeches of Lysias and the Biographical Tradition." *Hermes* 109: 280–94.

———. 1987. *The Reconciliation Agreement of 403/402 B.C. in Athens: Its Content and Application. Hermes* Einzelschriften 53. Stuttgart.

Loraux, N. 1980. "L'oubli dans la cité." *Le temps de la réflexion* 1: 213–42.

———. 1986. *The Invention of Athens: The Funeral Oration in the Classical City.* Trans. A. Sheridan. Cambridge, Mass.

———. 1988. "De l'amnistie et de son contraire." In *Usages de l'oubli:* 23–47. Paris.

———. 1991. "Reflections of the Greek City on Unity and Division." In A. Molho, K. Raaflaub, and J. Emlen, eds., *City-States in Classical Antiquity and Medieval Italy:* 33–51. Stuttgart.

———. 1993. *The Children of Athena: Athenian Ideas about Citizenship and the Division between the Sexes.* Trans. C. Levine. Princeton.

———. 1997. *La cité divisée: L'oubli dans la mémoire d'Athènes.* Paris.

———. 1998. *Mothers in Mourning: With the Essay of Amnesty and Its Opposite.* Trans. C. Pache. Ithaca, N.Y.

———. 2000. *Born of the Earth: Myth and Politics in Athens.* Trans. S. Stewart. Ithaca, N.Y.

Lotze, D. 1964. *Lysander und der Peloponneische Krieg.* Berlin.

———. 1967. "Der Munichion 404 v. Chr. und das Problem der Schaltfolge im athenischen Kalender." *Philologus* 111: 34–46.

Lowenthal, D. 1985. *The Past Is a Foreign Country.* Cambridge.

McCoy, W. 1975. "Aristotle's *Athenaion Politeia* and the Establishment of the Thirty Tyrants." *YCS* 23: 131–45.

MacDowell, D. M. 1962. *Andocides: On the Mysteries.* Oxford.

———. 1963. *Athenian Homicide in the Age of the Orators.* Manchester.

———. 1975. "Law-Making at Athens in the Fourth Century B.C." *JHS* 95: 62–74.

———. 1978. *The Law in Classical Athens.* Ithaca.

———. 1990. *Demosthenes against Meidias (Oration 21).* Oxford.

Maier, C. 1988. *The Unmasterable Past: History, Holocaust, and German National Identity.* Cambridge, Mass.

Markle, M. M. 1985. "Jury Pay and Assembly Pay at Athens." In Cartledge and Harvey, eds.: 265–97.

———. 1990. "Participation of Farmers in Athenian Juries and Assemblies." *Ancient Society* 21: 149–65.

Mathieu, G. 1914. "Survivances des luttes politiques du Ve siècle chez les orateurs Attiques du IVe siècle." *RP* 38: 182–205.

Meier, C. 1990. *The Greek Discovery of Politics.* Trans. D. McLintock. Cambridge, Mass.

Merkelbach, R. 1977. "Egotistic and Altruistic Motivation in Historiography: An Excursus to the Papyrus of Theramenes." In J. D'Arms and J. Eadie, eds., *Ancient and Modern: Essays in Honor of Gerald F. Else:* 111–17. Ann Arbor, Mich.

Merkelbach, R., and Youtie, H. C. 1968. "Ein Michigan-Papyrus über Theramenes." *ZPE* 2: 161–69.

Meyer, E. 1993. "Epitaphs and Citizenship in Classical Athens." *JHS* 113: 99–121.

Miller. 1993. *Humiliation and Other Essays on Honor, Social Discomfort, and Violence.* Ithaca , N.Y.

Millett, P. 2000. "Mogens Hansen and the Labelling of Athenian Democracy." In P. Flensted-Jensen, T. Nielsen, and L. Rubinstein, eds., *Polis and Politics: Studies in Ancient Greek History Presented to Mogens Herman Hansen on His Sixtieth Birthday:* 337–62. Copenhagen.

Minow, M. 1998. *Between Vengeance and Forgiveness: Facing History after Genocide and Mass Violence.* Boston.

Missiou, A. 1992. *The Subversive Oratory of Andocides: Politics, Ideology and Decision-Making in Democratic Athens.* Cambridge.

Missiou-Ladi, A. 1987. "Coercive Diplomacy in Greek Interstate Relations (with special reference to *presbeis autokratores*)." *CQ* 37: 336–45.

Moore, S. 1978. *Law As Process: An Anthropological Approach.* London.

Morris, I. 1987. *Burial and Ancient Society: The Rise of the Greek City-State.* Cambridge.

———1992. *Death-Ritual and Social Structure in Classical Antiquity.* Cambridge.

———. 1994a. "The Athenian Economy Twenty Years after *The Ancient Economy.*" *CP* 89: 351–66.

———. 1994b. "Everyman's Grave." In Boegehold and Scafuro, eds.: 67–101.

———. 1996. "The Strong Principle of Equality and the Archaic Origins of Greek Democracy." In Ober and Hedrick, eds.: 19–48.

———. 2000. *Archaeology As Cultural History*. Oxford.

Morris, I., and Raaflaub, K. A., eds. 1998. *Democracy 2500? Questions and Challenges*. *AIA* Colloquia and Conference Papers 2. Dubuque, Iowa

Mosley, D. J. 1973. *Envoys and Diplomacy in Ancient Greece*. *Historia* Einzelschriften 22. Wiesbaden.

Mossé, C. 1962. *La fin de la démocratie athénienne: Aspects sociaux et politiques du déclin de la cité grecque au IVe siècle avant J.-C.* Paris.

———. 1973. *Athens in Decline, 404–386 B.C.* Trans. J. Stewart. London.

———. 1978. "Le theme de la *patrios politeia* dans la pensée grecque du IVe siècle." *Eirene* 16: 81–89.

———. 1987. *Le procès de Socrate*. Brussels.

Munn, M. 2000. *The School of History: Athens in the Age of Socrates*. Berkeley.

Munro, J. 1937. "The End of the Peloponnesian War." *CQ* 31: 32–38.

———. 1938. "Theramenes against Lysander." *CQ* 32: 18–26.

Murphy, T. 1989. "The Vilification of Eratosthenes and Theramenes in Lysias 12." *AJP* 110: 40–49.

———. 1992. "Lysias 25 and the Intractable Democratic Abuses." *AJP* 113: 543–58.

Murray, O., and Price, S., eds. 1990. *The Greek City from Homer to Alexander*. Oxford.

Nader, L., and Todd, H. F., Jr., eds. 1978. *The Disputing Process: Law in Ten Societies*. New York.

Nagy, G. 1990. *Pindar's Homer: The Lyric Possession of an Epic Past*. Baltimore.

North, H. 1966. *Sophrosyne: Self-Knowledge and Self-Restraint in Greek Literature*. Ithaca, N.Y.

Nora, P., ed. 1984–97. *Les lieux de mémoire*. 3 vols. Paris.

Nouhaud, M. 1982. *L'utilisation de l'histoire par les orateurs attiques*. Paris.

Ober, J. 1989a. *Mass and Elite in Democratic Athens: Rhetoric, Ideology, and the Power of the People*. Princeton.

———. 1989b. "The Nature of Athenian Democracy." *CP* 84: 322–34.

———. 1993. "The Athenian Revolution of 508 / 7 B.C.E.: Violence, Authority, and the Origins of Democracy." In Dougherty and Kurke, eds.: 215–32.

———. 1998. *Political Dissent in Democratic Athens: Intellectual Critics of Popular Rule*. Princeton.

Ober, J., and Hedrick, C., eds. 1996. *Demokratia: A Conversation on Democracies, Ancient and Modern*. Princeton.

Ober, J., and Strauss, B. 1990. "Drama, Political Rhetoric, and the Discourse of Athenian Democracy." In J. Winkler and F. Zeitlin, eds., *Nothing to Do with Dionysos? Athenian Drama in Its Social Context*: 237–70. Princeton.

O'Donnell, G. 1986. "On the Fruitful Convergences of Hirschman's *Exit, Voice, and Loyalty* and *Shifting Involvements:* Reflections from the Recent Argentine Experience." In A. Foxley, M. McPherson, and G. O'Donnell, eds., *Development, Democracy, and the Art of Trespassing: Essays in Honor of Albert O. Hirschman:* 249–68. Notre Dame, Ind.

Oliver, J. H. 1935. "Greek Inscriptions: Laws." *Hesperia* 4: 5–32.

Ollier, F. 1933–43. *Le mirage spartiate.* 2 vols. Paris.

Osborne, M. J. 1981–83. *Naturalization in Athens.* 4 vols. Brussels.

Osborne, R. 1985a. "The Erection and Mutilation of the Hermai." *PCPS* 211: 47–73.

———. 1985b. "Law in Action in Classical Athens." *JHS* 105: 40–58.

Osborne, R., and Hornblower, S., eds. 1994. *Ritual, Finance, Politics: Athenian Democratic Accounts Presented to David Lewis.* Oxford.

Ostwald, M. 1986. *From Popular Sovereignty to the Sovereignty of Law: Law, Society, and Politics in Fifth-Century Athens.* Berkeley.

Paine, R. 1994. "Masada: A History of Memory." *History and Anthropology* 6: 371–409.

Patterson, C. 1981. *Pericles' Citizenship Law of 451/0 B.C.* New York.

Pearson, L. 1941. "Historical Allusions in the Attic Orators." *CP* 36: 209–29.

Perelli, C. 1994. "Memoria de Sangre: Fear, Hope, and Disenchantment in Argentina." In Boyarin, ed.: 39–66.

Perlman, S. 1961. "The Historical Example, Its Use and Importance As Political Propaganda in the Attic Orators." *Scripta Hierosolymitana* 7: 150–66.

Perrin, B. 1904. "The Rehabilitation of Theramenes." *AHR* 9: 649–69.

Pesely, G. 1989. "The Origin and Value of the Theramenes Papyrus." *AHB* 3: 29–35.

Piérart, M., ed. 1993. *Aristote et Athènes.* Paris.

Powell, C. A. 1979. "Religion and the Sicilian Expedition." *Historia* 28: 15–31.

Raaflaub, K. A. 1994. "Democracy, Power, and Imperialism in Fifth-Century Athens." In Euben, Wallach, and Ober, eds.: 103–46.

Rahn, P. J. 1981. "The Date of Xenophon's Exile." In G. S. Schrimpton and D. J. McCargar, eds., *Classical Contributions: Studies in Honour of Malcolm Francis McGregor:* 103–23. Locust Valley, N.Y.

Raubitschek, A. E. 1941. "The Heroes of Phyle." *Hesperia* 10: 284–95.

Reden, S. von. 1995. "The Piraeus—A World Apart." *G&R* 42: 24–37.

———. 1998. "The Well-Ordered *Polis:* Topographies of Civic Space." In Cartledge, Millett, and von Reden, eds.: 170–90.

Rhodes, P. J. 1972. *The Athenian Boule.* Oxford.

———. 1980. "Athenian Democracy after 403 B.C." *CJ* 75: 305–23.

———. 1981. *A Commentary on the Aristotelian Athenaion Politeia.* Oxford.

———. 1984. "*Nomothesia* in Fourth-Century Athens." *CQ* 35: 55–60.

———. 1991. "The Athenian Code of Laws, 410–399 B.C." *JHS* III: 87–100.

———. 1993. "'Alles eitel gold'? The Sixth and Fifth Centuries in Fourth-Century Athens." In Piérart, ed.: 53–64.

Rich, J., and Shipley, G., eds. 1993. *War and Society in the Greek World.* London.

Roberts, C. 1938. *Catalogue of the Greek and Latin Papyri in the John Rylands Library.* Vol. 3. Manchester.

Roberts, J. T. 1982. *Accountability in Athenian Government.* Madison, Wis.

———. 1986. "Aristocratic Democracy: The Perseverance of Timocratic Principles in Athenian Government." *Athenaeum* 64: 355–69.

Roberts, S. 1976. "Law and the Study of Social Control in Small-Scale Societies." *Modern Law Review* 39: 663–79.

———. 1983. "The Study of Dispute: Anthropological Perspectives." In J. Bossy, ed., *Disputes and Settlements: Law and Human Relations in the West:* 1–24. Cambridge.

Robertson, N. 1990. "The Laws of Athens, 410–399 B.C.: The Evidence for Review and Publication." *JHS* 110: 43–75.

Romilly, J. de. 1995. *Alcibiade.* Paris.

Rosavich, V. 1987. "Autochthony and the Athenians." *CQ* 37: 294–306.

Rosenberg, T. 1995. *The Haunted Land: Facing Europe's Ghosts after Communism.* New York.

Rosenzweig, R. 1983. *Eight Hours for What We Will: Workers and Leisure in an Industrial City, 1870–1920.* Cambridge.

Rousso, H. 1991. *The Vichy Syndrome: History and Memory in France since 1944.* Trans. A. Goldhammer. Cambridge, Mass.

Roy, J. 1998. "The Threat from the Piraeus." In Cartledge, Millett, and von Reden, eds.: 191–202.

Ruschenbusch, E. 1956. "Der Sogenannte Gesetzescode vom Jahre 410 v. Chr." *Historia* 5: 123–28.

———. 1958. "πάτριος πολιτεία: Theseus, Drakon, Solon und Kleisthenes in Publizistik und Geschichtsschreibung des 5. und 4. Jahrhunderts v. Chr." *Historia* 7: 398–424.

———. 1966. "Ephialtes." *Historia* 15: 369–76.

Ste. Croix, G. E. M. de. 1972. *The Origins of the Peloponnesian War.* London.

Salmon, P. 1969. "L'établissement des Trente à Athènes." *AC* 38: 497–500.

Sartori, F. 1951. *La crisi del 411 A.C. nell'Athenaion Politeia di Aristotele.* Padua.

Savage, K. 1994. "The Politics of Memory: Black Emancipation and the Civil War Monument." In Gillis, ed.: 127–49.

Sayer, J. 1997. *Ghost Dancing the Law: The Wounded Knee Trials.* Cambridge, Mass.

Schwartz, B. 1982. "The Social Context of Commemoration: A Study in Collective Memory." *Social Forces* 61: 374–402.

———. 1987. *George Washington: The Making of an American Symbol.* Ithaca, N.Y.

———. 1991. "Social Change and Collective Memory: The Democratization of George Washington." *American Sociological Review* 56: 221–36.

Schwartz, B., Zerubavel, Y., and Barnett, B. 1986. "The Recovery of Masada: A Study in Collective Memory." *Sociological Quarterly* 27: 147–64.

Schwartz, E. 1889. "Quellenuntersuchungen zur griechischen Geschichte." *RhM* 44: 161–93.

Seager, R. 1967. "Thrasybulus, Conon and Athenian Imperialism." *JHS* 87: 95–115.

———. 1973. "Elitism and Democracy in Classical Athens." In F. C. Jaher, ed., *The Rich, the Well Born, and the Powerful:* 7–26. Urbana, Ill.

Sealey, R. 1975. "Pap. Mich. Inv. 5982: Theramenes." *ZPE* 16: 279–88.

———. 1982. "On the Athenian Concept of Law." *CJ* 77: 289–302.

Shapiro, H. A. 1998. "Autochthony and the Visual Arts in Fifth-Century Athens." In Boedeker and Raaflaub, eds.: 127–51.

Sickinger, J. 1999. *Public Records and Archives in Classical Athens.* Chapel Hill, N.C.

Sinclair, R. K. 1988. *Democracy and Participation in Athens.* Cambridge.

Spence, I. 1993. *The Cavalry of Classical Greece: A Social and Military History with Particular Reference to Athens.* Oxford.

Stark, C. 1975. "Brothers at / in War: One Phase of Post–Civil-War Reconciliation." *Canadian Review of American Studies* 6: 174–81.

Stone, I. F. 1988. *The Trial of Socrates.* Boston.

Strauss, B. 1983. "Aegospotami Reexamined." *AJP* 104: 24–35.

———. 1986. *Athens after the Peloponnesian War: Class, Faction, and Policy, 403–386 B.C.* Ithaca.

———. 1987. "A Note on the Topography and Tactics of the Battle of Aegospotami." *AJP* 108: 741–45.

———. 1992. "Ritual, Social Drama and Politics in Classical Athens." *AJAH* 10: 67–83.

Stroud, R. 1971. "Greek Inscriptions: Theozotides and the Athenian Orphans." *Hesperia* 40: 280–301.

Sturken, M. 1997. *Tangled Memories: The Vietnam War, the AIDS Epidemic, and the Politics of Remembering.* Berkeley.

Thomas, R. 1989. *Oral Tradition and Written Record in Classical Athens.* Cambridge.

———. 1992. *Literacy and Orality in Ancient Greece.* Cambridge.

———. 1994. "Law and the Lawgiver in the Athenian Democracy." In Osborne and Hornblower, eds.: 119–33.

Thompson, E. P. 1975. "The Crime of Anonymity." In D. Hay, P. Linebaugh, and E. P. Thompson, *Albion's Fatal Tree: Crime and Society in Eighteenth-Century England:* 255–344. London.

Todd, S. C. 1985. "Athenian Internal Politics, 403–395 B.C., with Particular Reference to the Speeches of Lysias." Unpublished Dissertation. Cambridge.

———. 1990a. "*Lady Chatterley's Lover* and the Attic Orators: The Social Composition of the Athenian Jury." *JHS* 110: 146–73.

———. 1990b. "The Purpose of Evidence in Athenian Courts." In Carledge, Millett, and Todd, eds.: 19–39.

———. 1990c. "The Use and Abuse of the Attic Orators." *G&R* 37: 159–77.

———. 1993. *The Shape of Athenian Law.* Oxford.

———. 1996. "Lysias against Nikomachos: The Fate of the Expert in Athenian Law." In Foxhall and Lewis, eds.: 101–31.

———. 2000. *Lysias.* Austin.

Todd, S. C., and Millett, P. 1990. "Law, Society and Athens." In Cartledge, Millett, and Todd, eds.: 1–18.

Tuplin, C. 1993. *The Failings of Empire: A Reading of Xenophon Hellenica 2.3.11–7.5.27.* *Historia* Einzelschriften 76. Stuttgart.

Usher, S. 1965. "Individual Characterisation in Lysias." *Eranos* 63: 99–119.

———. 1968. "Xenophon, Critias and Theramenes." *JHS* 88: 128–35.

———. 1999. *Greek Oratory: Tradition and Originality.* Oxford.

Vernant, J.-P., ed. 1968. *Problèmes de la guerre en Grèce ancienne.* Paris.

———. 1980. *Myth and Society in Ancient Greece.* London.

———. 1983. *Myth and Thought among the Greeks.* London.

Vidal-Naquet, P. 1996. *The Jews: History, Memory, and the Present.* Trans. D. Curtis. New York.

Vlastos, G. 1983. "The Historical Socrates and Athenian Democracy." *Political Theory* 11: 495–516.

Voeglin, W. 1943. *Die Diabole bei Lysias.* Basel.

Wagner-Pacifici, R., and Schwartz, B. 1991. "The Vietnam Veterans Memorial: Commemorating a Difficult Past." *American Journal of Sociology* 97: 376–420.

Walbank, M. B. 1978. *Athenian Proxenies of the Fifth Centurey B.C.* Toronto.

———. 1982. "The Confiscation and Sale by the Poletai in 402 / 1 B.C. of the Property of the Thirty Tyrants." *Hesperia* 51: 74–98.

Wallace, R. 1989. *The Areopagos Council, to 307 B.C.* Baltimore.

———. 1994. "Private Lives and Public Enemies: Freedom of Thought in Classical Greece." In Boegehold and Scafuro, eds.: 127–55.

Wallach, J. 1988. "Socratic Citizenship." *History of Political Thought* 9: 393–413.

Walters, K. R. 1976. "The 'Ancestral Constitution' and Fourth-Century Historiography in Athens." *AJAH* 1: 129–44.

———. 1983. "Perikles' Citizenship Law." *CA* 2: 314–36.

Wankel, H. 1988. "Die Datierung des Prozesses gegen Timarchos (346 / 5)." *Hermes* 116: 383–86.

Weissenberger, M. 1987. *Die Dokimasiereden des Lysias (orr. 16, 25, 26, 31).* Frankfurt.

Whitehead, D. 1980. "The Tribes of the Thirty Tyrants." *JHS* 100: 208–13.

———. 1982 / 83. "Sparta and the Thirty Tyrants." *Ancient Society* 13 / 14: 105–30.

———. 1983. "Competitive Outlay and Community Profit: φιλοτιμία in Democratic Athens." *C&M* 34: 55–74.

———. 1984. "A Thousand New Citizens." *LCM* 9: 8–10.

———. 1993. "Cardinal Virtues: The Language of Public Approbation in Democratic Athens." *C&M* 44: 37–75.

Winkler, J. 1990. *The Constraints of Desire: The Anthropology of Sex and Gender in Ancient Greece.* New York.

Wooten, C. 1988 / 89. "The Earrings of Polemarchus' Wife (Lysias 12.19)." *CW* 82: 29–31.

Worthington, I. 1991. "Greek Oratory, Revision of Speeches and the Problem of Historical Reliability." *C&M* 42: 55–74.

———, ed. 1994. *Persuasion: Greek Rhetoric in Action.* London.

Wylie, G. 1986. "What Really Happened at Aegospotami?" *AC* 55: 125–41.

Yerushalmi, Y. 1989. *Zakhor: Jewish History and Jewish Memory*. Seattle.

Young, J. 1993. *The Texture of Memory: Holocaust Memorials and Meaning*. New Haven, Conn.

Zerubavel, Y. 1994. "The 'Death of Memory' and the Memory of Death: Masada and the Holocaust as Historical Metaphors." *Representations* 45: 72–100.

———. 1995. *Recovered Roots: Collective Memory and the Making of Israeli National Tradition*. Chicago.

INDEX